THE ARCHAEOLOGY
OF THE
ROMAN ECONOMY

THE ARCHAEOLOGY
OF THE
ROMAN ECONOMY

Kevin Greene

University of California Press
Berkeley and Los Angeles

Frontispiece
Limestone carving (120×74cm) on a grave
memorial of the second or third century AD from
Trier, Germany, illustrating several aspects of the
food trade. A large barrel (containing wine?) is
chained to a heavy ox-cart, possibly leaving a
country estate. In the upper half, an olive-oil
amphora and barrel stand in front of a counter, on
which stands a funnel; a series of graduated
measuring jugs hangs above it. A transaction is
being completed at a table, above which game
birds are shown. (Photograph by courtesy of
Rheinisches Landesmuseum Trier; Cüppers 1983
226, no. 182)

University of California Press
Berkeley and Los Angeles, California

© Kevin Greene 1986
First Paperback Printing 1990

Library of Congress Cataloging-in-Publication Data 1990
Greene, Kevin.
    The archaeology of the Roman economy.

    1. Rome — Economic conditions.   2. Excavation
Archaeology — Rome.   I. Title.
DG85.G74   1986   330.937   86-7024
ISBN 0-520-07401-7 (alk. paper)

Printed in the United States of America

08   07   06   05   04   03
12   11   10 9   8   7   6   5   4

The paper used in this publication meets the minimum
requirements of ANSI/NISO Z39.48-1992 (R 1997)
(*Permanence of Paper*). ∞

Contents

List of illustrations

Acknowledgements

First, I must thank the undergraduates at Newcastle who have taken my option, 'Roman trade, technology and transport', which grew from a small part of a general undergraduate course on the archaeology of the Roman empire. It was the enthusiasm with which each year-group selected and explored different aspects of this enormous subject (with little need for encouragement) that inspired me to write this book, in order to convey its essence to a wider audience. Several past and present students as well as colleagues have helped me by reading and commenting on drafts of chapters; they are Fiona Bayliss, John Chapman, Karen Griffiths, Corinne Ogden, Eleanor Scott and Mark Wood. Help with the compilation and typing of the bibliography came from Wendy Dennis, Cathy Rutherford and Pat Southern. Julia Greene carried out much of the editing and indexing, with back-up assistance from Soheila Luft.

Whilst the Department of Archaeology of the University of Newcastle was a congenial setting for the writing and research involved in this book, other parts of the university provided excellent technical resources. I made extensive use of the Computing Laboratory's facilities and advice about the text processing and database programs involved in the production of my text and bibliography. The Audio-Visual Centre Stills and Graphics Sections prepared the majority of the illustrations, and I wish to thank Ian Munro in particular for his work on the design and production of diagrams and maps. Many individuals and institutions also contributed illustrations; they are acknowledged individually in the captions.

Batsford have been as helpful and tolerant as ever with this project, and I thank Peter Kemmis Betty and Alison Bellhouse, as well as Graham Webster, who has offered prompt and detailed advice throughout. Prof. Keith Hopkins provided a timely boost to my confidence in the latter stages by commenting on parts of the manuscript.

Foreword

I began research into Roman pottery in 1969, studying finds from the site of a Neronian legionary fortress at Usk in south-east Wales (Greene 1973). Alongside earthenware kitchen vessels, made on the site for the use of the garrison, were more specialised forms from other parts of Britain, and imported fine table and drinking wares decorated with coloured slips or even lead-glazes. Study of museum collections and publications showed that some of these had enormous distributions, stretching from the upper Danube to Britain. My publication of the fine wares in the Usk excavation report series (1979) included a brief discussion of their transport and trade, which was completely undocumented in Roman written sources. It was natural that an awareness of the economic implications of pottery should generate a broader interest in the archaeology of the economy as a whole.

Whilst my first book was a detailed report on pottery, with a short account of its significance in the Roman economy (Greene 1979), my second was a general account of the methods of archaeology (Greene 1983). This new book combines elements of both, and examines the use of archaeological methods in the context of the Roman economy. It is unashamedly exploratory and selective; particular emphasis is placed upon the methodology of archaeological research. Occasionally, references are made to earlier or later periods of prehistory or history, as a reminder that comparisons can be extremely informative, whether they produce similarities or contrasts; space does not permit the inclusion of more than a small number. Relatively little reference is made to Roman literary sources, because this is a book about archaeology as much as the Roman economy. I hope that general readers will want to explore the relevant historical sources for themselves; they are much more accessible than archaeological publications, and will in any case be well known to ancient historians.

Chronological table

814 BC: traditional date for foundation of Carthage

753 BC: traditional date for foundation of Rome

750 + BC: foundation of Greek colonies in Italy and around west Mediterranean

510 BC: expulsion of Etruscan kings; beginning of Roman republic

*c.*400 BC: capture of Etruscan city of Veii; Roman control of Etruria and Latium

290 BC: Roman control of Italy complete

264–241 BC: first war against Carthage; Roman control over Sicily, Corsica and Sardinia

218–201 BC: second war against Carthage; Roman control over parts of Spain

*c.*200 BC: Roman control over north Italy up to the Alps

168 BC: Roman control over Macedonia (northern Greece)

149–146 BC: third war against Carthage; Roman control over part of Africa

146 BC: Roman control over Greece

120 BC: Roman control over southern France

100 BC: Roman control over Cilicia (Turkey)

67 BC: suppression of piracy in east Mediterranean

64 BC: Roman control over Syria

58–51 BC: Julius Caesar campaigns in France, Britain and Germany

49–44 BC: civil war; Octavian emerges as victor

31 BC: Octavian assumes title *Augustus*

30 BC: Roman control over Egypt

27 BC–AD 14: beginning of Roman empire; reign of first emperor, Augustus. Conquest of Spain and Alps completed; new territories occupied in Germany and beyond Alps, as well as Judaea, Cyprus and parts of Turkey.

31 BC–AD 68: Julio-Claudian dynasty (Augustus, Tiberius, Caligula, Claudius, Nero)

AD 40s: Britain, Lycia and Pamphylia (Turkey), Thrace (Balkans), and Mauretania (North Africa) added to empire

AD 69–117: Flavio-Trajanic dynasty (Vespasian, Titus, Domitian, Nerva, Trajan)

AD 105–115: Dacia (Romania), and eastern provinces of Armenia, Assyria and Mesopotamia added to empire

AD 117: maximum expansion of Roman territory reached

AD 117–138: Hadrian reigns; consolidation of frontiers begins (eg Hadrian's Wall)

AD 138–193: Antonine dynasty (Antoninus Pius, Marcus Aurelius, Commodus)

AD 193–235: Severan dynasty, established after civil war

AD 235–284: Succession of short-lived emperors, intermittent civil war

AD 250 +: growing numbers of attacks on empire by Germanic barbarians

*c.*AD 270: province of Dacia abandoned

AD 284–305: reign of Diocletian, as part of Tetrarchy, a system of four rulers

AD 306: Constantine put forward as emperor by troops in Britain

AD 306–324: collapse of Tetrarchy, rise of Constantine

AD 324–337: sole rule of Constantine

AD 330: foundation of 'new Rome' at Constantinople

AD 378: major defeat of Roman army by Goths at Adrianople; emperor Valens killed

AD 395: formal division of eastern and western halves of the empire on death of Theodosius

AD 410: sack of Rome by Visigoths

AD 476: end of western Roman empire

ONE

Introduction

APPROACHES TO THE ROMAN ECONOMY

The French historian Fernand Braudel has written an impressive three-volume survey of the fifteenth to eighteenth centuries entitled *Civilization and Capitalism* (1981–1984); volume one bears a particularly significant title: *The structures of everyday life: the limits of the possible*. Nowhere in the volumes is there any historical narrative, for it is Braudel's belief that history consists of an understanding of the interrelationships between an endless series of factors which make up the ever-changing structure of life, and impose the limits which condition the form of human actions and institutions.

> It remains for me to justify one last choice: that of introducing everyday life, no more no less, into the domain of history. Was this useful? Or necessary? Everyday life consists of the little things one hardly notices in time and space. (op.cit. 29)

Braudel describes these everyday themes of material culture as 'parahistoric languages – demography, food, costume, lodging, technology, money, towns – which are usually kept separate from each other and which develop in the margin of traditional history' (ibid. 27). He relies largely upon written evidence for his books, but the aspects of life to which he has devoted such detailed attention are very much those which interest archaeologists, notably those like diet, lifestyle, and the significance of everyday objects. In some respects, Braudel has conducted retrospective anthropology from written sources.

The related disciplines of sociology and anthropology have also changed the terms upon which the past may be approached. Historians and archaeologists have long recognised that their ideas spring from their own limited experience of and information about the world; anthropology

provides an opportunity to counteract these limitations by examining different lifestyles and institutions in widely differing environments. Ethnography concentrates on the study of the material culture and artefacts of people; thus, a combination of anthropology, ethnography, archaeology and history should make up an ideal battery of research tools for investigating the Roman empire, particularly its economy. There is an attractive convergence between the thinking of Braudel and that of ethnoarchaeologists like Binford or Hodder, who believe that small items of everyday life, such as burial practices or forms of pottery and metal objects, reflect wider aspects of society, for instance social structure and religious beliefs. This is comforting for archaeologists, who have no choice other than to study these material traces; in historical periods, they have the added luxury of being able to compare the implications of archaeological research with the written evidence for the peoples involved (Binford 1978; Hodder 1982).

The limitations of archaeology

Archaeology uses fieldwork and excavation, and the comparative study of sites and objects to compile information about the past. In prehistoric periods there is nothing else; in historical times such studies must be fully integrated with evidence from written sources. A growing number of scientific techniques assists archaeologists in their task. Thus, to study agricultural systems, there are methods of locating, recording and excavating the sites of farms, studying the bones and plant remains recovered, and analysing the potential of the soils in relation to the geography of a settlement pattern. Populations can be studied from skeletal remains, which reveal traces of their diet, diseases and mortality. Technology

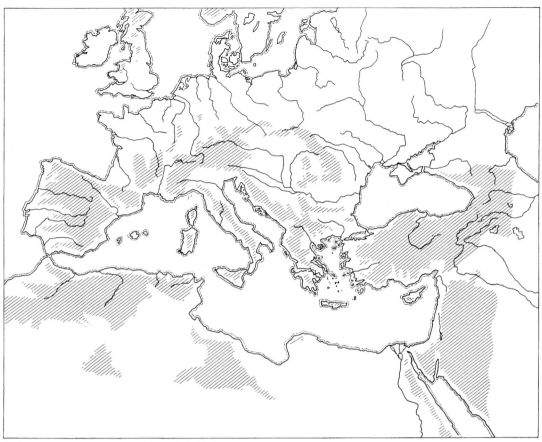

can be investigated by means of analyses of metals, building stone or pottery, and trade can be detected from the distribution of artefacts away from their sources. All of this information can be placed into the general context of the climate and other prevailing environmental conditions.

What archaeology cannot do is achieve certainty. All of the known sites and artefacts are merely a surviving sample of what once existed – and not necessarily a representative sample. Thus, it may be dangerous to generalise the results of particular studies from one region to another, or from one century to the next. This uncertainty and a suspicion of scientific gadgetry has no doubt convinced many historians that the results of archaeology can be used only when they happen to illuminate a safely established historical point, or to provide a picturesque illustration for a publication. This book is aimed in part at historians of all periods, in the hope that archaeology can be examined in its own right, and that its results can be judged in a fairly familiar

1. The territory which eventually formed the Roman empire contained much hilly and mountainous land (the shaded area exceeds 500m), particularly around the Mediterranean. To the south and east lay deserts, but to the north lay Britain, Gaul and the fertile plains bounded by the Danube and the Rhine. The fundamental differences between the core provinces and the periphery have profound implications for the economy of the empire, particularly where transport and agriculture are concerned. (Audio-Visual Centre, University of Newcastle upon Tyne).

historical setting. Conversely, prehistoric archaeologists may like to examine how their subject fares in a period which has abundant written records. Finally, all students of economic history should benefit from gaining a better perspective on the ancient world, and realise the complexity of a period which, in works devoted to more recent centuries, is usually dismissed in a brief opening chapter full of easy generalisations.

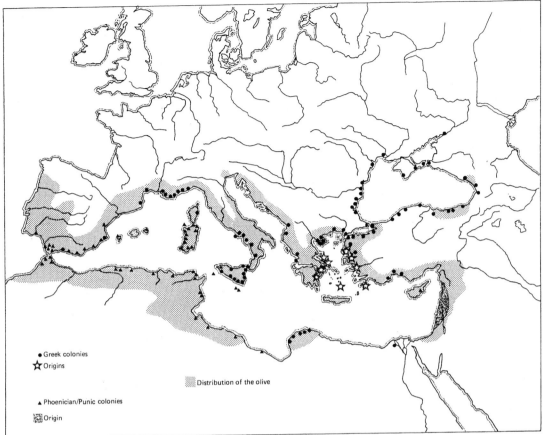

· Greek colonies

☆ Origins

Distribution of the olive

▲ Phoenician/Punic colonies

Origin

THE STUDY OF THE ROMAN ECONOMY

Justification

Most accounts of the Roman empire, like those of other periods, follow a rigid historical arrangement, and concentrate upon political and military history, derived primarily from documentary sources. Some chapters on the army, towns, villas, trade and similar themes tend to appear around half way through such books, often physically dividing the early empire from the late. They may well have the atmosphere of an interval, to which light relief may be added by the use of attractive illustrations of Roman ruins or photogenic artefacts. However, some writers have gone out of their way to write specifically social or economic histories, for which the political and military events form a framework for events or processes of more fundamental significance. Whether ancient or modern periods are involved, this approach is open to accusations of determinism – the reduction of the rôle of individuals in favour of amorphous trends of which they were unwittingly a part.

2. Pre-Roman Mediterranean civilisations: from the eighth to the sixth centuries BC, Greek and Phoenician or Punic cities almost encircled the Mediterranean and the Black Sea, from homelands around the Aegean and the Levant. It is noticeable that they coincide to a large extent with the areas of 'Mediterranean polyculture' (the cultivation of cereals, grapes and olives). This combination of crops seems to have been an important element in the development of civilisation (Chapter 4). Rome was not yet distinguishable from other settlements in Italy, and until c.500 BC it was overshadowed by the Etruscans, who occupied much of northern central Italy. (Audio-Visual Centre, University of Newcastle)

Still more dangerous is the possibility of seeing a single factor as explaining vast historical processes – slavery, money, agriculture or climate are ready candidates.

Different ages choose different interpretations of the past, which may reflect the aspirations or fears of their own times rather than any historical reality. Unfortunately, the preoccupations of historians are usually only made clear by the application of hindsight. In the latter half of the twentieth century, sociology and economics have reached a commanding position in the interpretation of the contemporary world, and exert a powerful influence over political decision-making. However, post-war hopes that explanation would lead to understanding and thus to control of the processes involved have diminished in the 1970s and 1980s.

Naturally, historians and archaeologists have been influenced by this atmosphere, and social and economic explanations of the past have multiplied in relation to more traditional political accounts. One of the first rules of scholarship is to assess the biases to be expected in the opinions of writers, whether ancient or modern; thus, to understand the development of attitudes to the Roman economy, it is necessary to examine the backgrounds of the writers involved. Michael

Rostovtzeff's *Social and economic history of the Roman empire* was first published in 1926; the author was a Russian émigré with direct experience of the Russian Revolution and American capitalism;

3. The expansion of Roman power began slowly after the end of Etruscan superiority around 500 BC; it became more rapid in the fourth century, and the whole Italian peninsula came under Rome's control by 264 BC. By 146 BC, Rome had taken possession of Sicily, Corsica, Sardinia, and parts of Spain and north Africa, as a result of three wars with Carthage. Further provinces were acquired in Greece and Asia Minor by 100 BC, and by AD 50 the whole of the Mediterranean coast was in Roman hands, as well as most of Europe up to the Danube and the Rhine. The maximum extent of the empire was reached in the second century AD, when it stretched (in modern terms) from Scotland to Egypt, and from Morrocco to south Russia. Most of this territory remained intact until the fifth century AD. (Audio-Visual Centre, University of Newcastle)

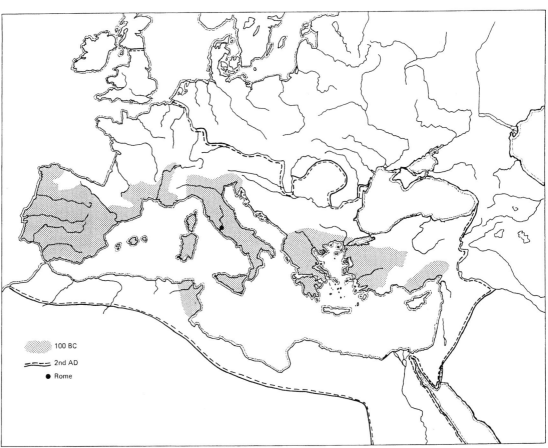

100 BC
2nd AD
● Rome

Tenney Frank, editor of the five-volume *Economic survey of ancient Rome*, lived through the Wall Street crash and the great Depression of the 1920s; Moses Finley, a long-term student of the interaction of social, economic and political affairs, reacted against the excessive optimism of the 1960s in his published series of lectures *The ancient economy* (1973).

The rôle of archaeology

The study of history has been an essential component of economics for several centuries, in order to provide a sufficient time perspective for the identification of long-term trends, and the analysis of causes and effects. This situation is a close parallel to the current view of archaeology held by many American exponents, who regard it as the 'past tense' of anthropology. In the nineteenth century, a blend of archaeology and anthropology provided the inspirations for theories of social evolution, notably those of Engels and Marx, based on the advance of technology and its economic consequences. Because of its emphasis on 'modes of production', Marxist thinking and contemporary anthropological research continue to provide fertile ground for the development of historical and archaeological thought. However, the weighty political implications of Marxism or other schools of economics place a great burden upon historians, archaeologists and anthropologists – the accuracy of the information upon which they are based is absolutely critical. Here, archaeology can play an important rôle in bringing its full range of investigative powers to bear upon periods or problems for which historical documentation is inadequate.

An excellent example of the potential of archaeology is the study of early medieval Europe and the Mediterranean, a period which involved the economic effects of the end of the Roman empire and the rise of barbarian kingdoms in the west, and Islam in the east. For half a century, debate centred upon the propositions of Henri Pirenne that the economics and thus the actions of Europe were conditioned by the impact of the Arabs. The comparatively small amount of evidence – most of it documentary – was simply rearranged by different protagonists. However, the accumulation of archaeological evidence has been growing ever faster, and is now of sufficient quality and quantity for there to be a real opportunity to test existing and new theories. The books produced by Hodges and Whitehouse (1982; 1984) demonstrate the new direction that early medieval archaeology and history have taken. Unlike the static number of surviving historical documents, the archaeological information will continue to grow, and cannot be ignored by any historian of that period. The immediate impact of archaeology in the Roman period is proportionately smaller because of the greater number of contemporary historical sources, but the principle remains the same: archaeology can provide new information about existing questions, and illuminate aspects of Roman life which were never recorded or whose documents have failed to survive.

If early medieval archaeology seems of marginal relevance, perhaps the potential of industrial archaeology may be more convincing. One of the classic questions of economic history concerns England's Industrial Revolution. Did society produce the revolution, or technology? Was there in fact a sudden revolution, or a more gradual evolution? Many detailed questions of technology, demography and agriculture cannot easily be answered from inadequate historical sources, particularly if a long-term view back into the Tudor or even medieval periods is required (Hodges 1973). However, these are just the kinds of issues which archaeology may profitably explore, as Platt's (1978) survey of medieval England demonstrates.

Finally, the relevance of an archaeological study of the Roman empire may be called into question; I believe that justification is straightforward. One profound issue is the assessment of Roman technology and agriculture, with related aspects of military activity and urbanisation. The improvements in the understanding of such issues brought about by archaeological information are fundamental to further interpretation of their social implications. A concerted effort on behalf of many disciplines is necessary to advance the understanding of the economy of the Roman empire. The thinking exercises involved in the task can only be of benefit in a world of differential economic development, technological and demographic change, and varying relationships between states, societies and their economies. Perhaps there is as much to be learned from the question of why the Roman empire did not experience an Industrial Revolution as why eighteenth-century England did.

MODELS OF THE ROMAN ECONOMY

There has been a sudden growth in interest about ancient economies amongst ancient historians, stimulated to an extent by Finley's *The ancient economy* (1973). It has resulted in several notable publications which have made the progress of the study accessible to a wide audience; archaeologists neglect the development of thinking at their peril. In particular, Keith Hopkins has not only advanced the discussion of the Roman economy, but has conveniently summarised the position which research had reached by the early 1970s – the 'new orthodoxy' (1983, xi–xiii). His publications have the added benefit of being set out in the form of discussions of models, which make the differences between assumptions, evidence and implications comparatively clear. The most concise statement of Hopkins' views appears in his introduction to a collection of papers, *Trade in the ancient empires* (Garnsey *et al.* 1983, ix–xv). Hopkins' model is an extension to the 'new orthodoxy' established by M. I. Finley and A. H. M. Jones, whose view of the economy can be summarised fairly briefly.

The Finley/Jones model

Finley and Jones reacted against the 'modernizing' tendencies of historians like Rostovtzeff, who made simplistic equations between aspects of antiquity, such as towns or coinage, and their modern counterparts. Against the tendency of archaeology to study manufactured and traded goods like pottery or metalwork, they both stressed their view that agriculture was the dominant form of economic activity in the Roman empire.

Agriculture was pre-eminent, but most of its products were consumed locally, not traded. With a few exceptions like Rome or Alexandria, towns were where rich landowners lived, and provided centres for administration and state religion, modest crafts and local markets. They were centres of consumption, financed from taxes and rents, rather than trade or industry. Inter-regional trade was small in volume, because of poor transport and the lack of specialisation resulting from the uniform farming conditions which existed around the Mediterranean. Because there was no mass-market, the small amount of long-distance trade that did exist was restricted to luxuries. Traders and craftsmen were modest in their operations, and of low social status; any who did make fortunes promptly bought land, and became 'respectable' landowners to whom commerce was a side issue. Land brought status, and status involved displays of wealth by private consumption and expenditure on public benefactions – never productive investment.

While accepting the basic validity of the Finley/Jones model, Hopkins has introduced a significant modification. He contends that there was genuine economic growth, which increased surplus production by means of political change, and technical or social innovations (1978; 1983, xiv–xv). The period of growth was the late first millennium BC and the first two centuries AD; its results were felt in production, consumption and trade. Hopkins' proposition that there was a trend towards greater surpluses is set out in seven clauses (ibid. xv–xxi) which provide a useful framework for the examination of the relevance of archaeology to the study of the economy of the Roman empire.

1 Agricultural production rose, and more land was cultivated. Hopkins notes the relevance of pollen analysis and the study of settlement patterns. Here, archaeological evidence is of profound and growing significance.

2 Population in the first two centuries AD was greater than 1000 years earlier or 500 years later. A combination of literary evidence and archaeological research into settlement and mortality is relevant here.

3 A greater proportion of workers was involved in non-agricultural production and services, both in the towns and countryside. Excavation of rural and urban workshops and the study of their products is important here.

4 High division of labour promoted increased production, and a high-point in the distribution of luxuries and more mundane goods occurred in the first two centuries AD. Very detailed quantified archaeological studies of finds from occupation sites, and centres of manufacture of items like pottery or brick (particularly those where items were stamped with workers' names) can allow exploration of this clause (fig. 4).

5 Production *per capita* rose, in both agriculture and other spheres, as a result of a wide range of stimuli including taxation, slavery, business practices, prolonged peace and technical devel-

opments. The application of archaeology is limited to the last of these factors.

6 The intensity of exploitation increased because of the amount and proportion of production which was diverted in the form of taxes or rents. Evidence for this must rely primarily on documents and inscriptions.

7 In core-provinces, the levying of money taxes, which were spent on the frontiers (to pay armies) or in Rome (for state activities), stimulated long-distance trade, means of transport, production of goods for sale, the use and volume of coinage, and the importance of towns. Archaeology can assist in the study of each of these results of taxation and expenditure, although literary evidence is needed to establish the level and nature of taxation.

Thus, it can be seen that archaeology has a major part to play in the analysis of at least five out of Hopkins' seven clauses. Clause 7 is undoubtedly the most important element in Hopkins' proposition, and he has devoted detailed articles to the effects of Roman taxation and expenditure (1980; 1983b). It demands a more optimistic view of Roman economic activity than Finley or Jones were prepared to allow, without in any way destroying their model, and furthermore implies a clear rôle for archaeology:

Above all we need to know the volume and value of trade in the classical world. We need to know what was traded and the routes along which food, goods and metals flowed. How much did the volume, value, content and direction of trade change over time and between regions during classical antiquity? (1983, xxi)

Lest archaeologists are over-eager to heed this call for their valuable and growing sources of information, Hopkins displays a perceptive caution over the use of archaeological studies (ibid. xxii) which centres upon the problem of generalising from those goods such as pots which survive well, to those such as textiles which do not: 'The answer to

---

4. A good example of the value of archaeological evidence is provided by the classification and quantification of amphorae (large clay containers) from excavated deposits of different dates in Ostia, the port and town at the mouth of the river Tiber, for they reveal the changing pattern of Rome's exports and imports. Most amphorae of republican date, when Italian exports still flourished, were from Italy itself. In the first century AD, large quantities of oil, wine and fish sauce were imported from Spain and Gaul, whilst north African amphorae became increasingly important from the second century, reaching a dominant position after AD 200. The results of this study correlate closely with changing patterns in the location of shipwrecks in the western Mediterranean (Parker 1984). Thus, archaeology on land and under water can be integrated with historical evidence about Italian and provincial agriculture and trade, but, unlike the literary evidence, the quantity of archaeological evidence is growing rapidly. (Audio-Visual Centre, University of Newcastle; based on data from Panella 1981 68–69 tav. 15 and Carandini and Panella 1981 491, fig. 29.1)

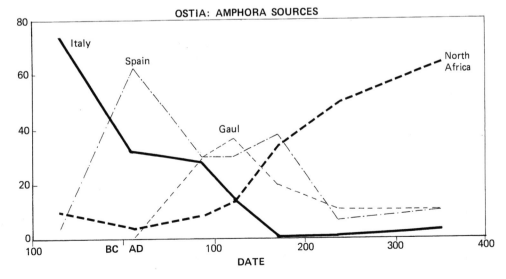

OSTIA: AMPHORA SOURCES

% of amphorae from each source

Italy
Spain
Gaul
North Africa

DATE

this question is surprisingly critical for the study of the ancient economy'. The tendency of archaeology to rely more and more upon scientific aids and mathematical methods makes it harder for historians without archaeological training to answer this question. One of the most important objectives of this book is to increase the critical awareness of the workings of archaeology amongst non-archaeologists.

Literary evidence

Historians may find that the chapters which follow pay scant attention to literary sources. In defence, it may be pointed out that Frank's *Economic survey* (1933–1940) ran to five volumes whilst paying comparatively little attention to archaeology. Translations of important authors such as Pliny the Elder or Columella are readily available, whilst inscriptions are considered in Frank's volumes. A detailed commentary on all of the major Roman texts which concern the economy, incorporating all of the relevant archaeological information which qualifies their validity, would be a long-term undertaking for a well-financed team of scholars.

FURTHER READING

The development of the ancient Greek economy forms an important background to this chapter; see Finley's collection of papers on this theme (1983), and Austin and Vidal-Naquet's *Economic and social history of ancient Greece* (1977). The latter is a source-book containing translations of documents and inscriptions; equivalents for the Roman empire are Lewis and Rheinhold (1966), and Levick (1984), which is wider in scope than its title, *The government of the Roman empire*, implies. Crook's *Law and life of Rome* (1967) provides a useful perspective on the setting of the economy.

The study of the economy has developed steadily since archaeological information has become available for study and recognised as an important source of information. Frank published *An economic history of Rome* in 1927, before editing a vast five-volume *Economic survey* which appeared from 1933–1940. Rostovtzeff's *Social and economic history of the Roman empire* (a sequel to a study of the Hellenistic world) appeared in various editions and languages from 1926 before the definitive English version of 1957. It contains lavish illustrations of artistic and archaeological evidence relating to its theme.

The more critical post-war view of the economy is represented by a number of significant papers by A. H. M. Jones, gathered together in a single volume in 1974. Mossé's *The ancient world at work* (1969) and Finley's *The ancient economy* (1973) rounded off this phase, but Frederiksen's review of the latter (*J. Rom Stud* 1975) should be read for a different perspective. Duncan-Jones attempted to wring some quantitative evidence out of the Roman sources (*The economy of the Roman empire* (1974)), while remaining in the Jones/Finley camp. Martino's *Storia econimica di Roma antica* contains detailed footnote references to ancient sources, as well as good guides to relevant modern publications at the end of each chapter.

The impact of the economic anthropology contained in *Trade and market in the early empires* (edited by Polanyi and others in 1957) is most clearly seen in the daunting but illuminating *The shape of the past* by Carney (1975), whilst rumbling discontent about the use of ancient literary evidence is epitomised in Hopkins' 'Rules of evidence', a review published in 1978, the same year as his *Conquerors and slaves*, which made full use of a sociological approach to Rome and its economy. Finley's challenging pessimism over archaeological evidence stimulated a series of Cambridge seminars by ancient historians and archaeologists, some of which make up *Trade in the ancient economy*, edited by Garnsey *et al.* in 1983; this book demonstrates the vigour of the subject in the 1980s.

TWO

Transport in the Roman empire

ROME AND THE SEA

According to tradition, Roman power was first established on the coast of the Mediterranean when Ostia was founded near the mouth of the Tiber in the seventh century BC. The Etruscans had already traded with Greece and its colonies in southern Italy and Sicily since the eighth century BC. These cities, with their ports and mercantile systems, all came under Roman authority by 200 BC (figs. 2–3). However, this legacy of seaborne trade brought conflict with the Phoenicians based in Carthage; Rome consequently developed naval power in order to combat piracy, and to attack the Carthaginian monopoly of trade with areas such as the north African coast. A large Roman fleet was constructed by 260 BC, and after three periods of war the city of Carthage was finally destroyed in 146 BC.

By 44 BC, the whole Mediterranean coast was in Roman hands except for Egypt and Africa west of modern Tunisia. Fleets of warships continued to play an important rôle in the civil wars of the first century BC, and in the suppression of any piracy which might threaten communications over such a vast area. However, Octavian secured sole power by his defeat of Mark Antony at the battle of Actium in 31 BC, and became the first emperor, Augustus. Within a century, the remaining independent territories with Mediterranean coasts were absorbed, and naval requirements were restricted to the needs of transport, communications, and local patrolling. Thus, in the course of five centuries, Rome grew from an inland town on a navigable river, the Tiber, into the capital of an empire which entirely surrounded the Mediterranean. During the empire, attention can be focused on merchant ships, built without any provision for defence.

THE STUDY OF ROMAN TRANSPORT

The geographical complexity of the Roman empire is as important in the understanding of transport as it is in other aspects of the economy such as agriculture or settlement patterns (fig. 1). The coasts of the Atlantic Ocean formed the western boundary, Britain was an island, and the frontiers of most of the provinces between Germany and Romania were determined by the courses of two great European rivers, the Rhine and the Danube. The eastern provinces related in a variety of ways to the Black Sea and Red Sea, or to two more great rivers, the Euphrates and the Nile. From Egypt in the east to Morocco in the west, north Africa was a narrow band of fertile land between the Sahara desert and the Mediterranean, without any significant rivers. Thus, generalisations about transport are almost impossible, because each region relied in different proportions upon roads, rivers and the sea.

Since transport was one of the most important influences upon the Roman economy, it is essential to gain an understanding of its speed, cost and availability, whether on land or water. The quality and quantity of literary and archaeological evidence relevant to transport both vary throughout this enormous area, and provide a series of insights rather than a general understanding. We must also make a distinction between long-distance and local transport, for whilst transport systems obviously control the extent of long-distance trade, they are perhaps even more important at a local level, particularly where bulky agricultural products are concerned. Where no direct evidence for transport can be found, traded goods may be studied in order to assess the means by which they might have been distributed.

Literary and artistic evidence

Greek and Roman writers such as Strabo and Pliny the Elder described trade routes in many parts of the empire, whilst large numbers of inscribed altars, tombstones and other epigraphic sources provide instances of individual merchants, sailors, or companies involved in transport. Inscriptions on gravestones were not written for literary or historical purposes, and provide interesting but often indirect insights into the framework of transport or its organisation. In 1914, Villefosse used the *tituli picti* (painted inscriptions) found on discarded amphorae heaped up on the *Monte Testaccio* in Rome to link oil and wine imported into Rome to traders known from their memorials in Narbonne. Similar relationships continue to be revealed through underwater archaeology today; Rougé has explored the implications of inscriptions from Lyon, as well as inscribed lead tags which once acted as seals or customs certificates on merchandise (1964). Much still remains to be gained from this approach (e.g. Christol 1971).

Circumstantial accounts of actual sea voyages occur in the writings of authors as diverse as Lucian and St Paul, which include valuable references to ships and their fittings, as well as navigational practices. Diocletian's *Edict* on prices includes figures relating to several means of transport (Hopkins 1982), and therefore allows interesting comparisons between Roman, medieval and modern costs to be made. For instance, there is encouragingly close agreement between the ratios of sea to river to land transport costs known from eighteenth-century England and those deduced from less reliable Roman sources (below p. 40).

Ships and vehicles are relatively common in Roman art, but are bedevilled by the problem that few artists – then or now – could be expected to give a faithful rendering of sails and rigging or suspension and steering (frontispiece). These matters are very important, for ineffective navigation and traction have been held responsible for some of the supposed shortcomings of the Roman economy (below pp. 28, 39). The geographical distribution of these representations is extremely uneven; scenes including vehicles pulled by horses, mules and oxen are relatively common in eastern France and its neighbouring countries, but are totally absent from Britain and Spain. Exceptionally, very convincing representations are found, such as the well-known graffito of a large merchant vessel in Pompeii, which has given its name to the 'House of the ship Europa' (fig. 8).

Archaeological evidence

Archaeological research and excavation have identified various kinds of artefacts, from humble pots to complete marble columns, whose geographical distributions can be studied in order to deduce trade routes. The growth of underwater archaeology since 1950 has made a dramatic contribution to our knowledge, through the location, recording, and in some cases actual excavation of Roman wrecks and their cargoes, preserved from decay in water-logged sea-bed deposits. The basic problems and possibilities have been discussed by Basch (1972) and Parker (1973); the number of wrecks dating to before AD 1500 known from the Mediterrean now exceeds 800, and the majority belong to the Roman period (Parker 1984, 99). This large database is a good subject for computerised recording and analysis, and the benefits of this approach are beginning to be apparent (Parker and Painter 1979; Parker 1984).

It is fairly obvious that well-preserved wrecks can tell us a great deal about the intricacies of ship construction (figs. 6–7), but it must be emphasised that even on wreck sites where the hull has completely disintegrated and the cargo has been scattered, valuable insights can still be gained into the trade in metals, oil, wine and fish products, thanks to the good chances of the survival of large items such as amphorae or ingots. With a notable recent exception from Guernsey, wrecks of sea-going ships are virtually unknown outside the Mediterranean. Well-preserved river boats have been discovered in the silts of important trade routes such as the Rhine, however, such as the collection salvaged in advance of building work in Mainz (fig. 11a; Rupprecht 1984). These excavated remains provide a basis for comparison with the river craft which are illustrated in Roman wall-paintings, carvings and mosaics from the same region (Ellmers 1978). Roman roads have been intensively studied, but information about vehicles is much poorer than that about ships, because their remains are unlikely to be found in conditions favourable to the preservation of timber.

The study of ships, harbours, vehicles and roads is also of considerable interest from the point of view of the level of technical achievement which they represent. Surprises are frequent; it was recently observed that a wreck found off the Tunisian coast contained a sophisticated rotary water-lifting device, part of which was driven by a cog-wheel whose cogs were of a sloping shape hitherto considered an innovation of the late seventeenth century AD (Kapitän 1983). The history of the bilge-pump would be sadly incomplete but for the study of material from shipwrecks (Foerster 1984). Even when the technology of transport was low, its very existence and the amount of capital and effort invested in it are of great interest in the general interpretation of the Roman economy.

SHIPBUILDING: THE BACKGROUND

Most boats built before the advent of iron hulls and steam propulsion were based on underlying principles of construction which are still in use in many parts of the world today. There has not been a single line of development, of course, but there are limits to the number of ways in which effective boats can be built. Various forms have been invented and developed separately in many parts of the world at different times, according to local needs and materials. Greenhill has defined four basic forms of construction: the raft boat, the skin boat, the bark boat and the dug-out (1976, 91–5). These will be discussed in order to place Roman craft into perspective, and to determine which forms are found in the Roman empire.

Rafts

These simple but effective craft are usually made from small buoyant timbers or bundles of reeds in areas where large tree trunks are not available; their form is also important if the deck area of a boat is more useful than its volume (Greenhill 1976, 97–115). Deck planking, bracing timbers, sides, cabins and masts for sails can all be added to increase the size and sophistication of a raft, and empty jars or inflated skins can be attached to improve buoyancy. Related to rafts are 'raft boats', which also rely on the buoyancy of their timbers, but have an internally concave hull and a deck rather than being a simple floating platform. This form of construction is not only suitable for small river craft, but is the predecessor of ancient Egyptian and Far Eastern sea-going ships (Greenhill 1976, 100, 106).

Casson has suggested that the *utricularii* ('blad-dermen') recorded on inscriptions from the Danube area in the early second century AD operated rafts with inflated skins (1971, 5), although others think that the term refers to the transporters of liquids in skin containers (Künow 1980, 6). It is very likely that rafts of wood or bundled reeds were common in Roman Egypt, and that timber rafts fulfilled a variety of rôles on inland waterways elsewhere in the empire. Because of the simplicity of their construction, their remains would be less distinctive than the timbers of other forms of boats, and thus escape recognition when accidentally found; however, fragments of a more sophisticated type of raft have been recovered from a site in France (Lagadec 1983; below p. 20).

Skin boats

A particularly important form of vessel construction is represented by skin boats (Greenhill 1976, 116–123). A complete animal skin can, of course, be made airtight and inflated as an aid to the buoyancy of a raft, or used on its own and propelled by paddling. A true skin boat is constructed by making a wooden or basketwork frame over which a number of separate hides are fitted, in the manner of the round Welsh coracles or longer Irish curraghs still in use in the twentieth century. The seaworthiness of much larger versions of this form has been demonstrated by the successful Atlantic crossing in 1976 by a replica of an early medieval Irish skin boat (Severin 1978). Julius Caesar was clearly impressed by the Celtic craft which he had encountered during campaigns in Gaul and Britain in the first century BC; when in military difficulties at Lerida in Spain in 49 BC, he ordered his men to build:

> ... ships of the kind that his experience in Britain in previous years had taught him to make. The keel and the first ribs were made of light timber, the rest of the hull was wattled and covered with hides. (*Civil Wars* I, 54; Loeb translation 77–9)

Caesar's boats were large enough to carry his army across a river at night to take up new positions, and required 'coupled carts' to transport them.

Knowledge acquired in constructing the framework of skin boats may have produced valuable ideas about effective methods of providing internal strengthening for log boats or even fully plank-built vessels. Unfortunately, the remains of wattles and light timbers would prove even more difficult to recognise archaeologically than the remains of rafts, for they would differ little from elements used in timber buildings. It is probable that skin boats continued to be important in Britain after the Roman conquest, and their use might easily have spread to areas of Gaul, Germany or Spain where cattle-raising was important, and a good supply of hides was available. In some part of the world large sheets of bark rather than hides have provided a tough, watertight hull material akin to hide; these are of importance in North America (Greenhill 1976, 124–8), but are unlikely to have existed in the Roman empire.

Log boats

The log boat (Greenhill 1976, 129–152) is such a simple craft that it takes little imagination to envisage the technical progression from a floating tree trunk to a fully hollowed 'dug-out' canoe. The maximum size of tree available need not limit its size, for trunks can be joined together to achieve greater length. An idea with important repercussions is to split a log boat lengthwise, and to insert planks in order to increase its width; the height of the sides can also be raised by attaching planks. With suitable strengthening frames and waterproofing, a substantial vessel can be constructed from a hollowed log which avoids the problems of forming a junction between the bottom and sides of the hull. In practice, large curved planks were probably made from split logs rather than by splitting an actual dug-out boat (McGrail 1981, 24). Expanded log boats merge into the general category of planked boats defined by McGrail (ibid. 5). As well as still being in use in many 'primitive' boat-building areas of the world, the log boat is well known on the Rhine from the medieval period to the present day (Ellmers 1978, 3).

Casson has conveniently collected many Roman literary references to log boats, which are widely attested in Italy and the rest of the Roman world (1971, 8). Our knowledge of Roman log boats has been advanced by the finding of six vessels in the silts of the old course of the Rhine near the fort of Zwammerdam in the Netherlands (fig. 11b and cover; de Weerd 1978). They illustrate a range of utilitarian craft of different sizes and complexity. Three are simple dug-out logs, ranging in length from 5.5 to 10.4m (18 to 34ft); one had been heightened by the addition of a wide plank. The remaining vessels are much larger (20.25, 22.75 and 34m [66ft 5in, 74ft 8in and 111ft 7in] in length), and are best described as barges. All three incorporate large curved planks derived from logs, between which six or seven planks have been inserted in order to construct wide, flat-bottomed craft; their sides were also heightened by a broad plank. The floors of the barges were formed from broad longitudinal planks, joined together by a series of lateral timbers nailed to them from above; in places, natural branches were used to link the lateral timbers to the vertical sides of the craft. Curved log-derived planks provided a simple method of forming the angle between the bottom and sides of the barges, which required no joining and waterproofing.

An interesting hybrid boat was recently found at Flavigny, on the upper reaches of the Moselle in France (Lagadec 1983). A long dug-out log, like a narrow canoe, had two raised sections with sockets, which may have carried one end of a horizontal platform. The craft would have consisted of a platform floating on two long logs (206, fig. 8), and would have been ideal for the shallow and uneven flow of the upper waters of the river.

Planked boats

This general term includes by far the greatest variety of craft (McGrail 1981, 5). Most of the world's traditions of building large vessels, even when derived from rafts or log boats, involve the use of considerable numbers of planks. There are, of course, many different ways of fixing them together to form a hull, including sewing, joinery and nailing, and the individual planks may overlap or meet smoothly edge-to-edge. The essential difference between large Greek and Roman Mediterranean ships and most of the larger ships of the medieval and modern periods lies in the approach to hull construction.

SHIPBUILDING TECHNIQUES

Like large primitive log boats or Egyptian raft boats, Greek and Roman Mediterranean ships relied on a rigid shell into which internal frames and strengthening timbers were fitted *afterwards*. In contrast, a modern vessel is assembled around a rigid skeleton of shaped frames fixed to a keel; the 'shell' of the hull is made up of steel plates rivetted onto the frames. Although the concept of skeleton-first hull building had become standard in Europe by the fourteenth century AD, the shell-first approach is still widely used for the construction of small craft in Europe and North America today, and large shell-first boats still abound in other parts of the world (Greenhill 1976, 60–88).

Shell-first construction

The principal consideration in the effective construction of a shell-first ship is that the shell itself should be rigid. Two rival techniques of achieving this rigidity have been used at various times in different parts of the world: planks may either overlap and be nailed, sewn or tied together (*clinker-built*), or be fitted edge-to-edge (*carvel*). The shells of Graeco-Roman ships in the Mediterranean were edge-jointed without any overlap. Deep mortises were cut into the opposing edges of their carefully trimmed planks, which could then be fixed together by tenons held firmly in place by wooden pegs (treenails); long copper nails were often added for further strength. Once the shell was complete, internal frames and strengthening timbers were individually shaped and fitted,

masts erected, decks constructed, etc. The lower part of the hull was sheathed in lead as a defence against wood-boring sea worms. Ancient descriptions and carvings, and modern studies of surviving traces of Roman wrecks all confirm the universality of this method of construction in the Mediterranean area (figs. 5–6).

In contrast, the shells of north European ships have been constructed from overlapping planks secured by iron nails up to modern times, and fragments of ships of Roman date suggest that this technique was already in use by then. A river barge and a sea-going ship of Roman date from London are quite distinct from Mediterranean finds, although the edge-jointed mortised construction was occasionally adopted in Britain (Marsden 1972). During the Roman empire there must have been an intensification of the cross-Channel trade which had already existed for many centuries before Roman power reached Britain and northern Gaul in the first century BC.

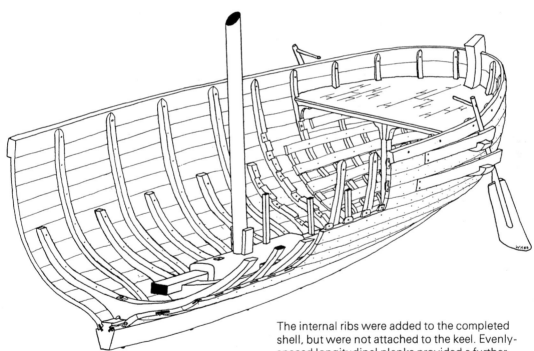

5. Diagram showing the construction of Mediterranean merchant ships during the Roman period. A heavy keel was laid, and a 'shell' was then built up from it by jointing planks edge-to-edge.

The internal ribs were added to the completed shell, but were not attached to the keel. Evenly-spaced longitudinal planks provided a further internal lining upon which cargo could rest. The main mast was planted firmly into the keel, and large steering oars were suspended from each side of the stern. Ships built around the coasts of Britain and Gaul were made in an altogether different fashion, from oak planks nailed together. (Drawing by William Hubbard)

Local traders probably used ships similar to those encountered by Julius Caesar when in 56 BC he crushed the sea-power of the Veneti, who inhabited what is now Brittany:

> Their keels were considerably more flat than those of our own ships, that they might more easily weather shoals and ebb-tide. Their prows were very lofty, and their sterns were similarly adapted to meet the force of waves and storms. The ships were made entirely of oak, to endure any violence and buffeting. The cross-pieces were beams a foot thick, fastened with iron nails as thick as a thumb . . . When our own fleet encountered these ships it proved its superiority only in speed and oarsmanship; in all other respects, having regard to the locality and the force of the tempests, the others were more suitable and adaptable. (*Gallic War* III, 13–14; Loeb translation, 155–7)

From Caesar's eye-witness account, it would seem that these Venetic ships may have borne a resemblance to the flat-bottomed, high-sided cogs of the medieval period, which also relied upon

6. It is easy to appreciate the 'shell-first' construction of Mediterranean merchant vessels from this ship found at the Bourse site, Marseilles. Part of the keel appears at the top left of the photograph, and an area of the ship's smooth shell is visible near the tractor. (Photograph by G. Reveillac, courtesy of Centre Camille Jullian, Aix-en-Provence)

nailed plank construction (McGowan 1981, 7). Caesar and Strabo's descriptions have received welcome confirmation from the remains of a merchant ship of the second century AD which has been rescued from the entrance of St Peter Port harbour, Guernsey. The flat-bottomed oak hull was well preserved, partly by a layer of burnt pitch, which had formed part of the cargo when the ship caught fire and sank. Conservation and reconstruction of the timbers will eventually allow a really detailed study of this ship, the first 'Celtic' sea-going vessel to have been discovered. Unlike north German and Scandinavian ships and boats in the 'Viking' style, the Guernsey ship had a smooth hull, with planks nailed to internal frames, rather than overlapping planks nailed to each other.

Strabo (*Geography* IV, 4, 1) adds a further detail about these Venetic ships which shows that they were waterproofed by caulking, rather than through the precise carpentry of the close-fitting planks of Mediterranean builders:

> . . . they do not bring the joints of the planks together but leave gaps; they stuff the gaps full of sea weed, however, so that the wood may not, for lack of moisture, become dry when the ships are hauled up . . . (Loeb translation, 235)

Regional traditions of pre-Roman origin must have survived in a similar fashion all around the Mediterranean, as well as on the many rivers of the empire (Graeve 1981; Casson 1971, 329–31, 338–43; Merzagora 1929). Unless the size or function of local ships required radical modification, there would have been no reason for traditional designs to change. The fact that Caesar was happy to admire and even imitate the planked ships and skin boats which he encountered in Celtic Britain and Gaul demonstrates that the technology of the Romans was not necessarily superior to that of their neighbours, whether 'civilised' or 'barbarian'. It is also known that the technology of Celtic carts and carriages was very influential, for many Roman vehicles bore names of Celtic derivation. Influences are likely to have been reciprocal; for instance, Höckmann has discussed the Roman and Celtic elements involved in the late Roman ships found in Mainz on the middle Rhine (1983).

SKELETON CONSTRUCTION

Research continues into the origins and date of adoption of skeleton construction for the building of large ships in Europe. It seems to have been the normal technique for Mediterranean galleys and sailing ships by the medieval period, whereas the contemporary clinker-built cogs and hulks of northern Europe were still built shell-first (McGrail 1981, 36–39). However, the distinction between these types of construction is not completely clear-cut (Greenhill 1976, 60–88). Some Mediterranean Roman ships show that the lower planking could be fitted to internal timbers before the construction of the rest of the shell (e.g. Madrague de Giens, Tchernia *et al.* 1978, 89–96,

and p. 26 below). The Venetic ships described by Caesar and Strabo, as well as the large river craft in use on the Rhine (below fig. 11), relied heavily on planks nailed to an internal framework. By the Byzantine period, more reliance was being placed on internal frames. In the hull of wreck no. 2 found at Yassi Ada off the southern coast of Turkey, edge-jointing had been simplified and iron nails were extensively used instead of treenails, and skeleton construction was employed for fixing the upper planking to the frames (McGrail 1981, 41–2; Doorninck 1972).

It is apparent that the ability to build skeleton-first, shell-first or hybrid ships was widespread in both Mediterranean and northern provincial areas. Greenhill has stressed that the most important factor determining the choice of technique may have been the scale of organisation of shipyards rather than the ability of the shipbuilders (1976, 73, 298). A shell-first ship can be constructed without a precise design by experienced builders; the internal frames need only be roughly prepared, and can be trimmed and fitted individually into a completed shell. In contrast, if a keel and ribs are to be completed first, it is necessary to have a much more detailed concept and precise plans of the finished vessel, because all of the main timbers have to be cut to the correct shape in advance.

However competent Roman ship-builders may have been, skeleton-first ships do have undeniable advantages (McGrail 1981, 43). Strength increases in direct relation to the size of the timbers, lower quality planks can be used, and old or damaged planking may be repaired more easily. A critical factor – of no interest to the Romans – was that gun-ports could be pierced through the planks of the hull without reducing its strength. Greenhill considers that the way in which the great Voyages of Discovery followed the widespread adoption of skeleton construction in the fifteenth century was a result of several factors, both technical and psychological. The sailing-power derived from the adoption of three-masted rigging, combined with the intrinsic strength of skeleton ships, gave rise to a sense of confidence that was reinforced by the superiority of their cannons' fire-power over anything likely to be encountered outside Europe (1976, 288–9). Earlier ships, both Graeco-Roman and medieval, would have been capable of crossing the Atlantic or rounding Africa, but at much greater risk, and with less certainty of a commercial return cargo.

ROMAN MERCHANT SHIPS

Roman ships are clearly divided into long ships, a term restricted to slender military galleys built for speed, and round ships, an all-embracing term for ships with proportions more suitable for carrying cargoes (Morrison 1980). The distinction was by no means new, as illustrations of Greek warships and merchant vessels make clear (Casson 1971, figs. 81–2). Warships were of marginal importance in the Roman imperial period because of the lack of seaborne military competition. In the Mediterranean, load-carrying merchant ships had a long history, for the Aegean, Crete, the east Mediterranean coast and Egypt were linked by sea-going timber sailing ships by 1000 BC (Morrison 1980, 9–13; Graeve 1981). Egyptian shipbuilding technology is physically attested by the oldest surviving ship in the world, which was buried beside the pyramid of Cheops *c*.2530 BC; it is 43.4m (142ft 6 in) long, 5.5m (18ft) broad, and the hull is 7.9m (26ft) deep (Jenkins 1980). Artistic representations show that sea-going galleys and sailing ships carrying a large rectangular sail existed in the second millennium BC (Casson 1971, 30–39), and the Cheops boat demonstrates the kind of skills available for the construction of sea-going craft. It is made up of edge-jointed planks strengthened by internal frames (Greenhill 1976, 161, fig. 111), although the shape is clearly derived from papyrus reed boats.

The wreck of a merchant ship dating from the fourth century BC, excavated at Kyrenia off the northern coast of Cyprus, demonstrates that Greek builders added a heavy timber keel to their ships (Katzev 1972; Morrison 1980, 57, pl. 42); this would increase strength and stability, particularly in conjunction with well-placed ballast. Greek and Roman ships continued to rely upon a large rectangular mainsail, with the addition of extra sails on small masts on very large ships. Little change took place during the Roman period except for the occasional adoption of a triangular 'lateen' sail, which would allow a ship to sail much more directly into the wind. Merchant ships illustrated on Roman carvings and mosaics have a distinctive profile with a low prow, a central main mast, and a high stern which would allow the steersman to look forward over the bow while operating the steering oar. The ratio of length to breadth of these vessels averaged 6:1, compared with the 10:1 proportions of warships. Viereck's general study of the Roman fleet (1975) includes many drawings of hypothetical reconstruction of transport and cargo ships as well as warships.

Occasional representations of merchant galleys show that they were much more robust versions of military vessels (Morrison 1980, 53, pl. 37; Casson 1971, pls. 138–140). They would have advantages of speed and manoeuvrability in calm conditions or in entering difficult ports, and could travel up large rivers to reach inland markets, thus eliminating the necessity to transfer cargoes to river boats. Larger crew requirements would perhaps be offset by the ability to transport perishable or high value cargoes and passengers with greater speed and flexibility. Unlike the ram of a warship, a pointed prow on a merchant galley or sailing ship did not have any aggressive purpose; it is simply one way of dealing with the constructional problems of finishing-off a straight keel, which is still employed in the design of many modern merchant vessels.

SIZES OF SEA-GOING MERCHANT SHIPS

A small number of vessels of excessive size sailed the Mediterranean (Casson 1971, 184–9; Duncan-Jones 1977), usually in the service of the grain supply; one, the *Isis*, was recorded in the literary works of the Greek writer Lucian in the second century AD:

> ... what a huge ship! A hundred and twenty cubits long, the ship-wright said, and well over a quarter as wide, and from deck to bottom, where it is deepest, in the bilge, twenty-nine (55 × 14 × 13m [182ft × 45ft × 44ft]). Then, what a tall mast, what a yard to carry! What a fore-stay to hold it up! How gently the poop curves up, with a little golden goose below! And correspondingly at the opposite end, the prow juts right out in front, with figures of the goddess, Isis, after whom the ship is named, on either side. And the other decorations, the paintings and the topsail blazing like fire, anchors in front of them, and capstans, and windlasses, and the cabins on the poop – all very wonderful to me. You could put the number of sailors at an army of soldiers. She was said to carry corn enough to feed all Attica for a year. And all this a little old man, a wee fellow, has kept from harm by turning the huge rudders with a tiny tiller. (*The Ship or the Wishes*; Loeb translation, 435–7)

It has been estimated that the *Isis* had a capacity of around 1200 tons, and the reception it received in Piraeus underlines the fact that it was exceptional (Casson 1950; Pomey and Tchernia 1978).

In contrast, most Roman merchant ships were small, the majority having an overall length of 15m (50ft) to 37m (120ft), and a capacity of 100 to 150 tons; again, Casson has collected and analysed figures from a variety of ancient and modern sources (1971, 170–3, 183–190). However, much larger ships were not uncommon, and vessels in the grain fleet might easily range from 300 to 500 tons, with a few (like the *Isis*) exceeding 1000.

For comparison, the largest ships travelling to the East Indies in the sixteenth to seventeenth centuries were 50m (165ft) long by 13m (42ft) broad, with a capacity of 1200 tons, and a major warship such as the *Duke of Wellington* built in 1852 measured 73 × 18m (240ft × 60ft). The imperial pleasure ships of the first century AD found in Lake Nemi, near Rome, measured 73 × 24 and 71 × 20m (240ft × 79ft and 234ft × 66ft) (Ucelli 1950). The largest timber ship ever built was the *Wyoming*, a schooner built in the USA in 1909 to compete with steam ships in coastal trade; it measured 100 × 15m (329ft × 50ft) and had a capacity of 3730 tons. In his discussion of the *Isis*, Casson remarked that 'The merchantman of 1200 tons first appears in any considerable numbers in the fleets of the East India Company around the end of the 18th and the beginning of the 19th century' (1950, 56). Pomey and Tchernia agree with this view, and conclude that the size of Roman merchant ships was not exceeded until the fifteenth century, and that the grain ships were not exceeded until the nineteenth; they stress the important implication that size was limited by demand rather than technical capability (1978, 250–251).

Steam powered iron-hulled ships appeared in the nineteenth century, but their greater size was partly a reflection of the need to carry bulky fuel as well as a cargo. Thus, it can be seen that the size and capacity of Roman ships was not exceeded until the introduction of steam power in the nineteenth century AD. Successful coastal trading from small wooden ships is still carried out around the Mediterranean to this day; nailed shell-first fishing boats still brave the North Sea in their hundreds.

CASE-STUDY: THE ROMAN SHIPWRECK AT MADRAGUE DE GIENS

This ship sank off the southern coast of France in the bay of Madrague de Giens, 20km (12½ miles) to the west of Toulon c.60–50 BC. It has been well excavated and fully published (Tchernia *et al.* 1978), and the extensive remains of the hull make it an instructive case-study. The survival of a large part of the ship's cargo allows good estimates of its carrying capacity to be made, and increases the interest of the wreck still further (fig. 7).

The excavation

The ship was protected from erosion and complete decay by a thick deposit of sediment. Its shallow depth (20m [65ft 7in]) and proximity to the coast allowed careful excavation to be carried

7. An underwater excavation across the middle of a cargo ship which sank off the south coast of France in the first century BC. In addition to revealing many details about the order of constructing its hull, the Madrague de Giens shipwreck allowed an estimate of its cargo capacity to be made, for wine amphorae were found in their original positions, carefully stacked in four layers. (Tchernia *et al* 1978 pl 13)

out over several years from 1972. Once the overall dimensions of the buried wreck had been defined by probing and magnetic surveying, a broad cross-section was opened across the middle of the vessel to study its cargo and construction. A large quantity of pottery was found in the bottom of the ship, including at least 1635 fine table vessels as well as coarser kitchen wares, but the main cargo consisted of amphorae, carefully stowed in three layers. They all had narrow pointed bodies and long cylindrical necks (form Dressel IB, 1.16m [3ft 10in] high); the points of the upper layers fitted between the necks of those below them, ensuring that the cargo was packed closely together, although it was protected from breakages by pine branches with their needles placed between the layers.

Many of the amphorae bore the stamp of Publius Veveius Papus, an estate owner whose name also occurs on stamps in the wine-producing areas around Terracina in southern Italy; the ship had presumably taken its last cargo on board at a port near this region (Tchernia *et al.* 1978, 42). Like the *Mary Rose* nearly 600 years later, it came to rest on the sea floor leaning to one side, and a substantial section of the upper part of the hull was consequently preserved by silt and tumbled amphorae. The standard size and systematic arrangement of the amphorae allowed their original number and thus the capacity of the ship to be calculated, despite the presence of some voids in the cargo which the excavators attributed to the work of Roman salvage divers (Tchernia *et al.* 1978, 29–31).

Cargo capacity

If no cargo other than amphorae was on board, it would have been possible to accommodate four layers of amphorae. Allowing for working space at each end of the ship, it could have carried between 5800 and 7800 amphorae, each weighing 50 kilos, giving a cargo of 290–390 metric tons, depending on whether three or four layers were carried. This result was found to agree well with that derived from methods of calculating cargo capacity from hull dimensions used in the eighteenth century AD. The cargo capacity places the Madrague de Giens ship into the upper range of Roman Mediterranean merchant vessels (see above p. 24), but it was by no means unusually large; the excavators pointed out that this size was not exceeded before the shipbuilders of Venice and

Genoa began to construct large vessels in the fifteenth century AD.

The construction of the hull

The exceptionally well preserved hull of the Madrague de Giens ship has been studied in great detail (op. cit. 75–99). A detailed analysis of its construction was possible through partial dismantling, lifting a length of the keel and its fittings, and even tunnelling beneath the hull. It was shown to conform to the standard shell-first method of building Graeco-Roman ships, but some elements of skeleton construction were also involved (stage 4 below). The Madrague de Giens ship was constructed in the following stages (Tchernia *et al.* 1978, 89–91, pl. 41):

1 The heavy keel was laid, and the first three planks of the hull were added to each side of it, smoothly edge-jointed by mortises and tenons.

2 Wide frames (extending both sides of the keel) were placed at intervals along the keel to form the framework for the lower parts of the hull; they were fitted onto long vertical metal spikes which had been hammered up through the thickness of the keel.

3 Individual frames were placed between those of phase 2, either side of but not actually joined to the keel.

4 The lower portion of the shell of the ship was constructed over the exterior of the lower frames fitted in phases 2–3, by the same edge-jointing technique as the lowest planks in phase 1; the treenails were hammered in from the exterior.

5 The upper part of the shell was constructed, independently of the frames, with treenails inserted from inside the hull.

6 Further internal frames were fitted inside the shell, to the full height of the hull; they were not joined to the lower frames.

7 A second skin of thinner planks was fitted to the exterior of the ship, and covered in lead; a layer of planks was also fitted inside, to cover the internal frames (Tchernia *et al.* 1978, pl. 39).

No evidence of the deck or superstructure of the ship survived, although a massive baulk of timber with carefully prepared sockets for the mast and its supports was found, carefully fitted onto the lowest frames of the hull. Study of the wood used to construct the ship has revealed that these frames and the mast-step were made from oak, as were the tongues of wood which joined the planks of the ship's shell, although a variety of different kinds of wood had been used to make the treenails which held them in place. The keel and the first layer of planks were made from elm, while the outer layer was of fir.

Thus, the wreck found at Madrague de Giens and its cargo demonstrate how much solid information is being contributed by underwater archaeology to the study of shipping, in this as well as other periods. Work on other wreck sites proceeds at a growing pace, and as a result we can look forward to a great improvement in our understanding of seaborne trade.

ROMAN SAILING, STEERING AND NAVIGATION

Evidence from carvings and other pictorial sources shows that Roman ships bore a large mast amidships to carry a rectangular mainsail (fig. 8); on large vessels, small masts might also be found near the stern and bow, the latter set forward at an angle (Casson 1971, pl. 145). The size and shape of the large rectangular sail could be altered quite easily, and the whole sail could be raised or lowered. This kind of rigging allowed the ship to run well before the wind, but tacking against it was laborious. The introduction of the triangular lateen sail improved the angle of tacking, allowing more headway to be made, but spare sails of different sizes had to be carried if varying wind strengths were to be coped with effectively. However, lateen sails became standard in the Mediterranean during the early medieval period, and survived into the eighteenth century as a part of more complex rigging.

8. A drawing of a Roman ship was scratched into the plaster of a house in Pompeii, which is now known as the House of the Ship *Europa*. It is a medium sized merchant vessel, and the drawing gives valuable information about the rigging. The details of the shape of the keel and the steering oar, not normally visible when the ship was afloat, show that the drawing was made by someone well acquainted with ships; it is therefore more reliable than most artistic representations which appear on carvings or mosaics. (Maiuri 1958)

In the early fifteenth century AD, three-masted ships carrying much greater amounts of sail were developed; multiple square sails on the first two masts provided power, and a lateen sail on the rear mast increased manoeuvrability (McGowan 1981, 10–17). The growth of three-masters coincided with the systematic use of the skeleton-first approach to hull construction. In the seventeenth century, schooner rig was introduced, which allowed very large sails to be aligned 'fore and aft' along the ship in the manner of lateen sails or those of a modern yacht. Such rigging greatly reduced the number of times a vessel would need to tack against the wind, and allowed much better use to be made of side and head winds, as well as reducing the size of crew required. Some of the last great merchant sailing ships of the later nineteenth and early twentieth centuries bore schooner rig on up to seven masts (Greenhill 1980, 38–9). Others maintained a dominance of square rigging, which was essentially a multiplication of the rectangular sails of antiquity, combined with fore-and-aft sails between the main masts (ibid. 40, 54–5).

Greek and Roman ships were steered by means of long oars hung alongside the stern, either singly or in pairs (figs. 5, 8); not until the late medieval period were rudders regularly fixed to a vertical stern post (e.g. McGrail 1981, 39, pl. 23). This change was not of great significance, for experimental work with steering oars has demonstrated that they are in no way inferior to rudders. Navigation was primitive, and good visibility essential, to the extent that the sailing season for open sea voyages lasted at the most from mid-March to mid-November. Charts took the form of lists of ports, rivers and promontories and distances between them, reflecting the predominance of coastal travel, but maps could be drawn from co-ordinates of latitude and longitude in the modern manner; the *Geography* of Ptolemy (second century AD) contains a discussion of the problems of projecting the spherical shape of the world onto a flat map (Lewis and Reinhold 1966, 309–310).

DURATION OF VOYAGES

Several records of the duration of voyages come down to us from Roman writers, but they should be viewed with caution when found as items of information in works such as Pliny's *Natural History* (19, 3–4; see Casson 1971, 283), for they are likely to represent particularly quick times considered worthy of note rather than averages. The voyages from Ostia to Gibraltar and to Narbonne lasted seven and three days respectively. It took nine days for the grain fleet to sail from Puteoli to Alexandria (1000 nautical miles), to take on a fresh load of Egyptian corn for the city of Rome. However, the return voyage lasted one or two months, because prevailing winds blew towards Egypt, causing the laden ships to beat north towards Cyprus and then west along the coasts of Turkey and Greece (1400 nautical miles). The *Isis* was on this route when it put into Piraeus for shelter, and was seen by Lucian, who recounted a very convincing circumstantial account of the voyage from Alexandria:

> When they left Pharos [the lighthouse at Alexandria], he said, the wind was not very strong, and they sighted Acamas [the western tip of Cyprus] in seven days. Then it blew against them from the west, and they were driven abeam to Sidon [32km (20 miles) north of Beirut]. After Sidon a severe storm broke and carried them through Aulon [literally the channel, meaning the passage between Cyprus and Turkey] to reach the Chelidonenses [Gelidonya, on the north coast of Cyprus] on the tenth day . . . I know the size of the waves there, especially in a sou'westerly gale with a touch of south; this, you see, happens to be where the Pamphylian and Lycian seas divide. The swell is driven by numerous currents and is split on the headland – the rocks are knife-edged, razor-sharp at the sea's edge. So the breakers are terrifying and make a great din, and the wave is often as high as the cliff itself. This is what the captain said they found when it was still night and pitch dark. But the gods were moved by their lamentations, and showed fire from Lycia, so that they knew the place. One of the Dioscuri [a deity who guided mariners] put a bright star on the mast head [St Elmo's Fire, still a sign of good fortune today], and guided the ship in a turn to port into the open sea, just as it was driving onto the cliff. Then, having now lost their course, they sailed across the Aegean beating up with the trade winds against them, and yesterday, seventy days after leaving Egypt, they anchored in Piraeus, after being driven so far downwind. They should have kept Crete to starboard, and sailed beyond Malea so as to be in Italy by now. (*The Ship or the Wishes*; Loeb translation, 439–441)

Underwater archaeology can reveal the wrecks of ships which were less fortunate than the *Isis*, and reconstruct their voyages from distinctive amphorae or other cargoes, but the atmosphere of Roman seaborne commerce can only be gained from literary sources such as this.

Casson has tabulated and analysed this and many other scattered pieces of evidence for the duration of journeys by sea, and has concluded that an average sailing speed in good conditions might be around five knots (8–9 kph: op. cit. 288). However, records of voyage times on major routes obscure the fact that most commercial journeys would have been loosely planned visits to a series of coastal ports, buying and selling on the way (Casson 1971, 337–8). As a comparison, Britain's coastal shipping (consisting primarily of cargoes of coal, corn and raw wool) was only exceeded by overseas shipping in 1906, long after substantial improvements in canals, roads and railways had taken place (Bagwell 1974, 63–4).

Trade with the East

We know nothing about the ships that traded with India and the East, benefiting from the knowledge of the alternating monsoon winds to travel thousands of kilometres across the open ocean, and back again later in the year (Dihle 1978). Strabo's description of the port of Alexandria emphasises the importance of this eastern trade, which was funnelled into the Red Sea:

> The advantages of the city's site are various; for, first, the place is washed by two seas, on the north by the Aegyptian Sea, as it is called (i.e. the Mediterranean), and on the south by Lake Mareia, also called Mareotis. This is filled by many canals from the Nile, both from above and on the sides, and through these canals the imports are much larger than those from the sea, so that the harbour on the lake was in fact richer than that on the sea; and here the exports from Alexandria also are larger than the imports . . . (Strabo, *Geography* 17, 1, 7; Loeb translation, 29–31)

> . . . in fact this is the only place in all Aegypt which is by nature well situated with reference to both things – both to commerce by sea, on account of the good harbours, and to commerce by land, because the river easily conveys and brings together everything into a place so situated – the greatest emporium in the inhabited world. (op. cit. 17, 1, 31; Loeb translation, 53)

The southward aspect of Alexandria is of particular importance in Strabo's description, for it had long been a source of enormous revenues from tolls paid on the luxury imports from the East. During the Roman empire, Alexandria was of importance primarily because it was the point at which the part of the vast requirements of grain was assembled and shipped to feed the population of Rome. The abundance of shipping which was involved in the transport of grain must have provided yet more opportunities for the carriage of small but valuable consignments of eastern luxuries to Italy and thence to the west, and the revenues from tolls probably increased. Trade with India seems to have reached a peak in the early empire (Raschke 1978), but it had already increased by the time that Strabo was writing in the first century BC:

> In earlier times, at least, not so many as twenty vessels would dare to traverse the Arabian Gulf far enough to get a peep outside the straits, but at the present time even large fleets are dispatched as far as India and the extremities of Aethiopia, from which the most valuable cargoes are brought to Aegypt, and thence sent forth again to the other regions; so that double duties are collected, on both imports and exports; and on goods that cost heavily the duty is also heavy. (op. cit. 17, 1, 13; Loeb translation, 53–55)

Indian and perhaps even Chinese ships must have reached the Red Sea (Ferguson 1978, 594–597); underwater archaeology may yet lead to the discovery of wrecks involved in the eastern trade.

PORTS AND HARBOURS

Artificial harbourworks are not essential to small ships, which can be beached and unloaded quickly. Harbours sheltered from storms and waves by moles, with vertical deep water quays, are, however, desirable for large vessels, especially those carrying cargoes which need careful loading, unloading and storage. The Greeks were first to provide large-scale moles and artificial basins, but Roman technology made a great advance with the use of concrete which would set under water. Remains of Roman harbours survive all around the Mediterranean (Lehmann-Hartleben 1923; Shaw 1972; Blackman 1982), but most of them were completed before the imperial period. In the later first century BC, the Roman architect Vitruvius included some information on harbours in his *De Architectura*:

> The masonry which is to be in the sea is to be constructed in this way. Earth is to be brought from the district which runs from Cumae to the promontory of Minerva, and mixed in the mortar, two parts to one of lime. Then in the place marked out, cofferdams, formed of oak piles and tied together with chains, are to be let down into the water and firmly fixed. Next, the lower part between them

under the water is to be levelled and cleared with a platform of small beams laid across and the work is to be carried up with stones and mortar as above described, until the space for the structure between the dams is filled. (op. cit. Book 5 chapter 12, 2–3; Loeb translation, 313)

The method described by Vitruvius employs hydraulic concrete made with *pozzuolana*, a volcanic ash found around the Bay of Naples and elsewhere. In the construction of the harbour of Portus, near Ostia, the emperor Claudius filled a large ship with hydraulic concrete and sank it in the desired position (Casson 1971, 188–9). For visible traces of Roman harbourworks and associated buildings, we must look at sites such as Leptis Magna in Tunisia (Bartoccini 1958) or Portus and Ostia (Meiggs 1960; White 1984, 107). However, although Ostia may be visible and Alexandria well documented (Fraser 1972), they are in their own ways unique, since they were involved in the imperial grain supply; indeed, they were two of the few ports capable of accommodating 'super-freighters' like the *Isis* (above p. 24). Leptis Magna and Carthage were subject to grand imperial rebuildings, in the latter case on the site of pre-Roman naval facilities (Hurst 1979). Typical harbours, like typical ships, were much smaller but more numerous, and have attracted less attention as a result; the potential that archaeology still has to contribute to their study is underlined by the research conducted at Carthage, Cosa or London (Hurst 1979; Brown 1951; Milne 1985).

Leptis Magna remains an excellent source of information on the details of a harbour, its fittings, and associated buildings, of which Bartoccini provided detailed drawings, photographs and reconstructions (1958). The port facilities and their associated warehouses along the Tiber in and around Rome itself have not yet been studied exhaustively; recent work has shown that they extended for at least 2km (1¼ miles) along both banks on a greater scale than hitherto imagined (Castagnoli 1980). In the provinces of the empire, excavations in the City of London have revealed magnificent timber waterfronts and quayside buildings (figs. 9–10), as well as remains of boats, and artefacts which help in the study of trading links. These can be interpreted in the light of literary information from other river-ports such as Lyon in France, where a rich collection of inscriptions has survived, which give

details of traders, shippers and organisations of river boatmen (Grenier 1937, 479–486). The lesson to be learned from the harbours of the Roman empire is that it is necessary to make allowances for the great variety of structures which must have existed, depending on local geographical circumstances, economic prosperity, and the attention of generous patrons (Spaar 1981).

TRANSPORT ON INLAND WATERWAYS

According to the geographer Strabo, writing at the time of Augustus, Gaul was laid out as if by the hand of Providence:

> The whole of this country is well watered by rivers, some of which flow from the Alps, the others from the Cevennes and the Pyrenees. Of these some flow into the ocean, the others into the Mediterranean. For the most part they flow through plains or hilly country with navigable rivers. The courses of the rivers are so excellently disposed in relation to one another that goods can be conveyed through from either sea to the other; for the cargoes must be conveyed over the plains for only a short distance and that without difficulty, while for most of the journey they travel by the rivers, in the one case going up into the interior, in the other going down to the sea. The Rhône is provided with special advantages in this regard; for it has tributaries joining it from many directions, as I have said, and it flows into the Mediterranean which is more advantageous than the Atlantic, and passes through the most fertile land in this part of the world. (*Geography* IV, 1, 2)

It is obvious from this quotation that river transport was seen as an integral part of trade and communications, because it could minimise the cost and effort of conveying a cargo. Independent support for this view is given by the large number of inscriptions from the city of Lugdunum (Lyon) recording guilds of river boatmen. The city is situated at the junction of the rivers Rhône and Sâone, only a short distance from the Loire, and altars and tombstones also testify to the number of traders based in the city (Grenier 1937, 479–486; Bonnard 1913). Lyon was the capital of the three provinces of Gaul, and its political importance is obviously a further reflection of its geographical location (Drinkwater 1975). River traffic was sometimes organised by the Roman army; on the Tyne, supplies for Hadrian's Wall must have been unloaded from ships onto river boats at the mouth of the river. The fort at South Shields was almost

9. Reconstruction model of the riverside wharves and warehouses whose remains have been uncovered in rescue excavations beside the Thames at Billingsgate, London. The prosperity of the port seems to have been shortlived, from the first to third centuries AD. A small merchant ship of Mediterranean type is also included (compare fig. 8), attended by a log boat. (Photograph by courtesy of Museum of London, Department of Urban Archaeology)

filled with granaries at one period when military campaigns were in progress in Scotland, and an inscription from the site records an army unit of *barcariorum* (bargemen), originally recruited from the river Tigris. They fulfilled the same rôle as the notorious keelmen of later centuries, who were only displaced when the river was channelled for large ships in the nineteenth century.

River boats

Riverine trade was already under active consideration by archaeologists more than 50 years ago, thanks to the plentiful inscriptions and pictorial evidence that has survived in Germany and France (Aubin 1925; Bonnard 1913). Our knowledge of Roman river boats has been advanced by the finding of several vessels in the silts of the old course of the Rhine near the fort of Zwammerdam in the Netherlands and at Mainz on the middle Rhine (fig. 11; Weerd 1978; Rupprecht 1984). These craft demonstrate how effectively river boats could be constructed for a wide range of purposes by developing the simple concept of the hollowed log, and expanding it in length and breadth to produce anything from a small fishing boat to a large cargo vessel. The shallow draught of the log-derived boats from Zwammerdam made them capable of travelling

10. The massive timbers from which the Billingsgate waterfront was constructed have survived in waterlogged ground conditions; the adjacent buildings were found to have been destroyed in a fire. (Photograph by courtesy of Museum of London, Department of Urban Archaeology)

11a and b. Roman river boats from the Rhine. Fig. 11a shows the elegant lines of a fourth-century craft excavated in advance of the building of the Hilton Hotel in Mainz, Germany; the light covering of snow emphasises the framework of the vessel. Fig. 11b is a view of the interior of a very different boat excavated at Zwammerdam in the Netherlands, also featured on the cover. It is a wide, flat-bottomed barge with near-vertical sides; clearly visible are the heads of the large nails which fix the cross timbers to the longitudinal planking of the bottom of the vessel. (Photographs by courtesy of Dr G. Rupprecht, Dr M. de Weerd)

far inland on shallow waterways, whilst their squared-off bows and sterns permitted passengers and/or goods to be landed on naturally sloping river-banks. The majority of the Mainz vessels had a rounder cross-section, more suited to open water and quays.

Ellmers has used the evidence of Roman carvings and other representations of river boats, together with knowledge of medieval and more recent practices, to demonstrate that these vessels could be sailed, rowed, punted, towed, or simply allowed to drift downstream with a current (1978, 10–11). The effect must have been similar to that of a medieval craft, the *Oberländer*, a model of which was illustrated by Aubin in 1925 (6 Abb 5).

CANALS

In recent centuries, canals have been constructed to link the major rivers of France and Germany, underlining the continuing desire to send cargo by water rather than road; indeed, a 'Canal Age' preceded the 'Railway Age' in Britain and elsewhere. In Roman times only the state could afford to build canals, and they were usually constructed primarily for strategic reasons (Smith 1977–1978). The *fossa corbulonis*, which joined the Rhine to the Meuse and avoided a sea journey between the mouths of the two rivers, is a good example of official canal building; although its 37km (23 miles) construction was primarily strategic in concept, it would also have offered advantages to traders. Canals affect the drainage patterns of rivers and lakes, as was realised at the time, and whether the primary purpose of the Car Dyke in Britain was for land-drainage or transport, or a mutually advantageous combination of both, has been the subect of debate (Simmons 1979; Salway 1981, 564).

There is no clear evidence to show whether any Roman canals involved locks; on the whole, canals simply extended or modified existing river routes (Singer 1956, 678–680), and pound-locks with sets of gates are not known to have appeared in European canal systems before the thirteenth century AD. The technology necessary to construct lock-gates and sluices certainly existed in the form of the dry docks used in Roman shipyards, but the literary sources which refer to canal building projects do not specifically mention them (White 1984, 112). Sluice gates were certainly used in association with dams in the wadis of Libya (Vita-Finzi 1961, pl. 2b), and in a rock-cut

channel connected with the republican harbour works at Cosa in Italy (Brown 1951, 95–7).

Selkirk has pointed out the problems of using the steep Roman roads of northern Britain for road transport, and has drawn attention to several Roman sites where a system of dams and by-pass canals with lock gates may have existed (1983). Excavation of some of these may clarify this question, together with more research into sea-level changes affecting river valley topography, and better knowledge of regional forms of river boats. Discussions of river versus road transport tend to underestimate the likely use of mules and human porters rather than waggons on steep inclines; however, the effectiveness of small waterways is not fully appreciated. Eckoldt has discussed the means by which small waterways can be utilised by the judicious use of locks and dams, or equally through simple channelling and dredging of their beds (1980; 1984).

One important aspect of canals in recent centuries was that, in addition to facilitating long-distance transport of heavy goods, they brought larger numbers of purchasers and producers into contact. Dyos and Aldcroft consider this to have been their most important function in Britain's Industrial Revolution, and they have published comparative maps demonstrating that canal building brought extensive areas of Britain into easy reach of water transport between AD 1700 and 1790 (1971, 84). Britain's spate of canal building in the eighteenth and nineteenth centuries, although soon overshadowed by the railways, was motivated by the needs of growing industries for fuel and raw materials, but the canals also facilitated the distribution of industrial products. Such far-reaching effects of canals are very instructive, and must be taken into account when comparisons are made between modern European internal trade and that of the Roman period.

One of the letters written to the emperor Trajan by the younger Pliny, during his period as governor of the province of Bythinia in modern Turkey in AD 112–13, underlines the Roman consciousness of the advantages of artificial waterways, and the appreciation of the significance of transport costs in the Roman empire:

Pliny to the emperor Trajan:

> In consideration of your noble ambition which matches your supreme position, I think I should bring to your notice any projects which are worthy

of your immortal name and glory and are likely to combine utility with magnificence. There is a sizeable lake not far from Nicomedia, across which marble, farm produce, wood, and timber for building are easily and cheaply brought by boat as far as the main road; after which everything has to be taken on to the sea by cart, with great difficulty and increased expense. To connect the lake with the sea would require a great deal of labour, but there is no lack of it. There are plenty of people in the countryside, and many more in the town, and it seems certain that they will all gladly help with a scheme which will benefit them all . . .

Trajan to Pliny:

I may perhaps be tempted to think of connecting this lake of yours with the sea, but there must first be an accurate survey to find how much water the lake contains and from what source it is filled, or else it might be completely drained once it is given an outlet to the sea. You can apply to Calpurnius Macer for an engineer, and I will send you out someone who has experience of this sort of work. (*Letters*; Loeb translation, 217–21)

Pliny died during his term of office in Bythinia, and there is no evidence of his scheme ever having been put into effect. It should be noted that Pliny's rationale was not entirely commercial; the extent to which Trajan would enjoy reflected glory from this project obviously weighed heavily.

TRANSPORT ON LAND

Roman roads

The Causeways and Roads, or Streetways of the *Romans*, were perfect solid Buildings, the Foundations were laid so deep, and the Materials so good, however far they were oblig'd to fetch them, that if they had been vaulted and arch'd, they could not have been more solid: I have seen the Bottom of them dug up in several Places, where I have observ'd Flint-stones, Chalk-stones, hard Gravel, solid hard Clay, and several other Sorts of Earth, laid in Layers, like the Veins of Oar in a Mine; a Laying of Clay of a solid binding Quality, then Flint-stones, then Chalk, then upon the Chalk rough Ballast or Gravel 'till the whole Work has been rais'd six or eight Foot from the Bottom; then it has been cover'd with a Crown or rising Ridge in the Middle, gently sloping to the Sides, that the Rain might run off every Way, and not soak into the Work: This I have seen as fair and firm, after having stood, as we may conclude, at least 12 or 1600 Years, as if it had been made but the years before.' (Defoe 1724–6, 520–1)

Despite the elder Pliny's opinion that roads had the undesirable effect of introducing vice, the Roman empire is particularly famous for its network of high-quality metalled roads, many of which are perpetuated by the routes of major highways to this day. The building of new turnpike roads was in its early stages in England when Daniel Defoe travelled in the early eighteenth century, but his enthusiasm for the improvements which were beginning to have an effect can be appreciated in the light of the fact that the new properly metalled roads increased the speed of travel two or threefold (Bagwell 1974, 41–3).

Roman roads varied considerably in their quality and size, depending on their strategic and economic importance. Following the writings of Siculus Flaccus (a surveyor in the first century AD), Chevallier has outlined a simple classification which underlines this variability (1976, 65–6):

1 Public and military roads, built by the state.

2 Local roads, financed regionally by town councils.

3 Minor roads, built by landowners for private use.

The first category was usually constructed by armies consolidating advances into newly conquered territory, and was maintained to ensure that large-scale troop movements and the official post system could travel quickly and effectively from the frontiers to the administrative centres of the empire. Such roads are often distinct on maps, radiating out from important cities or stretching along frontiers. The eight great roads which connected Rome to Latin settlements in the fourth and third centuries BC are an early example (Cornell and Matthews 1982, 39), whilst Augsburg demonstrates the same phenomenon north of the Alps (ibid. 140). Augsburg was initially important in the military occupation of the territory between the Alps and the Danube in the first century AD, and then became the civilian capital of the province of Raetia, and sat astride important roads which led over the Alps from Italy to the Danube frontier, as well as a major east-west route from Austria to France.

Chevallier's simple classification of roads makes an interesting comparison with that used in fieldwork in Turkey; French has developed a far more pragmatic but extensive range of categories into which surviving traces can be placed, from roads proper to simple 'courses' (1980, 703). These have been studied in detail, and 'models' of the development of road networks have been proposed by French, with the partial assistance of dated milestones. Several thousand Roman milestones survive from all around the empire; they are usually cylindrical, and frequently bear the names of the reigning emperors (Chevallier 1976, 39–47). They were often inscribed at the time of construction, or more often on the occasion of repairs, and underline the importance of road maintenance. Their elaborate inscriptions also make it clear that road repairs were something with which the government was keen to be associated in the popular mind. Military units, provincial and local government officials, and indeed private benefactors are commemorated on milestones, in addition to emperors (Lewis and Reinhold 1966, 153–5; Chevallier op. cit. 42–5).

Maps were available which would facilitate the planning of long journeys along major roads; like sailing charts (above p. 28), they aimed not at cartographical accuracy, but at providing an idea of the distances between settlements on highways. A medieval copy of a map of this kind, known as the *Peutinger Table* (lavishly illustrated and annotated in Cunliffe 1978, 216–225) shows a stylised layout of the empire, with rivers, seas, and names of areas; place-names appear at regular intervals along roads, which are drawn with a kink to indicate the end of a measured stage. A long series of lists of places and distances without a map also exists, known as the *Antonine Itinerary* (ibid. 34–37). Such maps and lists must have existed in all administrative and military centres, and would have been important in running the imperial post system, and in organising levies of agricultural produce as taxation. They are a land-traveller's parallel to the maps of Ptolemy or the *Periplus* of the Red Sea trade routes. A more specialised late Roman document known as the *Notitia Dignitatum* lists military units and their garrison posts throughout the empire; like the Peutinger Table, it survives only as a medieval copy. These and other documents (e.g. Chevallier 1976, 47–64), combined with inscriptions such as milestones, and literary accounts of journeys mentioning place-names and distances, have long been used by archaeologists as a key to the identification of Roman settlements.

Road construction

The poet Statius described the building of the *via Domitiana* in the later first century AD:

The first task here is to trace furrows, ripping up the maze of paths, and then excavate a trench in the ground. The second comprises refilling the trench with other material to make a foundation for the road build-up. The ground must not give way nor must bedrock or base be at all unreliable when the paving stones are trodden. Next the road metalling is held in place on both sides by kerbing and numerous wedges. How numerous the squads working together! Some are cutting down woodland and clearing the higher ground, others are using tools to smooth outcrops of rock and plane great beams. There are those binding stones and consolidating the material with burnt lime and volcanic tufa. Others again are working hard to dry up hollows that keep filling with water or are diverting the smaller streams. (*Silvae* IV, 40–55, quoted in Chevallier 1976, 83)

Details of construction vary throughout the empire, according to local climatic and geological conditions, the importance of the road, and the intensity of its traffic. Once again, Chevallier has made a convenient collection of evidence from a range of archaeological and literary sources (op. cit. 86–95). Road building also involved the cutting of inclines through hilly country, and the construction of bridges (ibid. 93–106). The majority of bridges were wholly or partly constructed in timber, but many stone bridges survived in use into recent centuries and provided models for later architects and engineers. It seems likely that the Romans gained much of their knowledge of road construction from the Etruscans in central Italy, for Etruscan roads and drainage schemes already involved cuttings, tunnels and bridges. Potter excavated a road near Narce in Etruria (fig. 12), where stone paving was superimposed in Roman times on the course of a deeply rutted Etruscan road (1979, 107–8 and pl. 8a). There can be no doubt that the construction of major roads was extremely expensive; Pekary has concluded that their relative cost rivalled that of modern roads (1968, 93–97, 167).

ROMAN VEHICLES

Like ships and river boats, wheeled vehicles must have varied considerably in the Roman empire, and many traditional local types will have remained largely unchanged. Furthermore, as in boat-building, there are only a few basic ways of constructing a serviceable cart. Two and four wheeled vehicles appear in the archaeological record by 3500 BC, and the progression from solid to spoked wheels had been made by 2500 BC. Roman technology did not have any supremacy in this field; the Celts were skilled constructors of carts and chariots, as Julius Caesar discovered during his campaigns in Gaul and Britain.

Evidence

Our knowledge of vehicles is derived almost exclusively from carvings and literary references; Roman evidence indicates a range of vehicles from slow solid-wheeled carts drawn by oxen through to light horse-drawn passenger vehicles (literary evidence – Chevallier 1976, 178–81; Leighton 1972, 70–81; carvings – Vigneron 1968, pls. 57, 59–65, 67, 69). Carvings cannot indicate the full range, of course, and may not be accurate in portraying details of structure and harnessing, any more than the average carving of a ship can be expected to have been executed by an artist

who understood rigging. Art is subject to conventions and distortion, particularly on gravestones or memorials; Gabelmann has shown that everyday scenes involving transport became standardised (1983, 145), and therefore cannot necessarily be taken as an accurate reflection of practices in the locality in which such carvings are found. Because horses were expensive and prestigious, they may be shown on gravestones in circumstances where they were not used in real life, in order to imply a higher status for the deceased (Raepsaet 1982, 216).

The study of carvings is complicated by the uneven quality of their publication. Molin's study of a cart carrying a huge barrel, from Langres in France, includes a series of photographs of the same carving with different directional lighting, which enables fine details such as a braking system to be distinguished (1984). Literary evidence adds little to our understanding of technical details, although a late Roman legal document, the *Theodosian Code*, lists a number of different vehicles by name, specifying their legal carrying capacity for goods and passengers (Sin-

12. Early Roman stone paving on a road near Narce, in Etruria, Italy. The hard surface has clearly been placed on top of a layer of make-up to turn the deeply-rutted Etruscan track into a weatherproof road. (Photograph by courtesy of Dr T. Potter)

ger 1956, 514, 539–40; Künow 1980, 19). Insights into the atmosphere of road travel are common in literature, however, and it was clearly not a pleasant experience. Official regulations for the supply of requisitioned transport to soldiers and officials are also interesting. An inscription found in Turkey includes details of the forms available in an area with difficult terrain, and gives an idea of their relative cost, thanks to the unfortunate necessity of controlling abuses of the system (Mitchell 1976).

Construction

It is generally held that Roman vehicle design was unsophisticated; suspension was non-existent, and the idea of mounting the front axle on a pivot to allow easier turning was either unknown or exceedingly rare (Landels, 1978, 180). However, Röring has carried out important research as a background to the reconstruction of a Roman cart for the Rheinisches Landesmuseum, Köln (fig. 13; Röring 1983). He has drawn attention to the large number of passenger carts which were buried in graves in Bulgaria (Thracia), following an ancient burial custom. The iron and bronze fittings demonstrate that out of 41 remains of vehicles, 25 did in fact have suspension; even more important, many had separate front axles which pivoted on a massive iron spike (ibid. 81–83; Venedikov 1960, pls. 76–7). The rarity of these features in carvings results from uninformative side-views carved by stone-masons with little interest in technical details; it underlines the present and future contribution of archaeology to the elucidation of such problems.

In Britain, coaches did not begin to replace open wains for the carriage of goods or passengers until the seventeenth century AD; their method of suspension, by which the coach body was hung from leather straps, resembled that of Roman passenger vehicles (Röring 1983). Coaches suspended in this way had a high centre of gravity which was dangerous at speed; in 1804, horizontal elliptical springs were introduced which immediately doubled the carrying capacity of coaches. In rural districts, open carts without suspension remained in everyday use well into the twentieth century. Regional variations abound, and show a high level of competence in carpentry. Undoubtedly, the typical Roman farm cart showed similar variation, and was as skilfully and effectively made as the log boats and barges which plied the

13. Full-size reconstruction of a passenger cart, based on metal fittings found in a burial at Wardartal, Germany (Röring 1983). Goods vehicles would have been less elaborate, but this cart illustrates the quality of carpentry and metalworking available, as well as technical details such as suspension and a pivoted front axle. The vehicle should be compared with the carving of an ox-cart shown in the frontispiece, from which all details of harnessing and structure were omitted by the mason. Close scrutiny of archaeological discoveries is the only way in which our understanding of these crucial technical features is likely to improve. (Photograph by courtesy of Römisch-Germanisches Museum, Cologne)

inland waterways. It is sad that the lack of well-preserved finds from waterlogged deposits denies us more detailed knowledge of this important aspect of Roman land transport; the survival of complete wooden wheels in pits at the Roman fort at Newstead in southern Scotland gives hope that further discoveries may yet be made (Curle 1911, 292–293, pl. 69).

Traction and harnessing

Roman harnessing methods for horses have been strongly criticised by historians of transport since misleading experiments were publicised by Lefebvre des Noëttes (1931). In essence, it was argued that horses pulled against a neck collar which was poorly adapted from ox harnesses, and which so badly constricted their blood vessels and breathing, that only 25 per cent of their potential power was used (Landels 1978, 175, fig. 57). This inefficiency is contrasted with the effectiveness of using a padded collar, which became common by AD 1200, and allowed the horse to take the weight of the cart upon its chest. However, recent experimental work on ancient harnessing methods, using replicas of the kinds of harnesses known from carvings, has demonstrated that this idea is incorrect, and that perfectly good traction could be obtained (Spruytte 1983, 101–107; Raepsaet 1979). Indeed, the evidence of a carving from Langres, which is unusually detailed, shows mules with an effective traction point on their chests rather than their necks (Molin 1984, 114). Molin argues that the lack of sophisticated harnessing indicates a lack of a demand for really heavy haulage, rather than poor technical understanding.

An important adjunct to harnessing which is also normally assigned to the medieval period is the use of shafts or traces attached to the sides of an animal. However, examples do occur in Roman carvings; their use may have been more widespread than carvings suggest, for we have already seen that these reliefs do not present a reliable view of vehicle suspension or steering. Raepsaet has noted evidence for the evolution of technical improvements in horse yoking and harnessing during the Roman period in northern Gaul, an area with plentiful carvings (1982); what unknown developments may have existed in other areas (such as Britain or Spain) where neither literary nor pictorial evidence exists?

In fact, the general reliance upon oxen rather than horses for pulling very heavy loads made the development of better horse harnessing unnecessary. Horses were expensive, and used primarily for riding or the draught of light, fast vehicles. Oxen could be yoked together, or use a simple neck collar; they could be fed on fodder during journeys far more efficiently than horses (Landels 1978, 177–8), and their hooves, which splay naturally, were less likely to get bogged down in soft ground (Bagwell 1974, 35). For abnormal loads such as large columns or blocks of stone from quarries, enormous teams of oxen were harnessed together (Burford 1960–1). Mules were also important both for pulling vehicles and as pack animals; they are tougher and more tolerant than horses, require little sleep, and can easily manage 80km (49$\frac{3}{4}$ miles) in a day (Landels 1978, 172).

Pack animals

In 1935, Sion published a perceptive criticism of Lefebvre des Noëttes' analysis of Roman harnessing, and rightly pointed out the differences in terrain between northern Europe and the Mediterranean lands; the latter lacks both the level roads and plentiful grazing required for large cart horses, but favours pack animals. White has recently re-emphasised the importance of animals as beasts of burden rather than traction in the Roman empire and more recent times (1984, 128–129). During the First World War, mules were considered suitable for carrying loads of 200 pounds – although loads had to be divisible to fit into the panniers, of course (Landels 1978, 171–3). In the difficult terrain of areas such as central Italy or Greece, they were superior to ox-carts, for a string of 20 mules could carry as much as five wagon loads. Donkeys were also common in the Roman world, and were often bought in order to carry a load, and then sold along with the load at their destination.

THE COST OF TRANSPORT

Sometime around 200 BC, Cato summed up the cost and complexity of carrying large, heavy loads overland in an unusually precise manner:

> A mill is bought near Suessa for 400 sesterces and fifty pounds of oil. The cost of assembling is 60 sesterces, and the charge for transportation by oxen, with six day's wages of six men, drivers included, is 72 sesterces. . . . At Pompeii one is bought complete for 384 sesterces, freight 280 sesterces. (*On Agriculture* XXII 3; Loeb translation, 41)

Cato was giving a countryman's advice to his fellow farmers in Italy. Pompeii was 120km (75 miles) away from his estate, Suessa only 40 (25 miles), but transport can be seen to add substantially to the cost of his new mill. Much of the Roman evidence for carriage costs is similarly anecdotal, but modern analogies help to elucidate the relative importance of various means of transport. Detailed figures are available for transport costs in eighteenth-century England, and they can be used as a yardstick for checking the few diverse figures which do survive from the Roman period. Duncan-Jones (1974, 366–9) has converted these prices into ratios to allow direct comparison:

eighteenth-century England:
> sea: river: land – 1: 4.7: 22.6

Roman empire:
> sea: river: land – 1: 4.9: 28

Despite the diverse sources from which the Roman figures are drawn, there is such close correspondence that the order of magnitude is likely to be correct. An independent set of calculations has been made by Künow, incorporating unmade roads and strong river currents, in an estimate of the costs of trade with German tribes beyond the Rhine frontier (1980, 21–23). His ratios are:

> sea: river: land – 1: 5.9: 62.5

The discrepancy between land and sea is increased to such an extent that he proposes that goods were likely to have been taken by water from the Rhine around Denmark to the Baltic coast of north Germany, rather than eastwards overland beyond the Rhine. In doing so, Künow has destroyed the basis of a recent analysis of these goods by Hedeager (1977), which concluded that the great density of finds around the Baltic reflected special local circumstances related to social structures. It seems that a far simpler explanation is possible; Roman trade goods are common there because that is where merchants landed.

It is obvious from the detailed information available from the eighteenth century AD that even the most optimistic estimate of the cost of Roman land transport is likely to fall way behind the advantages of the sea or navigable rivers (fig. 14). Like Roman figures for the time taken by sea journeys (above p. 28), the cost ratios of road to river and sea transport which Duncan-Jones has derived from ancient sources may well be the best that could be hoped for rather than what was normally achieved. Because the cost of transporting goods on land was well over 20 times that of those carried by sea, it is obvious that no low-value bulky cargoes could have been traded profitably overland for any significant distances. Similarly, river journeys were nearly five times

less expensive than road transport; we should, therefore, not be surprised either by the enthusiastic account of the geography of Gaul given by Strabo (above p. 30), or by the practical and effective design of Roman sea-going ships or river craft. However, land transport in the less mountainous parts of the empire may have been substantially cheaper than the ancient figures imply.

THE TRANSPORT REVOLUTION

Roman roads must often have been congested with slow local traffic, and the need for maintenance will have been continuous. Their structure, consisting of layers of different materials on solid foundations, cambered and drained, and paved or metalled with cobbles or gravel, certainly allowed effective maintenance as long as the basic foundations remained intact and dry. The existence of a powerful central government, combined with local civic responsibilities, probably avoided some of the ludicrously uneven conditions of eighteenth-century English roads, where routes of major national importance could change from well-made turnpike roads to quagmires (Bagwell 1974, 35–8).

In a way, the development of the railways resulted from the poor quality of roads, for timber waggonways were laid down as early as the sixteenth century in order to provide a firm surface along which heavy carts could be pulled in all weather conditions. Increased demand for coal and other raw materials led to their expansion,

14a and b. The map shows a number of possible routes by which cargos could have been conveyed from the west Mediterranean to Britain. The graph (fig.14b) illustrates the effects of the different routes and means of transport on costs. The cost-index was compiled by Peacock (1978) according to the ratios derived from prices for sea, river and land transport recorded in Roman documents. In Roman times, the number of trading points along a particular route may have been an important factor, as well as its cost. Thus, although the longest route via Gibraltar is in theory the cheapest (about half of the cost of the shortest, via the Seine), the most expensive route via the Mosel and Rhine would make contact with the greatest number of major cities and military fortresses. The samian pottery production centres indicated on fig. 14b are discussed in Chapter 6; these routes undoubtedly influenced their location. (Audio-Visual Centre, University of Newcastle)

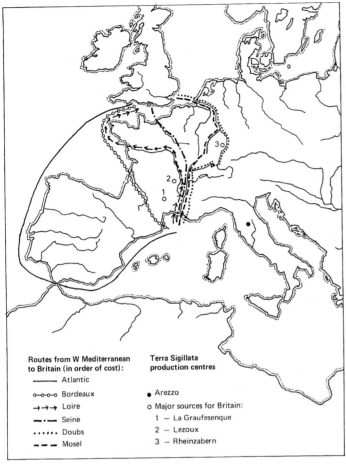

Routes from W Mediterranean
to Britain (in order of cost):

——— Atlantic

o–o–o Bordeaux

→→→ Loire

—·— Seine

••••• Doubs

– – – Mosel

Terra Sigillata
production centres

● Arezzo

o Major sources for Britain:

1 — La Graufesenque

2 — Lezoux

3 — Rheinzabern

TRANSPORT FROM THE WESTERN MEDITERRANEAN TO BRITAIN

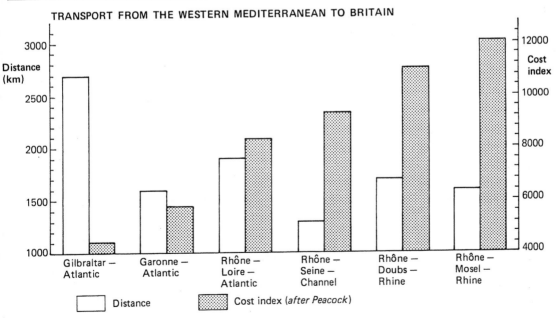

☐ Distance   ▨ Cost index (after Peacock)

and in some cases the wooden rails were strengthened with iron flanges to reduce wear and to guide the horse-drawn carts. The provision of solid iron rails and steam power simply completed a long series of developments, none of which actually involved technology beyond the reach of the Romans. Indeed, when in 1725 Ralph Wood decided to bridge a rocky gorge near Tanfield in County Durham with a stone arch to carry a waggonway from the Durham coalfields to the Tyne, he could find no contemporary experience to draw upon. He was forced to imitate Roman bridge design to construct the Causey Arch, a dramatic stone bridge with a single span of 30.48m (100ft) and a deck height of 24.38m (80ft), now safely preserved as the oldest surviving purpose-built 'railway' bridge in the world.

Most of the price difference between land and water transport can be explained by the factors of speed and labour; in 1776, Adam Smith expressed the advantages of coastal shipping in relation to the cost and effort of land transport in his *Wealth of Nations*:

> Six or eight men, therefore, by help of water-carriage, can carry and bring back in the same time the same quantity of goods between London and Edinburgh, as fifty broad-wheeled wagons, attended by a hundred men, and drawn by four hundred horses.

He added the further fact that the men and horses would also require maintenance, and that the horses and wagons would suffer considerable wear and tear (op. cit. I iii; Campbell and Skinner 1976, 32–3).

The following figures, which indicate the maximum weights that could be carried in the eighteenth century by various means other than by sea, emphasise the improvements associated with the Industrial Revolution (Bagwell 1974, 13):

- packhorse (on bridlepath): 2–3 cwt
- team of horses pulling heavy wagon on soft road: 1 ton
- team of horses pulling heavy wagon on hard road: 2 tons
- single horse pulling waggon on iron-railed coalfield waggonway: 8 tons
- single horse towing barge on river: 30 tons
- single horse towing barge on canal: 50 tons

In the following century George Stephenson's colliery locomotive, working at Killingworth in Northumberland in 1824, demonstrated that the improvement in the exploitation of the horse was far outstripped by the effectiveness of steam power, for it was capable of pulling fourteen 3-ton wagons. In fact, it was the building of railways which undermined coastal shipping for the first time, and led directly to the development of steam-powered iron-hulled cargo ships, which could compete with trains thanks to their ability to sail on reliable schedules in all but the very worst weather.

CONCLUSIONS

For the first and last times in its history, the whole circumference of the Mediterranean coast formed part of a single political system during the Roman empire. The hinterland, particularly on the north side of the empire, was accessible by road, river or a combination of the two, whilst Britain and the coasts of Gaul and Spain were open to the Atlantic. Ships and boats of a variety of sizes and specialised designs operated on the sea, along the coasts, and on the rivers, whilst carts or pack animals travelled along an extensive network of official and private roads. These means of transport were of a quality which at the least equalled, and in most cases exceeded, that of their medieval counterparts. Indeed, many of their features would not be matched again until the eighteenth century AD, when transport costs are known to have been generally similar.

The achievements of Roman imperial administration and defence demand the availability of an effective and flexible transport system; I feel that its existence is amply confirmed by archaeological discoveries. On one hand, some of the supposed deficiencies of land and sea travel have been shown to be illusory. On the other, its success is reflected by the distribution of traded goods, such as pottery, over wide areas to many levels of society, a phenomenon for which archaeology is the principal source of evidence (Chapter 6). The extent of rural settlement also implies active and effective local transport systems, by which agricultural products could be converted into the cash necessary for the purchase of goods or the commissioning of elaborately decorated buildings. Raepsaet has suggested that the vitality of the north Gaulish villas permitted efficient use of horses, and actually led to technical improvements in methods of traction. A view centred upon the Mediterranean may well underestimate the possibilities for transport in the less hilly fertile areas of Britain and Gaul; according to Sion (1935, 683), their climate, rivers and iron resources favoured the expansion of technology in later centuries, when they themselves had become centres of political power.

The transport systems of the empire worked best in the first two centuries AD, before internal and external insecurity, combined with financial instability and political restrictions, reduced the possibilities for long-distance trade. The peak in the number of Roman shipwrecks in the Mediterranean occurs in the first century AD, and declines rapidly from the third to the fifth (Parker 1984, 110, fig. 4). However, the literary evidence for the supply of grain to Rome in the fourth century AD still demonstrates the sophistication that a centralised state could bring to transport (Tengström 1974); the *cursus clabularium* in North Africa possessed scores of carts and oxen. The rôle of official shipping of bulky goods such as marble or grain should not be allowed to detract from the significance of independent trade, for the very existence of such channels of communication would have helped to support private transport and trade. Indeed, although such shipping was officially directed, it was actually carried out by private contractors (Casson 1980; Rickman 1980) who were able to combine these operations with their own, as the shippers' offices in Ostia show (Frank 1937). Literary evidence appears to show, however, that the shipping of the state's grain and oil became burdensome rather than profitable in the course of the second century AD (D'Escurac 1976, 204).

It has long been recognised that transport costs could cause a radical restructuring of agriculture. Yeo used recently excavated fragments of Diocletian's *Edict* to make the point that grain arriving in Rome from Egypt and Africa would have undercut cereals grown in Italy itself, if they had to be transported by road (1946, 241–242). This, he believed, caused a redirection of agricultural efforts into intensive wine and oil production or cattle raising. However, Yeo did not explore the possibility that the wealth and dense population of the countryside, which has been revealed by surveys since he wrote, might provide sufficient motivation for specialisation in cash-crops.

A comprehensive and effective infrastructure of transport and communications is an essential precondition for any revision of the negative assessments of Roman economic activity which have prevailed in recent years. The wealth of archaeological information for high levels of trade, agriculture, settlement and monetisation must now be taken seriously, and I believe that the archaeological contribution to the study of transport fulfils this precondition in a very satisfactory manner.

FURTHER READING

Geography is an essential component in understanding the history of the empire and its development, as well as its transport systems; the excellent *Atlas of the Roman world* compiled by Cornell and Matthews (1982) is a good starting point. Many of the ancient sources were incorporated into Charlesworth's pioneering *Trade routes and commerce of the Roman empire* (1926), and more recently into Casson's *Travel in the ancient world* (1974); the source-books of ancient texts cited at the end of Chapter 1 should also be examined. Contacts outside the empire were also important to the economy; see, for example, Warmington's *The commerce between the Roman empire and India* (1974), and Glodariu's *Dacian trade with the Hellenistic and Roman world* (1976). Shipping and transport costs in general have been discussed in two articles by Hopkins; 'Models, ships and staples' is included in the stimulating collection of papers edited by Garnsey *et al.* (1983), whilst 'The transport of staples' is rather inaccessibly located in the papers of the *Eighth international economic history congress*, Budapest 1982. The latter includes detailed lists of figures from Diocletian's *Edict on maximum prices*.

Maritime activity of pre-Roman and Roman date in the Mediterranean and neighbouring regions is examined in great detail in Casson's *Ships and seamanship in the ancient world*, and more readably in Rougé's *Ships and fleets of the ancient Mediterranean* (1981). The impact of underwater archaeology is clear from a lavishly illustrated collection of studies edited by Bass in 1972, *A history of seafaring based on underwater archaeology*, or from a lively periodical, the *International journal of nautical archaeology*. The French magazine *Les dossiers de l'archéologie* devoted an issue to this subject in July/August 1978 (no. 29). The most comprehensive guide to ship and boat construction is Greenhill's *The archaeology of the boat* (1976), whilst a very concise account can be found in the National Maritime Museum's series, *The ship: Rafts, boats and ships from prehistoric times to the medieval era* (McGrail 1981). In the same series is Morrison's *Long ships and round ships* (1980), which deals with the Graeco-Roman period. The problems of the bewildering variety of water craft have been placed on a new theoretical basis by McGrail's article 'Towards a classification of water transport' in *World Archaeology* 16.3 (1985) 289–303.

Lehmann-Hartleben's *Die antiken Hafenanlagen des Mittelmeeres* (1923) remains important for the study of ports and harbours, and Blackman has recently produced an up-to-date survey, 'Ancient harbours in the Mediterranean' (1982). Meigg's *Roman Ostia* remains a significant and comprehensive study of an individual port, its city and relations with Rome, whilst Bartoccini's *La porta romana de Leptis Magna* (1958) is full of technical information about harbour construction.

The study of land transport is well served by Chevallier's *Roman roads* (1976); excellent illustrations of roads and their associated engineering works and architecture can be found in *The Roman road in Italy* by Sterpos (1970), or in *Les dossiers de l'archéologie* 67 (October 1982). Many Roman vehicles featured in carvings are included in the latter, and in Vigneron's *Le cheval dans l'antiquité* (1968). A thorough examination of the origins and development of vehicles up to the Roman period has been published by Piggott: *The earliest wheeled transport* (1983).

The many and varied traders who used the trade routes of the empire are typified by those known from inscriptions in Europe, which have been studied and discussed in *Die Händler im römischen Kaiserreich* by Schlippschuh (1974), whilst a wider historical and geographical background is included in Rougé's *Recherches sur l'organisation du commerce maritime en Méditerranée* (1964).

The history of transport systems since the Roman period is well documented. Medieval maritime trade is featured in Unger's *The ship in the medieval economy* (1980), and land transport figures prominently in Leighton's *Transport and communication in early medieval Europe* (1972), which extends its cover back into the Roman period. Traders of the sixteenth and seventeenth centuries are considered in Ball's *Merchants amd merchandise* (1977), and in a wider context in Braudels *The wheels of commerce* (1982). The period of the Industrial Revolution is included in a vast number of books; *The transport revolution from 1770* by Bagwell (1974) is a clear account, and the emotive subject of the victory of steam over sail is discussed in a further excellent volume of *The ship: The life and death of the merchant sailing ship 1815–1965* by Greenhill (1980).

THREE

Coinage and money in the Roman empire

When the division of labour has been once thoroughly established, it is but a very small part of a man's wants which the produce of his own labour can supply. He supplies the far greater part of them by exchanging that surplus part of the produce of his own labour, which is over and above his own consumption, for such parts of the produce of other men's labour as he has occasion for. Every man thus lives by exchanging, or becomes in some measure a merchant, and the society itself grows to be what is properly a commercial society. (Adam Smith 1776; Campbell and Skinner 1976, 37)

Of all the subjects considered in this book, the study of coinage demands the most careful integration of different kinds of evidence. The archaeological side of numismatics is represented by new ways of analysing finds of coins from ancient sites, such as those developed by Casey and Reece (below p. 54). Fulford has attempted to detect patterns of trade from the distributions of coins from different mints (1978), whilst scientific studies have enabled subtle changes in the weight and purity of coins over time to be quantified (Walker 1976–1978). Theoretical economic archaeology, assisted by anthropology and history, can also provide new perspectives on ways in which economies can operate – with or without money in the form of coins. The study of surviving Roman literary sources is of prime importance, and it is interesting to note that scholars have reached radically different conclusions about the extent to which coins were used and understood in the Roman world, using essentially the same texts and coins (below p. 50). Before proceeding to the study of Roman coins themselves, this chapter will discuss some of the forms of economic activity and the origins of coinage which place Roman coinage in perspective.

TRADE, EXCHANGE AND MONEY

Adam Smith's *Wealth of Nations* contains a chapter entitled 'Of the Origin and Use of Money' (op. cit. 37–46), which is a well-informed and clear discussion of issues still debated by economic historians and anthropologists. Smith outlined the problems of barter, which relies upon achieving a balance between suitable surpluses and shortages that was probably rather difficult to achieve:

> . . . this power of exchanging must frequently have been very much clogged and embarrassed in its operations . . . every prudent man . . . must naturally have endeavoured to manage his affairs in such a manner, as to have at all times by him, besides the peculiar produce of his own industry, a certain quantity of some one commodity or other, such as he imagined few people would be likely to refuse in exchange for the produce of their own industry. (op. cit. 37–8)

Smith explained that metals held great advantages over other commodities such as cattle, for they required no maintenance or special storage, and could be divided to allow different sizes of exchange to take place.

After outlining the evidence of Pliny the Elder for early Roman use of metal bars as currency, Smith pointed out their principal drawback – the value of metals cannot be judged by eye as easily as that of agricultural produce; thus, precise weighing and tests of purity are necessary.

> To prevent such abuses, to facilitate exchanges, and thereby to encourage all sorts of industry and commerce, it has been found necessary . . . to affix a publick stamp upon certain quantities of such particular metals, as were in those countries commonly made use of to purchase goods (ibid. 40)

Thus, Smith envisaged a clear evolution from simple barter to specialised production of desirable trade goods, leading logically to the production of metal currency of guaranteed purity and standard weight as substitutes for goods or foodstuffs. However, for the sake of expediency, these could easily be abused by governments, whether Roman or of Smith's own time (43–4).

Adam Smith entered deeper waters in discussing what it was that gave things value (such as rarity or usefulness) and the problems of the fluctuation of standards of value. The problem remains today; commodities are valued and traded in terms of money values, but money is itself subject to the pressures of the market, and fluctuates in the same manner as a commodity. This is a serious matter for gold and silver coinage, whose values will fluctuate according to the market prices of the metals. If one gold coin is defined by the state as being worth 25 silver coins, what happens when the price of silver falls? As William Gladstone said in Parliament, '. . . not even love has made so many fools of men as the pondering over the nature of money', an observation quoted by Karl Marx in his own economic writings (Vilar 1976, 8).

Underlying most of Adam Smith's comments on coinage (and indeed barter) is the view that its primary function was for subsistence or commercial exchanges. However, a significant shift in thinking has occurred in recent decades, because of the realisation that social rather than purely commercial factors may be important in exchange. This has resulted from the work of economic anthropologists and historians, who have observed contemporary primitive societies, and analysed the economic structures of past societies of various dates and complexities. Some of the alternatives to commercial trade and exchange which they have identified will be examined here in order to place the Roman economy in perspective, for it is possible that similar systems could have existed in the Roman empire. It is also important to remember that comparatively primitive economic systems might have survived in areas of Europe and north Africa which had not experienced Greek or Carthaginian civilisation before their conquest.

Alternatives to commercial exchange

Adam Smith viewed the development of barter and coinage through the commercial lens of the eighteenth century. It is important to realise that notions of supply and demand, or profit and loss, which have been taken for granted by economists since the eighteenth century may be irrelevant in some societies. Simple primitive societies and also complex civilisations have existed without coinage or any system resembling a modern western economy. Debate continues amongst economists and anthropologists about how the great variety of known economic systems should be classified, but there is some concensus over three major forms: reciprocity, redistribution and the market. It may be useful to examine the meaning of these terms.

Reciprocity

Reciprocal exchange may include a wide range of goods, from foodstuffs between farmers and fishermen to gifts of luxury goods between rulers; in many cases examined by anthropologists, reciprocal exchange has had a social rather than commercial purpose. For example, Malinowski (1922) made a pioneering study of the 'Kula ring' which existed in islands scattered to the east of New Guinea, which were linked into a unified system through ceremonial exchanges of armrings and necklaces made from shells. Superficially, these objects resembled a form of currency, but they were in fact exchanged only between recognised partners; the arm-rings and necklaces circulated in opposite directions around the scatter of islands. They were never retained for more than one or two years, and their exchange was accompanied by elaborate ceremonials.

Malinowski classified the range of exchanges which he encountered into seven types (op. cit. 176–188). Only one had a purely commercial or utilitarian nature, and was conducted with haggling rather than ceremony; it involved specialised manufactured goods. Otherwise, all forms of exchange and gift-giving (of goods, foodstuffs or services) were inextricably locked into the pattern of social relationships, and equivalence rather than profit or loss was an essential element.

Redistribution

Redistributive exchange is less direct or personal than reciprocal exchange, and is associated with societies which have some form of centralised ruling power. Manufactured goods and agricultural produce are collected by this central power from a subservient population, and redistributed according to status, occupation, etc; the system can work either with or without money. Like reciprocal exchange, this form of economic activity is governed by the social structure of the community in which it operates, and naturally tends to stabilise and preserve its structure. The early empires of the Near East found this economy appropriate, as central authority was needed to construct and maintain elaborate irrigation systems upon which agriculture depended. This kind of system also simplifies the life of individuals involved in crafts, who can concentrate on their specialised activities without having to worry about subsistence farming as well. As long as their products were required by their rulers for redistribution to others, craft workers would obviously be provided with the essentials of life.

Another form of redistribution has been described as mobilised exchange (Carney 1975, 182); it takes place in an economic system where the produce of the economy is planned and collected for a specific purpose, usually war. It therefore has many features in common with redistribution, except that instead of products being shared back down to their producers, they are directed towards (in the case of war) the army.

The market

Market exchange is the form of economic activity most easily understood today. In a pure market system, prices are fixed according to supply and demand in the manner explored by Adam Smith and many modern economists. Until the workings of alternative forms of exchange became known from the writings of anthropologists, there was a tendency to assume that such 'price-fixing markets' were the normal outlet for surplus produce. The social factors involved in the exchange systems outlined above make it clear that this assumption is unjustified (fig. 15). Some recent writers have gone so far as to declare that 'true' markets are an exceptional form of trading, found only in modern industrialised western societies. It must be added that coinage is not necessarily an essential element of market systems; other forms of currency or even barter may fulfil the same rôle. Unlike the exchange systems outlined above, the market brings together individuals with goods to sell or money for purchases irrespective of their social relationships.

15. Do market buildings indicate a market economy? The public buildings of Roman cities were often constructed as a result of gifts from emperors or rich private patrons, and their size may reflect this social phenomenon rather than their true economic prosperity. This market hall and the many shops attached to Trajan's Forum in Rome have a very functional atmosphere compared with the vast basilica and courtyards which they adjoined, and their brick construction contrasts with the fine stones used in the ceremonial buildings of the forum. (Photograph: author)

Pluralism

Economic theorists do not believe that the exchange systems outlined above are completely separate, or that they ever occur in 'pure' form. They should be regarded as an aid to thinking, and used as 'models' of the ways in which economies might work. Snell has examined merchants' accounting systems in Mesopotamia, in a context usually thought of as a redistributive economy:

> Recent study has shown that the private as opposed to the royal or temple sector of the economy had a long history even in supposedly statist eras and in presumably capitalist eras the role of the crown continued to be important. (1982, 238)

We are at liberty to examine the Roman economy in terms of a mixture of all of these systems, and even to conclude that in fact none of them applies. Since the Roman economy obviously did involve the use of coins, the first task must be to scrutinise the nature and function of the coinage.

COINAGE

The origins: Greek coins

Money was first produced in the form of coins in Greek cities in Asia Minor in the seventh century BC. Small coins were made of electrum, an alloy of gold and silver which occurs naturally in the region. The metal discs were hammered into a die bearing animal or other decoration; the punches used for this purpose impressed symbols onto their reverse sides. The idea of marking a coin in this way (rather than using a plain ingot of metal) was probably adapted from the use of engraved seal-stones to indicate the source of the coin, whether minted by a city or an individual (Price 1983, 6). Coin production soon spread to other Greek cities around the Aegean, to Greek colonies in southern Italy by 500 BC, and from there to the western Mediterranean colonies. To allow easier estimation of their value, Greek coins soon came to be made from pure silver rather than electrum, and were formed between obverse and reverse dies, rather than simply bearing punch marks. Gold was rarely used, although it was utilised in the Persian empire, where the idea of making coins had been adopted from Asia Minor.

Roman coins

Bronze coins were first minted in the Greek areas of southern Italy, presumably because ingots of this alloy were a familiar form of currency amongst the native population of that region. For a long time, native Italian metal currency had included rough unstandardised pieces of bronze (*aes rude*), valued according to their weight. From the late fourth century BC, large cast bars of greater uniformity began to be made with simple decoration and other marks. They gradually replaced the irregular plain ingots, and remained in use for the first few decades after 300 BC, some by this time bearing the name of Rome.

True Roman coinage began around 289 BC, and a mint was established in the temple of Juno Moneta on the Capitoline Hill at Rome. Unfortunately, the details of the earliest Roman coinage are complicated rather than clarified by a passage in Pliny the Elder's *Natural History* (Sutherland 1974, 19). The first true coins were based on the *as*, an enormous bronze coin weighing one pound, which was subdivided into lesser denominations down to one twenty-fourth. They were much too large to be struck with dies, and were therefore cast; Pliny called them *aes grave* (heavy bronze). Silver coins also appeared in the third century BC, made in a Greek style but bearing the word ROMANO, although they were probably minted in the south of Italy rather than Rome. Further silver issues followed (some from Rome itself), and gold coins were issued near the end of the third century BC.

The *denarius* was to remain the principal silver coin until the third century AD. The first *denarii* seem to have been issued shortly before 211 BC, although the acceptance of this date requires the rejection of Pliny's date of 269 on the strength of archaeological and numismatic evidence (Sutherland 1974, 45–6). Henceforth silver became the standard of value rather than bronze, and the *as* and its subdivisions continued to decline in size and weight. One silver *denarius* was equivalent to ten bronze *asses*, and there were also half and quarter *denarii*, the *quinarius* and *sestertius*. A large issue of gold coins was minted around the same time, in three denominations. The changes made to Roman coinage in the late third century BC are normally seen as the result of financial pressures brought about by the war against Hannibal's Carthaginians.

Roman coinage was now set into a consistent pattern of gold, silver and bronze denominations which lasted throughout the republic and provided the foundations for the monetary system of the Roman empire. A modification occurred towards 100 BC, when the relationship between silver and bronze was adjusted so that one *denarius* was equivalent to 16 rather than 10 *asses*. Most coins were minted in Rome, with the exception of those issued from other centres during periods of civil war. The last republican coins merge into those of the reign of Octavian, victor of the final phase of the Civil War. He gradually assumed political powers which led to the adoption of his title Augustus, under which name he is acknowledged as the first Roman emperor, ruling from 27 BC. His reign was characterised by political stability, and among his acts was the establishment of a sound and well-structured coinage.

Roman imperial coinage

Large numbers of gold, silver and bronze coins were issued by Augustus from the mint of Rome and from others in the provinces, notably that of Lugdunum (Lyon) in Gaul. The system established during the reign of Augustus was as follows (fig. 16):

I AUREUS (gold) = 25 *denarii*
I DENARIUS (silver) = 4 *sestertii*
I SESTERTIUS (brass) = 2 *dupondii*
I DUPONDIUS (brass) = 2 *asses*
I AS (copper) = 2 *semisses*,
4 *quadrantes* (copper)

Less important were the *quinarius*, a silver half *denarius*, and the copper *semis* and *quadrans*, half and quarter divisions of the *as*. Gold and silver coins were minted in a fixed relationship to their bullion weight, so that one pound of gold produced 40 *aurei*, and one pound of silver 84 *denarii*.

Nero (AD 54–68) adjusted the weight relationships of the gold and silver coins by minting 45 *aurei* and 96 *denarii* to the pound, but otherwise the system remained unchanged for over 200 years. Some of the small copper coins dropped out of use, but no new coins were introduced until the reign

16. The system of coins established by the first Roman emperor, Augustus, lasted from the end of the first century BC until the third century AD. It consisted of pure gold and silver coins, accompanied by five brass and copper denominations. From the small *quadrans* up to the large *sestertius*, each coin had twice the value of its smaller counterpart. The relationships then widened, so that four *sestertii* were equivalent to the silver *denarius*, whilst the gold *aureus* was tarriffed at 100 times the value of a *sestertius*. The system thus included coins suitable for a wide range of transactions, from large payments in bullion to small change for everyday purchases. (Photograph by Audio-Visual Centre, University of Newcastle)

of Caracalla (AD 212–217), when a double *denarius* (known familiarly as the *antoninianus*) appeared. The portrait head on these coins bore a distinctive radiate crown to indicate its double value. The same means had been employed by Nero to emphasise the difference between the *dupondius* and *as*, which were of similar size, but whose different metal composition (brass and copper) became less obvious as they corroded. The Augustan system finally collapsed in the financial and political chaos of the later third century AD, and the subsequent reforms by Diocletian and Constantine gave rise to new coins with new names and relationships (fig. 17). The changes of the Late Empire are less well understood, but will be mentioned below (p. 61).

A MONETARY ECONOMY?

In 1970, Crawford published an influential article, 'Money and exchange in the Roman world', which reached two significant conclusions: first, that '. . . the use of coined money as a means of exchange was largely limited to the cities of the Empire'; second, that 'the Roman government had no policy concerning the supply of coinage and no monetary policy except in matters which directly affected its own interest or standing . . .' (ibid. 45, 48). These conclusions were based on a synthesis of evidence from literary, numismatic and archaeological sources, and were in accord with the general view of the Roman economy and the involvement of the state summarised in Finley's *The ancient economy* (1973). A few years later, Reece (1979) argued that the province of Britain remained locked into a tribal economy based on social interaction rather than cash-based exchanges for the first two centuries AD; this conclusion was reached under the influence of economic anthropology (Hodder 1979).

However, the pendulum of opinion has swung back in the opposite direction, as a result of momentum provided by both literary and numismatic evidence which demands different conclusions from those of Crawford and Finley. In his analysis of *The golden ass* (a Roman 'novel' of the second century AD by Apuleius), Millar emphasises the extent to which transactions at all levels were conducted in coinage in the Greek towns which provide the setting for the story: '. . . the towns in Apuleius function, not indeed as centres of production, but as the focus for organized exchanges of goods and the hiring of labour. All of this is conducted for cash; whatever else this may

be, it is certainly a fully monetized economy' (1981, 72). The countryside, too, was involved in similar activity: '. . . all the food-producing operations are specialized, and the products are exchanged for cash' (ibid. 73). Millar stresses the fact that *The golden ass* '. . . depicts levels of social and economic life which the vast mass of surviving Classical literature simply ignores' (ibid. 75). It is comforting to believe that Apuleius is the exception that proves the rule that we need not be unduly perturbed by a lack of agreement between the results of archaeological research into the economy, and those derived from Roman literary sources.

The same volume of the *Journal of Roman Studies* (1981) contained a paper by Lo Cascio which proposed that the Roman government not only had a consciousness of financial issues arising from coinage, but actively controlled the relationships between different denominations with considerable success from the time of Augustus to the early third century AD. The means of control included the limitation of mining operations, and adjustments to the supply, weight and purity of the gold, silver and bronze coinage, perhaps even with the needs of the economy as well as state finances in mind – in other words, through a monetary policy. Thus, in a little over a decade, numismatists and ancient historians have been able to present two opposing views of the Roman economy, one minimising rural coin use or the state's understanding of monetary affairs, the other proposing a thoroughly monetised imperial system in which the government strove to maintain the stability of coinage for economic reasons.

Obviously, archaeology cannot provide a final answer in this debate. In the introductory chapter, the importance of Hopkins' propositions about the Roman economy was stressed (above p. 14). His proposition that the pattern of taxation and expenditure in the Roman empire promoted long-distance trade is important for the study of coins. A fuller understanding of the rôle of coinage in taxation and long-distance trade may be gained from research into coins found on sites, and also the commodities like pottery and metalwork which might have been traded for cash (Chapter 6).

THE FUNCTION OF ROMAN COINAGE

Economists' definitions of money (which need not only take the form of coins, of course) normally include the following functions:

1cm

17. Coins of the third century AD reflect the financial troubles of their times. The *antoninianus* (top left) was made of impure silver, and was copied by large numbers of 'barbarous radiates' (top right), presumably because official supplies could not keep up with inflation. In the fourth century there were normally four sizes of bronze coins (bottom row), whose weight and size fluctuated considerably; the system was completed by pure gold and silver coins resembling those of Augustan times. Late Roman bronze coinage makes up the bulk of coins found on sites (see fig. 19). (Photograph by Audio-Visual Centre, University of Newcastle)

1 a medium for exchange;
2 a means of storing wealth;
3 a measure of value and standard for payments.

These aspects of money are not only relevant in a purely market economy, in which prices are fixed according to the forces of supply and demand, but can feature just as easily in exchanges which are made on a social basis. Thus, the existence of coined money in the Roman empire does not prove that it possessed a market economy; that

proof must be sought in a combination of historical sources and archaeological evidence. An important aspect of point 2 is that stored wealth can be used for social display; Painter has underlined the importance of various forms of bullion, such as gold and silver table ware, in this respect (1977).

Since Roman currency was largely derived from Greek coinage, it is obviously essential to investigate the reasons for the original development of coins in Asia Minor. It will be remembered that for a considerable period, Greek currency was minted only in precious metals, and therefore had a high value. Even in its smallest subdivisions it would have been more suitable for payments such as a day's wages rather than for the purchase of a loaf of bread (Price 1983, 5). Price concludes that the earliest coins were used in an almost ceremonial fashion to pay bonuses, which were gifts made on the completion of services (not necessarily paid for in currency at all):

> ... the personal nature of early electrum coins seems to require a specific function of this sort. The donor could be the state, or a monarch, or indeed a private individual. While it might be realised that the recipient could use the metal to acquire other

objects or to make any form of payments, he could equally keep it as indicative of wealth. This, after all, is the nature of a bonus. The coin type as the seal of origin represents the source of the bonus, the personal authority of the issuer . . . The place of such objects in the economy would grow as the practice of electrum bonus payments and gifts of coin became more widely adopted and as the coins circulated in other transactions. By the time Croesus of Sardes had within his kingdom the cities of the western seaboard such as Ephesus, the economy was ripe for the reform which brought gold and silver coinage into existence for the first time. It is then that the view of coinage as a medium for standardising payments to the state becomes attractive. With the existence of coins it would become normal to standardise in terms of coins . . . (Price 1983, 7–8)

Thus, Price sees the development of the use of coins in the Greek economy as an accidental result of a social practice. It proved so useful that coins are still universal in the developed economies of the twentieth century, despite the substitution of non-precious metals or even paper for metals of actual value. The principal difference between early Greek and modern currency is that none of the coins in circulation today is considered to have anything more than a token value, in contrast to gold sovereigns or Krugerrands which do not circulate, but are valued in terms of the fluctuating bullion price of the gold which they contain.

The distinction between bullion coins (worth the market value of their metal content) and token coins (which stand for a value defined in terms of something else) is fundamental. In 1757, the English Assay Master Joseph Harris stated this point long before any official coins were minted in base metals:

> Copper coins with us are properly not money, but a kind of token passing by way of exchange instead of parts of the smallest pieces of silver coin; and useful in small home traffic. (Whiting 1971, title page)

The relative importance of token and bullion coins in the Roman empire must therefore be considered with great care.

The other matter which requires careful study is the purpose for which Roman coins were issued. Their rather modern appearance, with higher and lower value denominations of different metals, portraits of the ruler on the obverse, and emblems and inscriptions on the reverse, is deceptive. It does not mean that we can immediately assume that they were primarily issued for use in everyday commercial transactions, from business deals down to daily shopping. This conclusion demands proof that coins were in plentiful supply, and that their purchasing power was appropriate for such purposes. Furthermore, we must ask whether the use of coins extended throughout society, or whether they were primarily restricted to the comparatively wealthy individuals living in towns. Most important, we must remember that coins are only one form of money, and that all manner of transactions can be carried out using other forms, from cattle to cowrie shells.

The use of Roman coins

Some clear evidence exists to show that Roman coin denominations were suitable for everyday transactions. In Pompeii, many skeletons have been found, along with their purses, which contain a good mixture of gold, silver and bronze denominations; this 'loose change' is easily distinguishable from larger collections of gold or silver coins, which were evidently savings that the victims were attempting to carry to safety (Breglia 1950, 57–59). Documents from Pompeii demonstrate that the bronze denominations had low purchasing power (ibid. 50–53). For instance, an *as* in the first century AD would buy half a pound of bread flour or a litre of cheap wine, but there were still half and quarter divisions of this coin, the *semis* and *quadrans*. Values were universally expressed in terms of coinage rather than bullion value in the Roman empire, and accounts were calculated in *sestertii*, the largest bronze coin. The finds from Pompeii underline the fact that Roman coinage in general use consisted primarily of *denarii* and *sestertii*; Reece has pointed out that a similar situation existed in eighteenth-century France, where around half of all the coins minted in each decade were gold or silver issues (1984, 202).

It is clear that monetary values were in use in peripheral provinces such as Britain as well as in Italy. For example, a fascinating inscription has been found on the base of a bronze statuette discovered in the Foss Dyke near Torksey, Lincolnshire (fig. 18):

DEO.MAR.ET/	AD SESTERN C/
NVB.AUG.COL/	CELATIUS AERAR/
ASVNI BRVCCI/	IVS.FECIT ET AERA/
VS ET CARATIVS DE/	MENTI LIB DONAV/
SVO DONARVNT/	IT FACTAM *III/

To the god Mars and the spirit of the emperor. Colasunius Bruccius and Caratius gave [this statuette] from their own resources at the cost of 100 *sestertii*. Celatius the bronzesmith fashioned it, and willingly gave the bronze, which he had made at the cost of 3 *denarii*. (Collingwood and Wright 1965, 91 no. 274)

No doubt Mars was expected to give full value in exchange for such a conspicuously priced dedication.

Roman coins are still cheap and plentiful today in the shops of coin dealers, and excavations or casual finds continue to produce large numbers from all around the empire. The existence of such quantities today does not necessarily mean that they were in plentiful supply throughout the whole empire for its entire duration. As we shall see, the survival of coins on archaeological sites or in hoards needs to be carefully scrutinised before any economic conclusions may be drawn.

ROMAN COINS FROM ARCHAEOLOGICAL SITES

Individual coins tell us little apart from the date at which they were issued. During the empire, the obverse of the coin usually bore a portrait of the reigning emperors, or occasionally relatives or revered predecessors, surrounded by a series of abbreviations of the parts of their names and titles. On the reverse side, there was usually a representation of a deity, a personification of a virtue (peace, plenty, etc.), or a piece of more blatant propaganda about a military victory or state occasion. The date of issue can be determined roughly through recognition of the portrait of the emperor, and more precisely from references to any offices which he held, such as consulships. Historical evidence from Roman writers or inscriptions may provide precise dates for the acquisition of these offices or honorific titles such as *pater patriae* (father of the country) or *Britannicus* (conqueror of Britain). In practice, there are abundant detailed reference books which allow virtually all Roman coins to be identified, catalogued and dated.

It is more difficult to establish the date of loss of a coin. At the time of writing this paragraph in 1985, the author's pocket contained a range of coins with the following dates of issue: 1947, 1969 (2), 1971 (3), 1975, 1976, 1977, 1979, 1980, 1983, 1984. If these coins were lost and not recovered, and then excavated at some time in the future, none would indicate the exact year of loss.

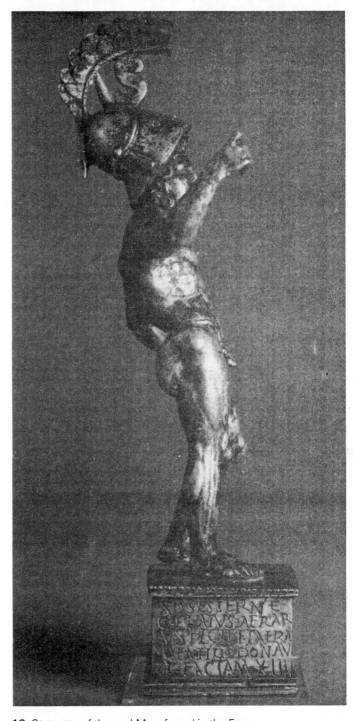

18. Statuette of the god Mars found in the Foss Dyke, Lincolnshire. The base bears an inscription giving precise details of the cost of the raw materials and manufacture of the statuette in *sestertii* and *denarii*, showing that the use of monetary values was well established in the provinces as well as in the centre of the empire. (Photograph by courtesy of British Museum, London)

However, if only one were lost and later excavated, there would be more than a one in two chance of it being at least ten years old. It might show a certain amount of wear to suggest that it was not new when lost, but more precision would be impossible. Before the decimalisation of English coinage in 1969, it was common for a pocketful of change to stretch back into the reign of Queen Victoria, and a range of 100 years was quite normal.

The situation in the Roman period was similar, particularly in the case of large bronze coins. Thus, in order to estimate the date of loss of a Roman coin, it is necessary to determine its date of issue, the amount of wear it has received, and the length of time that the particular issue survived in circulation. The last of these factors may be established from studies of coins found on archaeological sites which were only occupied for short periods (such as forts in Germany or Britain lying on dated frontiers), or in hoards (collections of coins concealed or lost in the Roman period and never recovered). A site of known date – for instance a fort on the Antonine Wall in Scotland – or a purse full of an individual's cash can provide a cross-section of the coins which circulated together during a restricted period. The absence of previously common types will suggest that these have gone out of circulation in the manner of the 'old' British pennies and halfpennies which were rapidly taken out of circulation by banks while new decimal coins were introduced in 1969.

The use of coins for archaeological dating purposes involves the concept of the *terminus post quem* (Greene 1983, 63–4). A single coin can only have been lost after its issue date, but how long after may be difficult to judge. A group of coins found together, whether as an excavated group or in a hoard, is dated by the latest coin in the group, for the deposit or container of the hoard could not have been sealed or buried until after the date of the latest coin which it includes. A knowledge of the circulation life of individual coins may help to ascertain the latest date that a particular type of coin would have been available to be lost or hoarded; this *terminus ante quem* and the *terminus post quem* of the issue date, will provide a likely chronological bracket.

There are always pitfalls, however. New coins may be hoarded for a long time and then re-enter circulation in an unworn freshly-minted condition. Some coins may be preserved long after their normal lifespan as talismans or as part of jewellery, particularly if made of gold or silver. The Merovingian king Childeric was buried in Tournai in Belgium in AD 481 with a large number of coins, as well as his personal effects; the coins ranged from Alexander the Great (fourth century BC), through many of the early Roman emperors, and up to late Roman rulers of Childeric's own lifetime. No doubt these coins (mostly gold *aurei* and *solidi*) had been in treasure chests for most of their lives, changing hands only occasionally through commerce, diplomacy, gift or theft (Lasko 1971, 32, figs. 19–20).

The quantification of coins from sites

Collections of coins from individual Roman sites often run into hundreds or even thousands of items. Some may have been found in proper archaeological excavations, but most will probably have been casual finds made during building work or other disturbance of Roman deposits; others will have no record of their origin. Superficially, a large collection of coins would seem to promise the possibility of charting the economic life of a site, as well as its period of occupation. Spells of prosperity might be marked by large numbers of coins, whose loss should reflect their former abundance, whilst lean periods should be indicated by shortages of coin finds. The existence of large coin collections from several similar classes of sites (such as towns, villas or military establishments) should allow comparisons to be made between them. Similarities between coin finds should help to establish 'typical' patterns to be anticipated on sites of the same kind, whilst contrasts may point to differences in their individual histories.

Unfortunately, detailed comparisons between many sites in Roman Britain have shown that the economic life of individual sites cannot be assessed so easily (Casey 1974; 1980). Casey has demonstrated the necessity of understanding the general history of Roman coinage before any conclusions can begin to be drawn about site histories. He has devised a method of presenting coins graphically by means of a histogram, which reduces collections of different sizes to a single standardised scale in order to allow direct comparisons to be made (fig. 19). The horizontal axis of his graphs represents time, but is divided into reigns of emperors or other significant periods of coin issue rather than straightforward years or decades. The total number of coins found on the site is standardised

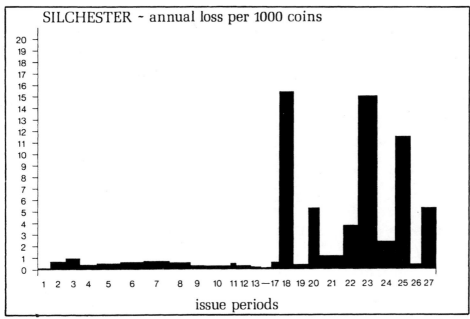

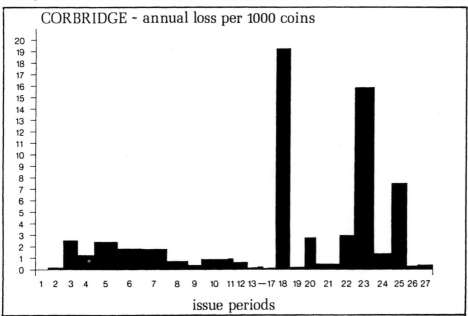

19. Standardised histograms of coins from two Romano-British sites, covering 27 periods of coin issues from the first to early fifth centuries AD. The general pattern is very similar, particularly after the collapse of the Augustan system of coinage in the third century. This was followed by successive reforms and debasements, which are responsible for the recurrent peaks and troughs of the right-hand part of the graphs (periods 18–27). The larger, higher-value coins of the early empire are comparatively rare on both sites, but are more prominent at Corbridge because it housed large military garrisons, and because the early levels have been extensively excavated. The final peak in period 27 is missing from Corbridge, because Roman control of the northern frontier ceased before the last official shipments of coins reached southern Britain. (Audio-Visual Centre, University of Newcastle; based on Casey 1980, 31, figs. 5–6)

to 1000 and the number assignable to each reign or issue period is determined by the following formula:

$$\frac{\text{COINS PER REIGN}}{\text{LENGTH OF REIGN}} \times \frac{1000}{\text{TOTAL FROM SITE}}$$

The vertical scale of the histogram indicates the number of coins lost each year out of every thousand found on the site. The division of the number of coins in each reign or issue period by its length in years balances out the distorting effects of short reigns with small issues of coins, or long reigns with large issues.

An unavoidable weakness in this method of presenting coin losses is that it does not take any account of the length of time for which coins circulated before being lost. Coins of the early empire in particular are likely to have been lost well after their date of issue. However, histograms of this kind are at least objective and standardised, so that direct comparisons can be made between them. The size of the coin collection should *always* be stated, for it would be nonsensical to use this graph to compare a collection of 50 coins with one of 5000. Even when two samples of comparable size are examined, small differences should not be taken too seriously, for no two collections will have been lost and recovered in exactly the same way; economic and historical judgements may only begin to be made when gross discrepancies occur. Such factors as different sample sizes, or differing proportions of coins derived from excavation rather than casual finds, must be taken into account. Even then, it is advisable to carry out statistical tests of significance in order to eliminate random variations.

It is salutary to realise just how few coins have actually been recovered from sites, compared with the numbers which once circulated there. John Casey has made this calculation for Corbridge in Northumberland (1974, 38). The site was founded in *c*.AD 85, and was occupied by a succession of forts for a century or more, before developing into a frontier town with a predominantly civilian population in the hinterland of Hadrian's Wall. The site has produced 1387 coins of the first two centuries AD, with a combined value of 26 *aurei*, the standard gold coin of the period. However, if the pay of the soldiers who were accommodated in the forts over the same length of time is calculated, the minimum amount of cash paid out on the site would have totalled 240,000 gold *aurei*, or 24,000,000 *sestertii* (the largest bronze coin).

This calculation demonstrates just how small our surviving samples of coins really are, and this fact should always be remembered when such information is used. The Roman town of Silchester in Hampshire has produced a collection of 8870 coins, which sounds impressive, but comes from a site which was a major urban centre for 300 years or more, and which has undergone extensive excavation since the late nineteenth century. It would therefore be unwise to claim that because only very small numbers of coins are found on many rural villas and farmsteads, their occupants were not involved in a cash economy except when visiting urban markets, as was suggested by Crawford (1970).

The histogram of coin losses from Silchester has a distinctive shape. The loss per 1000 coins per year remains below one up to AD 260, and then suddenly rises to over 15, only to fall back to around one again in AD 273. A series of similarly dramatic fluctuations occurs down to the end of Roman coinage in *c*.AD 402. Such marked periods of abundance and paucity cannot possibly reflect the amount of economic activity on the site, particularly when it is found that very similar results have been obtained from other Roman town sites in Britain. In fact, these fluctuations can be explained in relation to the quality and supply of coinage in general, rather than by any characteristics of the sites themselves. The great number of coins of period 18 (AD 260–273) represents a collapse of the currency, and its coins are mainly base double-*denarii* (fig. 17) which were rendered worthless by an attempt to reform coinage in period 19. A succession of similar declines and reforms makes up the pattern for the fourth century AD, combined with occasional periods of coin shortage caused by political and military factors (Casey 1974, 43–47).

Thus, quantified studies of coins from sites (and comparisons between them) demonstrate that an abundance of coins from a site is likely to indicate bad economic circumstances rather than good. The studies also underline a further factor; unlike hoards, site finds are merely the coins which people could afford to lose. A dropped *aureus* will have occasioned a careful search, and gold coins are therefore very rare finds. Debased third-century coins containing hardly any silver merited little effort to recover them, particularly when reforms of the coinage frequently rendered them worthless. The size of coins is also relevant, for small denominations are more easily lost than large ones. Even the small bronze coins of the early empire are larger than those of most of the fourth century, and commensurately harder to lose.

Reece has compiled a graph which shows the number of coin losses on a large number of Italian sites over the period of the empire. It approximates to a straight line, showing that the short-term fluctuations may conceal an overall stability. The period when losses were greatest was the third century AD (1984, 199, fig. 1). In the same article, Reece makes the important point that, although we know where many coins have been found, we do not know their exact context. Excavations in Carthage have allowed the stratigraphy of dated coins and pottery to be compared, and have shown that many fourth-century coins still circulated well into the fifth century. It will be a long time before information of similar quality is readily available from sufficient sites to allow valid comparisons to be made.

Great care is necessary in order to establish that Roman coins really were lost in Roman times, rather than having been brought to an area by modern collectors. Many eastern issues came into Britain as souvenirs in the pockets of soldiers who had served in the First and Second World Wars, and have acquired spurious local provenances as a result of finding their way into museums. Casey (1985) has shown that the long list of stray finds of coins from Scotland is so unlike reliably-excavated site assemblages that it cannot possibly represent ancient losses – and consequently has no historical or economic value. This is unfortunate, for Davies has recently demonstrated the importance of regional studies; coins found on native sites in Wales chart the entry of their inhabitants into a monetised economy, and their return to more primitive forms of exchange in the late Roman period (1983).

Coins and trade

Unfortunately, it is difficult to make detailed quantified comparisons between individual sites or classes of sites in different areas of the empire, because each region relied upon varying supplies from different mints. However, Hopkins has published a graph of coins from many different parts of the empire (1980, 113, fig. 4) which shows that from AD 40–180 there was a remarkable consistency in the supply of new silver coins through-

out the Roman empire, in samples taken from Britain, Germany, Italy, the Balkans and Syria. This evidence certainly supports his proposition that the economy of the empire was integrated by the effects which tax collection and state expenditure had in stimulating trade, particularly because the breakdown in uniformity in the third century coincides with an apparent decline in the vitality of towns and long-distance trade (ibid. 115). Thus, although we have concluded that site-finds of coins do not tell us much in detail about localised economic activity, coins in general provide a continuous commentary upon some more important factors in Roman economic life.

Fulford has made an interesting attempt to use coins as an indicator of subtle changes in the intensity and direction of trade in the late Roman period. Fourth-century coins are consistent in bearing an abbreviation of the name of the city in which they were minted, and the number of mints in operation was increased by the subdivision of the administration of the empire. As Casey's graphs have shown, late Roman coins are exceptionally common finds on sites. Thus, a large sample of coins exists which can be divided reliably into the products of specific mints. Fulford has studied the changing proportions of coins from different mints found on a number of sites in Britain, France and Germany (fig. 20); he proposes that even in this late period, trade (rather than purely official expenditure) was an important factor in their distribution. More archaeological studies of potential trade goods of the same period are needed to test his hypothesis (1978, 90).

INFLATION IN THE ROMAN EMPIRE

An issue that has a long history of discussion in coin studies is the relationship between changes in coinage and the rate of inflation of prices. This issue has regained topical interest in the 1970s and 1980s, but the irreconcilably conflicting views held by modern economists and politicians about the connections (if any) between state spending, interest rates, the money supply and prices should serve as a warning about the difficulty of drawing firm conclusions about the Roman period. Evidence that inflation was a problem in Roman times comes from a number of different sources, including contemporary literature, inscriptions, and even personal letters preserved on papyrus in Egypt. It is more difficult to establish the rate and severity of inflation, although this is what we

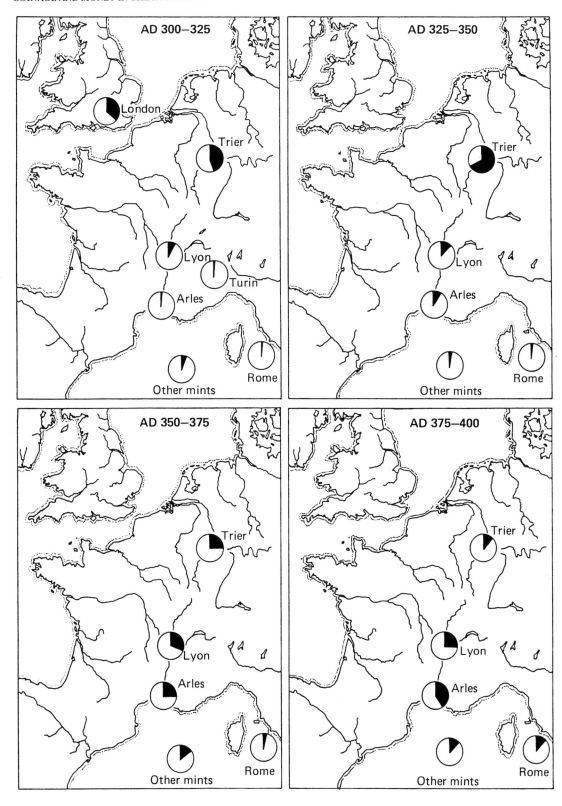

really need to know in order to estimate its effects on economic life.

Wages and prices

Two measurable sources of information about wages and prices may provide some guidance – army pay, and the price of wheat, although the former is more reliably documented than the latter (Duncan-Jones 1974, 10).

Army pay

Under Augustus (27 BC–AD 14), a legionary received 900 *sestertii* each year; under Domitian (AD 81–96), pay rose to 1200 *sestertii*, and under Severus (AD 193–211) to 1800/2000. After this date, the supply of provisions as part of wages complicates the estimate of army earnings. In the two centuries between Augustus and Severus, there was an increase of 100–120 per cent in legionary pay, a rate well below that of even the most budget-conscious modern governments.

Wheat prices

Since wheat was one of the essential commodities of the Roman world, its price (allowing for seasonal fluctuations) presumably reflects general changes in the value of money. The surviving evidence is sporadic. In Egypt, the second-century price was 25 per cent higher than that of the first century; in Ephesus (Asia Minor) the early third-century price was 100 per cent higher than that of the early second. Diocletian's *Edict* on maximum prices (AD 301) gives a price 200 per cent higher than its first- to second-century cost.

These separate pieces of evidence are not inconsistent with the impression given by legionary pay, that the rate of inflation was low in the early empire. Crawford believes that it really gathered momentum from the 260s (1975, 571), and that bronze coins continued to suffer rapid inflation in terms of gold, which rose from 48,000

denarii to 99,000 *denarii* per pound between the late third century and Diocletian's *Edict* of AD 301 (ibid. 584). The marked increase which seems to have occurred in the third century coincided with dramatic changes in coinage.

Inflation and coin denominations

In any monetary system which provides coins small enough for everyday transactions, a slow rise in prices will gradually render the smallest denominations too small for useful transactions. The English farthing (a quarter-penny) disappeared well before the decimalisation of coinage in 1969. At this date pennies became more valuable, for 100 'new' pennies made up one pound instead of 240 'old'. However, the high rate of inflation of the 1970s led to the withdrawal of the halfpenny coin in 1984, although it had in fact been worth more than one 'old' penny when first issued only 15 years earlier. Likewise, fifty-pence and one-pound coins were introduced in 1969 and 1983 to replace paper bank notes, because the fall of their purchasing power made paper an unsuitable medium for a heavily used unit of currency. Other countries have used more drastic methods in order to bring coins into line with inflated prices. In 1958, France simply knocked two decimal places off the franc, so that one new ('heavy') franc was equivalent to 100 old francs. The history of the Roman monetary system includes instances of both the disappearance of small denominations and the revision of values. Since Roman gold and silver denominations were isued according to their metal content rather than as token coins, further opportunities existed for adjusting the value of these coins by altering their weight and/or purity.

Changing uses of denominations

We have already seen how John Casey's quantified studies of coin finds from individual sites shed considerable light upon the general quality and availability of Roman coins, at least as far as their loss on sites is concerned. A different direction has been explored by Richard Reece, who has also compiled graphs of coins from sites, similarly divided up into reigns or periods of issue (Reece 1972). In addition to studying individual sites, Reece has conflated finds from large regions (Britain, northern France, southern France, northern Italy) in order to draw comparisons between them. For these regions, the proportions of different denominations of coins in the various

20. Changing sources of coins in fourth-century Britain; the percentage of coins from each mint is represented by the dark sectors of the circles. There was a gradual shift away from the northern mints during the course of the century, which may reflect general economic factors such as the direction of trade, rather than purely official monetary affairs. Comparisons of this kind are possible as a result of the detailed catalogues which have been compiled of coins found on British sites. (Audio-Visual Centre, University of Newcastle; based on Fulford 1978, 66, fig. 50)

reigns and issue periods have also been computed, so that their relative frequencies can be examined (Reece 1973).

In a series of complex graphic presentations, Reece has shown that in northern Italy between Augustus (27 BC–AD 14) and AD 275 the ratio of silver *denarii* to brass *sestertii* remained roughly in balance, and equal numbers of both occur on sites (op. cit. fig. 3). A very different picture is found in the case of the smaller bronze coins (*dupondii* and *asses*). Under Augustus, there were around six times as many of the small bronze coins as *sestertii*, and the two categories came briefly into balance around AD 160. By the 250s, however, the Augustan position had been reversed, and *sestertii* were much commoner than the smaller coins. Thus, if we follow the principle that the coins lost are the least valuable ones which will not be particularly missed, it is clear that the *sestertius* had declined from being a valuable bronze coin under Augustus to being the commonest. This is confirmed by the fact that its subdivisions had largely ceased to be issued, because their purchasing power was too small. The Augustan system had originally in-cluded two subdivisions of the *as*, the *semis* and the *quadrans*; these suffered the same fate as British farthings, halfpennies and 'new' halfpenny coins, and were rarely issued after the 60s AD. Thus, the progressive but gentle inflation indicated by army pay and wheat prices is reflected by the gradual decline in the purchasing power of bronze coins.

The decline of the denarius

Inflation seems to have gathered momentum during the third century AD, which provides some good examples of financial desperation, probably

21. Scientific studies of coins can reveal both metallurgical and historical information. For example, the silver content of the *denarius* declined drastically in the late second and third centuries AD. The comparative stability up to *c.* AD 150 and the accelerating debasement of the third century accurately reflect changes in political and military security undergone by the empire in the same period. (Audio-Visual Centre, University of Newcastle; silver content from Kent 1978, 357)

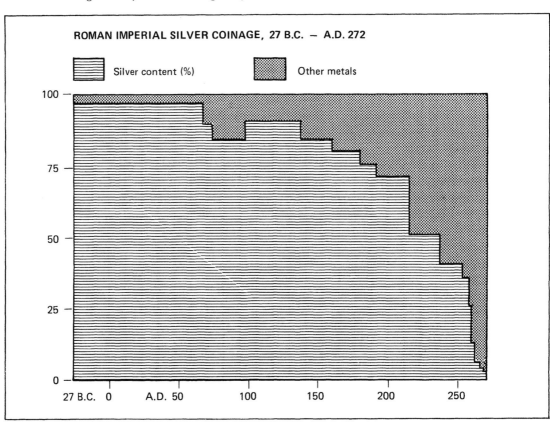

brought on by political and military difficulties. The debasement of the *denarius* is particularly dramatic; whereas under Augustus, it was made of virtually pure silver, the gradual decline in purity and weight of the second century accelerated in the third, until it became little more than a bronze coin with a small percentage of silver (fig. 21). Metallurgical analyses have added considerable detail to our knowledge of the speed and extent of debasement (Walker 1976; 1977; 1978).

Lo Cascio (1981) has argued that reductions in the purity of the *denarius* were part of a careful control of the relative values of gold and silver coins, which assisted the impressive stability of the first two centuries AD, witnessed by the graphs prepared for individual sites by Casey or the whole empire by Hopkins (above p. 55). In the third century, the motive for debasement is more likely to have been to gain short-term benefits for the Roman emperors, who were involved in successive struggles for the throne within the empire as well as attacks and invasions from enemies outside. Quite simply, old *denarii* collected in taxes could be melted down to make a larger number of new, less pure, coins, which would thus go further for paying the army and civil service. To make matters even worse, the emperor Caracalla (= Antoninus, AD 211–217) introduced a new coin, now called the *antoninianus*, which was in theory a double-*denarius*, but in fact only contained 50 per cent more silver than a single *denarius* (fig. 17). Once these coins had entered general circulation, however, the newer debased coins would not be accepted for goods or services at the same rate as the old, and a rise in prices was the inevitable result. Owners of older *denarii* would probably melt them down or hoard them, rather than exchange them for coins with the same theoretical face value, but a lower silver content. However, Crawford warns against overestimating the inflationary effect of these changes upon prices, since the coins were measured in terms of their silver content (1975, 567, 591).

The value of bronze denominations was also reduced by these debased silver issues, since it was defined by their relationship to the *denarius*. Since the bronze coins were token rather than bullion coins, they could be revalued by government proclamation, and the third-century emperor Aurelian made a valiant attempt to structure a currency reform around a new bronze *sestertius*

(Casey 1980, 13, pl. 2). Understandably, the steady reduction of the formerly pure silver *denarius* to the status of a bronze coin must have both increased inflation and hastened the demise of the traditional bronze coins; their place was taken by 'barbarous radiates', poor copies of the debased *denarii* which presumably filled the need for token small-change (Crawford 1975, 269–570). The lowest point in the debasement of the *denarius* was reached in AD 260, when the minting of even base silver coins ceased, to be replaced by copper coins with a silver surface coating which soon wore off in use (King and Hedges 1974).

Reforms of the coinage

The familiar denominations of the early empire disappeared in the later third century, and the history of coinage in the fourth century is both complex and imperfectly understood. Diocletian may have attempted to produce a new version of the Augustan system, but by AD 340, fourth-century coinage consisted of pure gold and silver coins, and enormous quantities of four different sizes of bronze coins without any silver content (fig. 17; Crawford 1975, 560–1). As Casey's histograms show, this phase is characterised by a series of currency reforms, represented by sudden reductions in the numbers of coins found on sites. Each one is followed by a deterioration in the size and weights of the new coins, leading to their increased occurrence as site finds until the same cycle was initiated by the next reform. The process ended with the virtual cessation of the issue of small bronze coins in the western parts of the empire in the early fifth century AD. However, the very existence of large quantities of fourth-century bronze coins indicates that they still fulfilled an important need; as we have seen above, Lo Cascio considers that (in the early empire at least) they were issued for the benefit of economic activity in general, and not merely for the selfish requirements of the Roman state.

THE RÔLE OF MONEY IN THE ROMAN ECONOMY

It can be argued that the Roman system encouraged the use of money in a market economy, because of the requirements of state expenditure for paying an enormous standing army and an elaborate civil service. After the initial stages of conquest of new areas, with their profits from

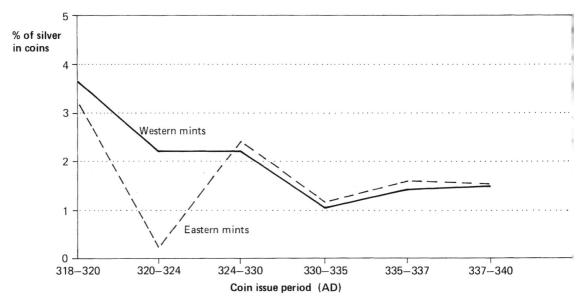

22. The average silver content of coins issued in the early fourth century AD by mints in the east and west of the empire was remarkably uniform, indicating close adherence to standard and careful preparation of alloys. However, the eastern mints departed from the norm in the period 320–324, at the time of civil war breaking out between the emperor Constantine and his eastern colleague Licinius, who may have reduced the silver content as an emergency measure in order to produce larger amounts of money to finance his attack on Constantine. A return to uniformity followed the defeat of Licinius. (Audio-Visual Centre, University of Newcastle; based on data from Barrandon and Brenot 1978, Barrandon *et al.* 1980)

captured spoils, the demands of garrisons, administrators and military and civil building works required money. An important objective would be to make provinces not merely self-financing but profitable in terms of tax revenue. Rather than impoverishing the subjects of new provinces, taxation (initially in produce, perhaps) would often have provided a stimulus to the use of money and markets. When subjected to taxation, farmers would need to maintain surplus production, and if taxation was demanded in the form of coinage, to market this surplus for cash. The idea that increased surpluses could not only pay taxes but could finance the purchase of other goods offered for sale in a market would not be lost on a wily country-dweller.

The ability to store and accumulate wealth from successful surplus farming might actually have allowed some landowners to increase the size of their holdings, and to achieve the political and social status which accompanied the rôle of estate owner in the Roman world. No doubt the most successful were those who were already prominent in pre-Roman society, but monetisation of the economy certainly provided new opportunities, without necessarily destroying the existing social structure. Native aristocrats in the provinces were often in receipt of large loans from rich Romans, with which they would strive to adopt the outward trappings of Roman civilisation, such as a country house with appropriate furnishing and decoration, along with wine and exotic cuisine. Such loans required repayment, and the motivation to produce agricultural surpluses and turn them into cash would, therefore, have operated at a high social level as well as amongst peasants.

The presence of an army of conquest and the attendant bureaucracy of provincial administration must have played a fundamental rôle in 'monetising' the less advanced western areas of the empire. A characteristic phenomenon in frontier areas is the growth of civilian settlements around forts; many of these subsequently developed into major towns even after the garrisons moved elsewhere. The rôle of the army in instigating quarrying for building stone, mining for precious and other metals, and in placing contracts for supplies and equipment will be discussed further in Chapter 6; the 'pump-priming' effects of introducing coinage into provincial economies cannot be ignored.

Millar's discussion of Apuleius' *Golden ass* (above p. 50) provides good testimony for the comprehensive use of coinage throughout the Roman social and economic system, at least near the Mediterranean in the second century AD. The extent to which relatively humble categories of pottery and other goods reached ordinary rural sites, and the very density of non-urban settlement patterns (Chapter 5 below), also argue for thoroughly monetised interactions. Hopkins' model of integration through taxation provides a logical framework for conceptualising the way in which this complex system operated. There is another view, however; Millett (1981) has proposed that the rapid penetration of samian pottery into rural sites in Britain may have been the result of the redistribution of prestige goods downwards from the higher levels of society which had access to (and probably controlled) the trade in luxury goods. In this instance, I believe that the literary evidence for coin use, whether from Apuleius or papyri from Egypt, favours an interpretation centred upon coinage rather than social relations; the significance of alternative economic systems must not be ignored, however.

ROMAN MONEY AND FINANCE

... it was the slow pace of the heavy metal money, its failure so to speak to keep the engine running, that created the necessary profession of banker, at the very dawn of economic life. He was the man who repaired or tried to repair the mechanical breakdown. (Braudel 1981, 475)

Although Roman coins have a rather modern appearance, it must not be forgotten that there is more to money than coins. We have already seen how economic anthropologists have described a variety of physical forms of money (above p. 46); in more complex societies, paper notes and less obvious forms such as bills of exchange can act in the same ways as coinage for making purchases and payments. Even abstract notions such as credit and barter are arguably forms of money, for they may fulfil the same functions. Beyond money, there is also the question of financial institutions such as banks, and the kinds of transactions which they make possible, which may have great influence over the potential for both internal and overseas trade. In the view of Braudel, a historian with particularly broad

perspectives on world history, systems of finance, banking and credit are a reflection of the complexity and needs of a particular economy. It follows that there is no simple 'evolution' of methods from one period to the next, and that improvements may have a limited life, and only operate in the context which generated them. Early forms of credit, mortgages, interest-bearing loans, cheques and bills of exchange were operating in Babylonia around 1000 BC, which had no direct influence upon later civilisations; in the absence of coinage, payments were made in ingots of metal or commodities (Angell 1930, 35, 197).

If Braudel is right in seeing necessity as the stimulus for development in financial affairs, a knowledge of the nature and extent of financial institutions in the Roman empire may provide a measure of the vitality of its economy, expressed by its needs. With the advent of coinage, and in particular the complicated Roman system of gold, silver and bronze denominations, money-changers were very important in converting one form of currency to another, and (perhaps intuitively) exchanging coins of different values and metal contents from different regions. In the Middle Ages and later, problems of exchange were far greater in divided or small states such as Italy or Holland which depended upon international trade; their currency was made up of many coins of various origins over whose quantity and purity of issue their governments had no control. The exchange bank set up in Amsterdam in 1609 was a product of these circumstances, but it introduced a novel solution, by converting all money into a standard accounting unit instead of any real coin subject to the whims of an individual government. Any kind of coins could be deposited, whether local or foreign, fresh or worn, pure or debased; their value was simply recorded on paper in terms of the independent standard value, which did not actually exist as a real coin denomination at all (Galbraith 1975, 15–16).

Once it had been converted to a standard, the ownership of money deposited in a bank could be exchanged between merchants without difficulty by means of paper transactions. Bankers with offices in a large number of ports or countries could thus enable payments to be made in local currencies in different places without any transfer of actual cash, an obvious help to merchants. The development of this form of banking was a prelude to the more imaginative kinds of uses to which money placed on deposit could be put, which developed rapidly in seventeenth-century England. Experience showed that deposits and withdrawals normally remained roughly in balance, leaving a large sum of money lying continuously idle. As long as sufficient cash was always on hand for meeting withdrawals, it was realised that this idle money could itself be lent out at interest. Soon, interest began to be paid on deposits to increase the amount available for lending, and the need to retain reserves in actual coin was further reduced by extending the possibility for payments to be made between individuals by the use of cheques and other paper transactions. Bank notes (first issued in Stockholm in 1661) acted as further substitutes for coinage, as they were more likely to circulate as money than to be brought back to the bank to be redeemed for cash.

The flaw in this kind of system is obvious, of course: if at any time doubt exists about the ability of a bank to honour its paper transactions in cash, its customers will immediately want their money, thus guaranteeing that their worst fears are rapidly fulfilled. The apparent enthusiasm with which western banks are willing to reschedule Third World debts is a modern symptom of this problem, as the confidence inspired by continued interest payments helps to conceal the extent to which capital reserves were over-stretched by high lending. Despite its inherent dangers, sophisticated banking is of great importance to trade and industry because it reduces dependence on cash, and encourages the use of credit. The supply of money thus increases, interest rates fall, and a continuous motive for finding productive investments exists.

BANKS IN THE ROMAN WORLD

Banking spread to Rome from the Greek world, where the multiplicity of local coinages from individual city-states had encouraged the establishment of exchange-banks. Much attention has been paid to the state banking system run by the dynasty of the Ptolemies in Egypt up to the time of its incorporation into the Roman empire. In addition to a centre in the royal capital at Alexandria there were large numbers of branches throughout Egypt. Their principal function was the collection of revenues and the making of state payments, but the bank also accepted deposits and made loans, and used a variety of written instructions for carrying out paper transactions. However, it ceased to exist when Augustus reorganised the administration of Egypt, thus

underlining its exceptional nature and difference from Roman practices.

The need for exchange-banks was limited by the existence of the well-organised and unified Roman system of coinage during the imperial period; the kinds of secondary developments from exchange banking seen in late medieval Europe were therefore unlikely to occur. Indeed, banking seems to have reduced in intensity and complexity as the economy suffered in the third century and later, although the legal framework of earlier times was preserved for posterity by Justinian's great codification of Roman law in the sixth century AD. Banks were not operated by the state but by private individuals, normally of the social class of the *equites*, whose level of wealth was high, but below that of senators. The predominant function of banks undoubtedly remained the important rôle of money-changing for small-scale local transactions such as market purchases or the paying of taxes. This is emphasised by a papyrus document which has survived from Oxyrhynchus in Egypt, which was occasioned by the reluctance of bankers to accept the coinage of the usurpers Macrianus and Quietus in AD 260:

> From Aurelius Ptolemaeus . . . strategus of the Oxyrhynchite nome. Whereas the public officials have assembled and have accused the bankers of the exchange banks of having closed them because of their unwillingness to accept the divine coin of the emperors, it has become necessary to issue an order to all the owners of the banks to open them and to accept and exchange all coin except the absolutely spurious and counterfeit – and not alone to them but to those who engage in business transactions of any kind whatever – knowing full well that if they disobey this order they will experience the penalties already ordained for them in the past by His Highness the Prefect. Signed by me. Year 1, Hathyr 281. (Lewis and Reinhold 1966, 442)

It is clear that in the Roman empire it was possible to deposit and lend money at profitable levels of interest, that bills of exchange could be used, and that large sums could be transferred between individuals or between places in different provinces by means other than transporting actual coins. Bankers also placed deposits out on short-term interest-bearing loan on behalf of their clients, but most loans seem to have been made for consumption or the purchase of land, rather than any kind of productive investment. Lopez has recently summarized a rather depressing view of Roman financial affairs, which echoes the more detailed discussions of Finley:

> Money changers and deposit bankers lent to merchants . . . but were hamstrung by the mediocrity of the business world, and never grew into anything that could be remotely compared to modern commercial and industrial development banks. Credit was a will-o'-the-wisp when it was not usurious pawnbroking; the prudent, conservative spirit of the Roman society could hardly conceive wealth otherwise than as a tangible collection of fields, houses, cattle, slaves, movable objects, or hard cash. (Lopez 1976, 10)

> There was endless moneylending among both Greeks and Romans . . . but all lenders were rigidly bound by the actual amount of cash on hand; there was not, in other words, any machinery for the creation of credit through negotiable instruments. The complete absence of a public debt is in this context a meaningful indicator. (Finley 1973, 141)

> . . . the imperial government . . . when wars and other emergencies forced it to spend more than it received through ordinary taxation . . . did not try to bridge the gap by borrowing from the citizens against the collateral of its immense assets. Extraordinary taxation and currency debasement were carried farther and farther, until all sources were exhausted and the Empire became disastrously insolvent without ever contracting any debts. (Lopez op. cit. 10)

CONCLUSION

In conclusion, it must be stressed that the Roman empire did not have paper, printing, or a system of numerals which could easily be used for accurate accounting, and double-entry book-keeping still lay in the future. It seems that the impression of modernity given by Roman coins is misleading; although England and America failed to achieve a regular system of state-issued token copper small-change until the nineteenth century AD, they had successfully developed comprehensive private and state banking facilities which could underpin their industrial economies at least a century earlier. However, the extent of monetisation of the Roman economy, even after the inflation and debasements of the third century, remains impressive. 'However distasteful the analogy may be to the purist, it does seem vital to point out that, in terms of its denominational range, the gold, silver and bronze of the early imperial coinage had no European parallel until the later medieval period. This fact must surely have considerable implications for the nature and achievements of the economies of both eras' (Fulford 1978, 90).

FURTHER READING

The most emphatic book on the inapplicability of modern economics to the classical world remains Finley's *The ancient economy* (1973). Textbooks on modern economics abound; an effective antidote is provided by Schumacher's *Small is beautiful: a study of economics as if people mattered* (1973). The rôle of 'primitive' economic systems in early states is described in *Trade and markets in the early empires*, edited by Polanyi *et al.* 1957. A clear sociological/anthropological account of such systems can be found in Belshaw's *Traditional exchange and modern markets* (1965) or in many textbooks of anthropology or prehistoric archaeology. The subject is discussed in more detail in Pryor's *The origins of the economy: a comparative study of distribution in primitive and peasant ecnomies* (1977). Alternatives to modern market exchange have also been discussed by an ancient historian (Carney, *The shape of the past*, 1975) and a medieval archaeologist (Hodges, *Dark age economics*, 1982). An impression of the vitality of this whole subject amongst prehistorians can be gained from a volume of papers edited by Sheridan and Bailey: *Economic archaeology: towards an integration of ecological and social approaches* (1981). An early exploration of alternatives to commercial exchange which is still worth reading is Grierson's paper 'Commerce in the Dark Ages: a critique of the evidence', *Trans Royal Hist Soc* (1959) 123–140.

Lavish illustrations with authoritative commentaries distinguish two 'coffee-table' books entitled *Roman coins* by Sutherland (1974) and Kent (1978). The potential and pitfalls of numismatics are elegantly summarised in a chapter which Crawford contributed to a useful book which he edited in 1983, *Sources for ancient history*, and many general methodological insights can be gleaned from Casey's concise account of *Roman coinage in Britain* (1980). The complexity of Roman monetary affairs is exemplified by Millar's paper on 'The aerarium and its officials under the empire' (*J. Rom. Stud.* 1964), whilst the contribution of new discoveries of inscriptions or papyri can be assessed from Erim and Reynolds' discussion of fragments of Diocletian's price *Edict* found at Aphrodisias in Turkey, in the same periodical (1970).

An important paper by A. H. M. Jones (originally published in the early 1950s), 'Inflation under the Roman empire', is included in a collection of his works, *The Roman economy* (1974). A paper by Hopkins stresses the rôle of taxation in the economy, 'Taxes and trade in the Roman empire' (1980), whilst the complexities of late Roman reforms can be appreciated from Goffart's *Caput and colonate* (1974). The interplay of political, military and financial problems was the theme of papers contributed to a conference on *Armées et fiscalité dans le monde antique* (CNRS 1977).

The post-Roman evolution of coinage in Britain is outlined very clearly in Sutherland's *English coinage 600–1900* (1973). The general economic setting of medieval and recent coinage is explored in a very readable manner in Cipolla's *Money, prices and civilization in the Mediterranean world* (1956), or in greater depth by Lopez's *The commercial revolution of the middle ages* (1976) and Braudel's wide-ranging *The wheels of commerce*, 1982. If the reader requires an entertaining (if somewhat alarming) demystification of the whole subject, Galbraith's *Money: whence it came, where it went* (1975) should serve the purpose well.

FOUR

Agriculture in the Roman empire

INTRODUCTION

> Almost everywhere a large part of the population was engaged in agriculture at a relatively low level, while industry depended on a backward technology and was rarely organised in large units. (Duncan-Jones 1974, 1)

Ancient historians are unanimous in accepting the importance of agriculture in the Roman empire, to the extent of contending that it was so important that no other form of economic activity could possibly be considered as significant (Finley 1973, 139; Jones A. 1974, 36–37). On the other hand, the Roman empire shows ample evidence for military power, sophisticated communications, imposing cities, lavish rural villas, metallic currency, and a wide range of goods such as pottery or metalwork which were traded over considerable distances. Are these phenomena consistent with an economy centred entirely upon 'low-level' agriculture, or do they suggest that it was in fact sufficiently productive to support a significant amount of non-agricultural activity? Comparisons with historical and anthropological evidence from medieval and modern times may well be instructive in answering this question. First, however, it is necessary to examine the state of current knowledge about Roman agriculture, using all possible forms of evidence.

Agriculture is perhaps the most complicated aspect of the Roman economy to study. A deceptive impression is given by the fact that some of its elements are extremely well documented in literary sources. Unfortunately, the documented areas (in both the technical and geographical sense) cannot safely be used to generalise about the agricultural economy of the empire as a whole. The rôle of archaeology is not much clearer; indeed, some of the most important

activities in the agricultural sector, such as the supply of grain to Rome, would be difficult if not impossible to establish from archaeological evidence on its own. Archaeology can do two main things: first, it can help to place agriculture into a general perspective, by examining the form and extent of rural settlement; second, it can give specific insights through the excavation of farming sites, with full attention to environmental evidence such as plant remains, animal bones and soils. The results of both approaches must of course be integrated with the surviving literary accounts of agriculture. Prehistorians may be shocked to find that in the publication of a British Museum symposium on Roman villas in Italy in 1980, it should still have been necessary for Potter to spell out something which has been a commonplace to them for at least 50 years:

> . . . villa-excavation is a complex business involving delicate chronological analysis, exploration of associated barns and field systems, and study of material both robust and ephemeral: seeds, bones and coarse-ware sherds have their story to tell as much as mosaics and architecture. (1980, 73)

This chapter will examine the ephemeral as well as the robust; plant remains, animal bones and soils can have far-reaching implications for the interpretation of individual sites or regions, general aspects of the economy, or even such fundamental themes as the origin of Mediterranean civilisation and the climatic history of the world. The aim of what follows is to provide a critical perspective on the kind of things some of these archaeological and scientific specialisms can (or, where appropriate, cannot) be expected to achieve. No attempt will be made to present a synthesis and discussion of Roman farming methods based on literary sources, for this service

has been performed in a comprehensive manner by K. D. White in a number of books and articles (e.g. 1967; 1970; 1975; 1977).

SOURCES FOR THE STUDY OF ROMAN AGRICULTURE

Literary sources

Extensive literature on Roman agriculture survives from a range of authors who wrote between the second century BC and the fourth century AD. It includes actual manuals of agricultural practices by Cato, Varro, Columella and Palladius, and, in addition, Pliny the Elder's *Natural History* also contains much information relevant to agriculture (White 1970, 18–31). The prevailing tone of the writers other than Palladius is one of more or less well-informed advice from one respectable Italian senatorial land-owner to another; Palladius, the latest of the writers in date, gives instructions, many of which are annotated summaries of the earlier writers. As any reader of modern books on gardening will know, they are not necessarily written by the best gardeners, and what is recommended in their pages is not always practical. Thus, valuable though it is to have the

23. Aerial photograph of a 'classic' Picardy villa, Estrées-sur-Noyes (Somme). The foundations have been revealed by ploughing, and they stretch for more than 400m. The large blurred rectangular patch at the far end of the complex indicates the location of the main residential building, while many further buildings lie along the sides of a large courtyard. An extensive excavation could sort out the structural history and dating of the site, but it would be a very costly project. The villa only shows up so well from the air because plough damage to the buried structures is so extensive; much information has already been destroyed, particularly about the latest phases of occupation, whose remains would be the first to suffer. (Photograph by courtesy of R. Agache)

luxury of several contemporary manuals on Roman agriculture, their worth must not be overestimated. They were written by (and for) a privileged few, from their own limited experience of some agriculturally favourable parts of Italy, combined with knowledge drawn from earlier Carthaginian and Greek writers (Martin 1971). Whilst they do demonstrate a range of possible

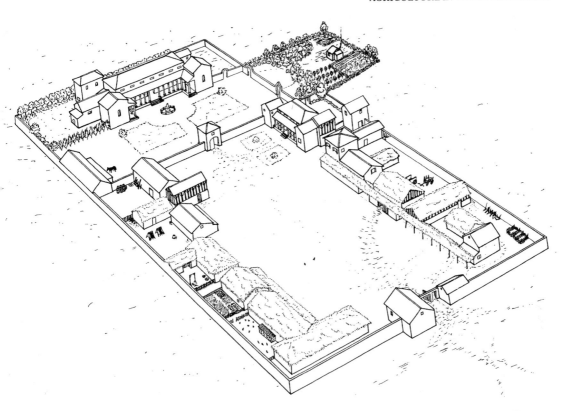

24. Reconstruction drawing of a villa complex similar to that illustrated in fig. 23. There is a marked contrast between the magnificent main residence and the working farm buildings beyond the walls of its gardens. It is usually assumed that sites with grand buildings were actually occupied by their owners (who probably also owned houses in neighbouring towns). The house in the corner of the courtyard might have belonged to an estate manager or bailiff. (Drawing by William Hubbard)

forms of agriculture, they are by no means comprehensive.

A second form of written evidence is provided by inscriptions on stone, which also have the advantage of being original documents, which have not suffered from errors made by the generations of copy-makers who preserved the literary works. In Egypt, an appreciable number of original documents written on papyrus has also survived (Lewis 1983). Useful evidence for the study of agriculture obtainable from these sources includes price lists and customs charges (Diocletian's *Edict*, Giacchero 1974; Fentress 1979, 208–209); boundary markers and maps of land divisions (Chouquer 1982); and details of legal arrangements for the restoration of waste land (Flach 1982; Peyras 1975; Lewis and Reinhold 1966, 179–184).

No attempt will be made in this chapter to discuss fundamental issues for which archaeology does not provide direct evidence, such as the use of slaves or tenants as a labour force (Kolendo 1976; Wiedemann 1981). The reader may be interested to investigate some questions which have been approached from opposite directions, using literary or archaeological sources; for example, Frayn relied almost entirely upon literature in her account of subsistence farming in Roman Italy (1979), but Applebaum used the plan of an excavated villa in Roman Britain to deduce its economy (1975). Spurr's study of millet cultivation is also entirely literary, and provides an excellent example of the information with which archaeological and botanical evidence should be compared. Very different is a discussion of the beneficial effects of a plant, medicago, in modern Libyan dry farming (Chatterton and Chatterton 1984); it is suggested that it may have been used to restore soil potential in the same way in the Roman period.

Barker has expressed strong personal views about the relationship between literary and archaeological evidence, conditioned by the fact that his main area of research has been in prehistoric archaeology:

> The archaeological data have to be studied in their own terms first, just like prehistoric data, and not simply worked into a historical framework from the outset, with dubious data from one discipline 'explained' by similarly dubious data from the other: in this case archaeological data will invariably tell you what you knew already – comfortingly, but quite spuriously, and expensively at that. (1985b, 132)

In his view, the real rôle of archaeological data is their potential for 'greatly enhancing our understanding of major social and economic processes in the classical world'. His discussion of the environmental remains from Benghazi on the Libyan coast includes an example – an evolving series of interactions between the city, rural settlements and nomadic peoples (1983, 35, fig. 9).

Before leaving the subject of literary evidence, the value of circumstantial details in the reference books of writers such as Columella or Pliny may be noted. Pliny the Elder tells an old anecdote which is intended to reinforce his views on the importance of well-managed hard work:

> Gaius Furius Chresimus, a liberated slave, was extremely unpopular because he got much larger returns from a rather small farm than the neighbourhood obtained from very large estates, and he was supposed to be using magic spells to entice away other people's crops. He was consequently indicted by the curule aedile Spurius Albinus; and as he was afraid he would be found guilty, when the time came for the tribes to vote their verdict, he brought all his agricultural implements into court and produced his farm servants, sturdy people and also according to Piso's description well looked after and well clad, his iron tools of excellent make, heavy mattocks, ponderous ploughshares, and well-fed oxen. Then he said 'These are my magic spells, citizens, and I am not able to exhibit to you or to produce in court my midnight labours and early risings and my sweat and toil'. This procured his acquittal by an unanimous verdict. (*Natural History* 18.8)

The whole point of the story would be lost if it were unthinkable that Chresimus should own these items of equipment on a small farm; such details are in many ways more interesting than the lists of essential tools and activities prescribed by Columella for the running of an ideal estate.

Art

Roman villas in many parts of the empire were decorated with paintings, or with mosaics, which because they were laid on floors and made of robust materials have a much higher survival rate than paintings. Many contain references to agriculture, sometimes by means of symbolic representations of the seasons, or less frequently by detailed scenes of farming activities (Précheur-Canonge 1961; Dunbabin 1978). Although the distribution of these is very uneven, they certainly bring the subject to life, and illustrate practices for which direct archaeological evidence has not been found, such as harvesting, ploughing and hunting. The tools involved are frequently quite distinct, and thus help in the interpretation of artefacts found in excavations (Rees 1979; Glodiaru 1977). Tools and other symbols of agriculture are particularly common on tombstones and religious carvings in Phrygia, Asia Minor (Waelkens 1977), whilst small metal models of farming implements have been found in Germany (e.g. Ternes 1976, 958, Abb 181, from Rodenkirchen). Sculptures from north-eastern Gaul have allowed a composite picture of a Roman reaping machine, the *vallus*, to be built up; it is described by Pliny the Elder, but no actual fragments have so far been identified (White 1967b; 1984, 61, figs. 47–48; Heinen 1976, 89–91, Abb 2a–b).

Archaeology

Over 50 years ago, Loeschcke provided an excellent example of the integration of literary, artistic and archaeological evidence in a study of wine production in the Mosel region (1932), an area outside the range of the Roman agricultural writers discussed above. Since Loeschcke's day, the quantity of carvings and inscriptions has remained static, but archaeology has expanded dramatically to become the principal means by which our understanding of agriculture can be increased. It is able to generate new and exciting areas of evidence both on a general scale by regional fieldwork, and on a detailed level through the location and excavation of individual sites such as villas or farmsteads. Furthermore, modern archaeology works hand-in-hand with many scientific studies which can advance our understanding of the environment in which Roman agriculture operated, such as geomorphology, soil science, climatology, palaeobotany and pollen analysis (Greene 1983, 141–147). Unfortunately for the study of the Roman economy, excavations carried out on many sites have been directed towards the study of architectural features; detailed investigations of outbuildings, soils, animal bones and plant remains are still rare. Scientific precision and thoughtful sampling are even rarer; a substantial excavation report (published in 1974) on an important villa in Britain contains the following preface to a specialist section on molluscs: '*Snails from Pit O, Room 7* (A very large number of snails were found in the pit, and about 100 were sent for examination)'.

Readers of excavation reports should not accept their conclusions without considering the complex range of factors which can distort their validity (Barker P. 1977). For instance, there are many technical difficulties involved in the excavation of rural sites. Insubstantial timber buildings will have decayed rapidly after their abandonment, and their remains are easily removed by ploughing. Masonry structures which underwent expansion and alteration over several centuries require sensitive stratigraphical study if their structural histories are to be dated correctly. The latest phases of their construction may have removed traces of earlier developments, and in areas without plentiful building stone the remains of their walls are likely to have been subject to disturbance by stone-robbing (Greene 1983, 79–80).

Perhaps the most difficult problem of all is that agricultural sites do not consist of settlements alone: an inseparable element in the understanding of agriculture is the study of field systems and the extent of the lands which they exploited. The physical structure, amenities and decoration of a villa, or the wealth of artefacts found on the site of a farmstead may reflect the prosperity of their inhabitants, but will not reveal the basis of that wealth. In Italy, agricultural activities were frequently carried out in sections of residential buildings; for example, olive and grape presses were located next to domestic facilities in the villa at Sette Finestre (fig. 35; below p. 91). In other areas, these functions might be located in subsidiary structures like the animal sheds and olive oil production unit at the farm known as 'LM4' in Libya (fig. 54; below p. 131). The boundaries of

land units such as villa estates are extremely difficult to define without detailed documentary evidence, which rarely survives before the medieval period in most areas of the Roman empire, although attempts have been made using varying amounts of information and guesswork (fig. 37; Peyras 1975; below p. 88).

Techniques of territorial definition and site-catchment analysis, derived from geography, can be applied to individual sites or distribution patterns of agricultural settlements, but they rest on many untestable assumptions (Higgs and Vita-Finzi 1972; Greene 1983, 167–171). Essentially, such studies define a theoretical territory around a site, and measure the proportions of different resources inside it. Applications to sites of the Roman period are rare, but Ellison and Harris found that Roman villas in Sussex possessed particularly favourable mixtures of good arable and grazing land (1972). Regional fieldwork studies such as those discussed in Chapter 5 involve many problems of interpretation, particularly where comparisons between different areas are attempted. It is well known that sites will only be revealed under special circumstances, whether by means of aerial photography or field-walking; for example, permanent pasture or afforestation will inhibit both (below p. 123). Thus, it would be possible for two areas whose settlement patterns were identical in the Roman period to appear quite different in archaeological surveys because of varying degrees or types of modern agricultural exploitation. In all cases, results from such surveys should be taken to represent a minimum view of the original extent of settlement. All of these aspects may be assisted by broad scanning techniques such as satellite imagery (Allan and Richards 1983).

Many of the surveys carried out in Italy have graded sites according to size, architectural complexity, and the range of datable types of pottery found. However, some excavation is essential to estimate the extent to which surface finds provide a reliable indication of the nature, extent and date of a buried site – in fact, results obtained on sites in Libya allow a degree of optimism (Barker G. and Jones G. 1984 29–31). A deeply plough-damaged site should provide plentiful surface finds of pottery and building materials, but if a prosperous early site was overlain by a mediocre later one, and damage was only superficial, surface remains would be unlikely to reflect the status of the earlier phase. However, such problems should not prevent the undertaking of such surveys, or the interpretation of their results, as long as non-archaeologists are fully aware of these technical factors and are suitably cautious in drawing conclusions from this kind of evidence. The problems involved will be discussed further in relation to individual cases in Chapter 5.

SCIENTIFIC EVIDENCE FOR ROMAN AGRICULTURE

Environmental archaeology has long been a well-established subdiscipline of prehistoric archaeology (Greene 1983, 131–149; Shackley 1983, 1985). Its rôle has, however, been taken more and more seriously in historical periods, because of a growing appreciation of its potential contribution to understanding the economic background to social and political events. It can provide specific information, such as demonstrating the function of a building; the classic example is the identification of remains of insects which infest grain-stores from a Roman riverside structure in York (Hall and Kenward 1976). On another level, soil science and plant biology can document long-term regional sequences of geomorphology and vegetation which have implications for the effects of climatic change and the impact on the landscape of human action such as deforestation and ploughing.

Cultivated plants: the background

The three most important agricultural products traded in the Roman world were grain, wine and olive oil; because of their ubiquity around the Mediterranean today, the plants which produced them are sometimes known as the 'Mediterranean triad', and their farming as 'polyculture'. Literary evidence demonstrates the importance of corn supplies to Rome, and the complex arrangements which ensured its transportation from Egypt and Africa; the thousands of pottery amphorae which carried wine and oil found on sites and in shipwrecks are a vivid record of their contents. However, the familiarity of these crops tends to diminish our concept of their significance. Work in the Near East and Greece by prehistorians has charted the domestication of various plants, and has assessed their significance for human settlement. The detailed accounts of different plant species which Jane Renfrew has been able to document, using samples from excavated pre-

historic sites (1973), underline the further, and as yet under-exploited, potential of botanical studies in the Roman period.

The cultivation of wheat and barley began in the Near East soon after 6000 BC, with the addition of lentils, peas, and flax for oilseed; fruit and nuts were gathered in the middle and late Stone Ages, including wild grapes and olives (Renfrew J. 1973, 202–203). The earliest farmers in south-east Europe were tied to permanent settlements by the need to plant, attend and harvest crops – a constraint not imposed by herds of animals. The objective was therefore to provide a storable surplus of large seeds which would provide essential foods throughout the year; diversification of crops helped to guard against failures (ibid. 28–29). Wild grapes and olives (ibid. 125–134) grew all around the coasts of the Mediterranean (fig. 2). Cultivation had begun before 3000 BC in Egypt and Syria, and is attested in Greece around 2500 BC. Although processing reduces the food-value of grapes and olives, they can be converted into wine and oil for long-term storage; finds of grape skins, stalks and pips from early Minoan Crete suggest wine-making, and olive presses are also known in Minoan Crete (ibid. 127, 134).

Polyculture and civilisation

There is profound significance in grape and olive cultivation as opposed to the gathering of wild fruits. These plants require different soil conditions from cereals and pulses, and are harvested later than those crops. Thus, an area of mixed land can produce two extra harvests with the same amount of labour; however, an investment of time is required to plant, grow and tend the vines and trees before they will produce crops. In Colin Renfrew's view, '. . . the development of Mediterranean polyculture was as important for the emergence of civilisation as was irrigation farming in the Near East' (1973, 229). He envisaged a spiral of development, as the demands of a growing population led to the exploitation of tree and vine crops, which in turn led to a higher level of production which could support more people, a proportion of whom could be engaged in work other than agriculture. The coincidence of Minoan and Mycenean civilisation with the areas of early olive and grape cultivation in Europe is therefore highly significant.

Colin Renfrew's exploration of the emergence

of civilisation around the Aegean does not lay emphasis upon single causes, but rather upon the 'multiplier effect' (1972, 476–504). The impact of polyculture in the Aegean area was only one of the factors whose cumulative effects transformed the region's society and economy into a civilisation. Specifically, it not only allowed greater exploitation of land and improved subsistence, but wine and oil became involved in complex social activities such as centralised storage and redistribution, leading to the literate 'palace economies' found in the Minoan civilisation (ibid. 304–307, 490). Such characteristics of civilisation tend to be taken for granted by classical archaeologists.

Graeme Barker has explored the significance of the cultivation of the 'Mediteranean triad' in Italy. In the Molise valley (on the east side of the Appenines), farming settlements gradually expanded from before 4000 BC until after 1000 BC, until even marginal land was thoroughly exploited. Then, the cultivation of olives and grapes coincided with a new expansion of settlements associated with changes in the whole structure of the economy (Barker G. 1981, 217). Barker discussed the relevance of two 'models' which might help to explain the observed changes: Renfrew's 'multiplier effect' (1972), and Boserup's ideas on the interaction of population growth and agricultural change (1965). He found a satisfactory answer in a combination of the two (ibid. 201–211). The 'multiplier effect', rather than contacts with Greek cities in the south of Italy, was sufficient to explain growth associated with polyculture in the first millennium BC. The contrast between this episode of transformation and the thousands of years of continuity which preceded it fitted fairly well with Boserup's model of the conservatism of agricultural systems, which only change when population pressures make it absolutely essential. Thus, population had risen to the extent which demanded change, whilst the form which the change took initiated the 'multiplier effect' and led to further growth.

First in Etruria, then in outlying regions like Molise, we can see how the new society had to be sustained by an agricultural system that brought with it a transformed world of commercial organisation and social differentiation. In an extraordinary reversal of rôles the prehistoric societies of central Italy changed in the space of a few centuries from a virtually Stone Age people . . . into the central nations of the Roman world. (Barker 1981, 219)

Plant remains on Roman sites

Botanical studies are crucial for the reconstruction of the early history of agriculture and the development of civilisation, whilst pollen analysis has a prominent place in the interpretation of the history of vegetation (fig. 52), as well as possible changes in climate. More specifically, the study of plants from individual sites can help to elucidate their economies as well as the general local environment. Samples must be recovered with care from significant datable deposits, with knowledge of the effects of different soil conditions upon preservation (Greene 1983, 141–144). Very wet or arid conditions favour the survival of actual seeds, stalks, etc, which can also be preserved as charcoal by burning. Such remains can be separated from samples of soil by some form of fine sieving, but pollen has to be isolated by more sophisticated laboratory methods.

The hot and dry conditions caused by the volcanic ash which buried Pompeii in AD 79 have allowed the survival of remarkable remains of fruit, nuts, beans and seeds. Together with the careful excavation of cavities left in the soil by the decay of roots, these remains demonstrate that sizeable areas of Pompeii were used as orchards, vineyards and market gardens (Jashemski 1979; below p. 94). Conversely, it was the permanently waterlogged conditions which preserved plant remains from a site near the Greek colony at Metaponto, in southern Italy (Carter et al. 1985); a water-basin at a spring sanctuary even contained offcuts from the pruning of vines and olive trees, whilst pollen analysis detected the introduction of intensive olive growing in the fourth century BC.

In Libya, plant remains and pollen found in dry conditions at Ghirza in the pre-desert included species that demand much more water than can be provided by normal rainfall (fig. 25). They help to confirm the intepretation of walls and cisterns in adjacent valleys as parts of a careful management system for the exploitation and storage of the little rain which did fall (Veen 1980–1981). Seeds from various plants including crops and weeds preserved in wet conditions in the Thames valley near Oxford show that low-lying grasslands were more permanently settled in the Roman period than in the preceding Iron Age, and that they were divided up by hedges (Robinson 1981). Rescue archaeology has con-

25. A selection of Roman plant remains from Ghirza, Libya, including a grain and internode of barley and a lentil (top), seeds from weeds associated with cultivation (centre – asphodel, marigold and mignonette), fig pips and a date stone. This material has survived thanks to arid conditions, and is particularly important because actual plant remains provide much more direct evidence of local crops than pollen. (Scale 7.5:1, except for date stone, which is 2.5:1; photographs by courtesy of M. van der Veen)

siderably increased the number of excavated plant remains; Jones has listed an impressive array of items from grapes and dates to cucumbers and coriander now known from Romano-British towns (Jones M. 1981, 97), many of them imported rather than home-grown. The military fortress at Novaesium (Neuss) on the lower Rhine in Germany has produced a catalogue of plant remains ranging from obvious items such as grain to numerous examples of medicinal herbs (Knörzer 1970). At nearby Xanten, Knörzer compared plant remains from military and civilian contexts, and found that the army had access to a wider range of soft fruits and pulses, which must have contributed to a healthy diet (1981, 158–160).

Plant remains may have most to offer archaeologists in the provinces of the Roman empire away from the Mediterranean where documentation is least adequate. The high degree of sophistication of animal and plant studies in Germany, the Netherlands and Britain allows comparisons to be drawn between prehistoric and Roman finds which are important in the understanding of the impact of the Roman conquest. Jones has discussed the question of change and innovation in British agriculture, which places the Roman period into an interesting perspective. A major

period of new crop introductions seems to have taken place, not at the beginning of the Roman occupation, but between 1000 and 500 BC (fig. 26), which was 'the main period of change between the early Neolithic and the 16th century AD' (1981, 104). The species involved are particularly suitable for growing on low-lying heavy soils, which began to be cultivated extensively from the early Iron Age, when ploughing was facilitated by the use of iron-tipped ploughshares. Superior 'eared' ploughs which could turn a furrow came

26. Introductions and innovations in British agriculture in the first millennia BC and AD. Jones used a wide range of types of evidence to compile this chart, some of it rather indirect. For instance, spike-rush is a plant characteristic of land that is wet in spring, while mayweed prefers clay soils; they provide supporting evidence for the occupation and cultivation of heavy valley soils. Most of the Roman innovations reflect increased intensity of planting and harvesting (plough coulters, large scythes and sickles, etc.) rather than new ideas, and they coincide with the late Roman period rather than the original conquest. (Audio-Visual Centre, University of Newcastle; based on Jones 1981, 116, fig. 6.4)

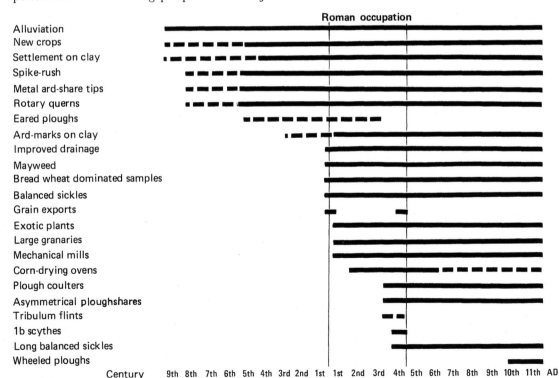

into use by the early Roman period at the latest (ibid. 112); more sophisticated ploughs may have been in use in the late Roman period, but direct evidence is scanty; large scythes and sickles were certainly in use.

Jones claims that the pattern of innovation in Romano-British agriculture demonstrates stagnation in the early empire, and investment in agriculture only in the late empire (Jones M. 1981). This is not compatible with a view of conquest and taxation stimulating production, and coin-based markets promoting 'capitalist' agriculture for profit. Whatever the truth of the matter, it can be seen that seeds and grains painstakingly recovered from samples of soil in the laboratory have implications which extend right to the heart of the economy and politics of the Roman empire. It is no longer sufficient to make lists of crops which appear in Roman literature and on sites; their growing conditions, yields and nutritional value all need careful evaluation. For example, the bread wheat which is universally cultivated today is easy to harvest and produces high yields of grain which separate easily from the ears. However, before the use of weedkillers and fungicides it was much less resistant to infestation and disease than other varieties of wheat such as emmer or spelt (Jones M. 1981, 107).

If the pattern of innovation and crop introductions is significant, so are the economic implications of crop yields. Research into prehistoric farming methods at Butser experimental farm in Hampshire (Reynolds 1979, 59) has achieved far greater returns of grain than had previously been considered likely. The economic implications are considerable; even on conservative estimates, Manning (1975) has calculated that the military garrison of Wales could have been fed without difficulty from local land, without recourse to the areas of south-eastern England traditionally considered to be the productive 'granary' which fed the 'highland zone'. In a recent review of this and other calculations, Scott (1983) took account of the Butser yields, and contrasted alternative high and low estimates for the amount of land required to supply the grain requirements of the army of Roman Britain; the results were over 80,000 ha (197,680 acres) or under 2000 (4942 acres), depending on which variables were selected. In isolation, such figures tell us little, but they do allow us to make better informed guesses when attempting to produce 'models' of how we think that the Roman economy worked.

Experimental farming

The crop-yields discussed above are just one result to have come from the Butser experimental farm (Reynolds 1979). Many hypotheses about buildings, methods, crops and animals have been tested, with remarkably clear-cut results. A good example relevant to Roman cereal farming is the case of T-shaped 'corn-drying ovens', a form of structure found on many sites and assumed to have been used for drying grain in advance of storage. A replica based on excavated remains proved totally unsuitable for this purpose, but did turn out to be effective for sprouting grain for malting and beer-brewing (Reynolds and Langley 1979). Thus, a further form of secondary agricultural production was suggested by the rejection of the original hypothesis. Brewing was significant enough to be commemorated on the gravestone of a woman from Trier in Germany (Binsfeld 1972); not all of the barrels known from sites and carvings need have contained wine. At the opposite end of the Roman empire, the experimental farm at Avdat in Israel has demonstrated the effectiveness of water-conservation methods in desert areas (figs. 27 and 60; Evenari 1971).

The study of animal remains

Studies of animal bones from Roman excavations have begun to demonstrate that they may be as informative in this period as in prehistory, where, like plant remains, they have been used for evidence of husbandry and diet for many decades (Greene 1983, 136–137). Barker has outlined the results of bone and other environmental evidence which contradict the supposed dominance of southern Italy by stock-raising (1978, 41–42); in Rome itself, a deposit dated to the fifth century AD has been published, which allows direct comparison with written records for the supply of meat to the city (Barker G. 1982, 85; Whitehouse 1981). The bones from the Schola Praeconum included large quantities of food debris amongst which pork, beef, and to a lesser extent lamb, were attested. A good idea of the balance of meat consumption and the sources from which meat was drawn can be gained from written records. The bones themselves allow further details to be added; for instance, the animals were as small as those found on prehistoric and medieval sites, showing that large 'improved' breeds are a very recent phenomenon (Barker G. 1982, 90). How-

27. Theories about ancient farming systems can be tested by modern scientific experimentation. At Avdat in the Negev desert, Israel, vines and fruit groves flourish thanks to water collected from the valley slopes (see also fig. 60). Exact measurements of rainfall, soil conditions and crop production allow estimates to be made of the potential of the area for agriculture and settlement in Roman times. Such experiments cannot answer all of the questions about early farming, but they do improve the quality of information upon which hypotheses can be built. (Photograph by courtesy of R. Burns)

ever, the narrow age-range during which the animals had been slaughtered implies that the fattening of the animals was very efficient, and that the quality of feeding was very high even when Italy was undergoing crises and invasions in the late Roman period (ibid. 88–89).

Many more sites in the north-western provinces of the Roman empire have properly excavated and published bone reports than around the Mediterranean. Large numbers of reports are important if comparisons are to be possible. Teichert has made a quantified examination of the frequent observation that cattle on Roman or 'Romanised' sites in Germany were larger than those on native sites (1984). He compared a large number of measurements from samples both sides of the Roman frontier, and demonstrated that, although the ranges overlap, cattle within the empire were of a consistently larger average size. However, the existence of some large cattle outside the frontier but near enough for trade implies that Roman stock or methods of husbandry were known in free Germany. The most significant observation is that the presence of large cattle is no longer attested north of the Alps after the end of the Roman occupation; Teichert concludes that the necessary knowledge of stock-raising did not exist amongst 'natives', or was lost in the confusion of the babarian migrations (1984, 101). An alternative interpretation is that the dis-

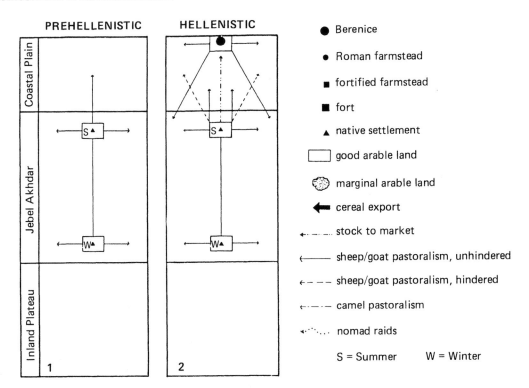

PREHELLENISTIC   HELLENISTIC

● Berenice

● Roman farmstead

■ fortified farmstead

■ fort

▲ native settlement

▢ good arable land

marginal arable land

← cereal export

←···· stock to market

←── sheep/goat pastoralism, unhindered

←--- sheep/goat pastoralism, hindered

←-·- camel pastoralism

←······ nomad raids

S = Summer   W = Winter

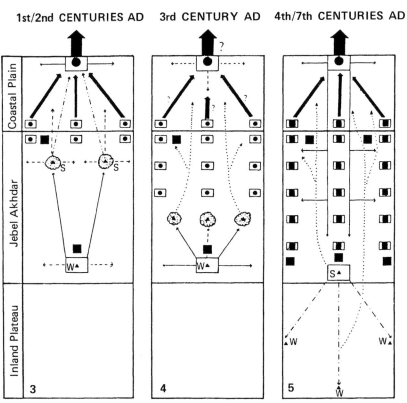

1st/2nd CENTURIES AD   3rd CENTURY AD   4th/7th CENTURIES AD

appearance of urban and military markets may have favoured a return to the selection of smaller, more manageable, animals.

In Britain, Maltby has published clear evidence for a complex butchery trade revealed by bones from Rowan towns (Maltby 1984). At Exeter, Silchester and London, deposits of cattle bones have been excavated which contain disproportionate numbers of bones from the extremities – skulls, jaws, lower leg – which result from the preliminary preparation of carcasses after slaughter. At Cirencester, 'secondary' butchery was indicated by cut and sawn bones found in pits adjacent to a market hall, which presumably contained rubbish from butchers' shops. At Gloucester, 'secondary' jointing of carcasses prepared elsewhere was still practised in the fourth century AD. Preliminary study of the age and sex of animals indicates specific production for meat rather than the eating of cattle which had already been used for milk production or traction, whose bones would reveal a wider age-range and include older animals. Female cattle are commoner in towns, presumably because they were easier to drive. Maltby's evidence does not show whether the meat supply had any official organisation, or whether it operated privately; the separation of stages of carcass preparation and butchery do indicate a level of complexity which must be accounted for in any interpretation of the economy. This evidence for the butchery trade is interesting in relation to a carving from Trier in Germany, which shows a butcher with a selection of joints and knives (Cüppers 1982).

---

28. Systems theory and theoretical modelling have exerted considerable influence upon prehistorians since the 1960s, but it is still rare to find applications in the Roman period. This example is based on bones and environmental evidence from excavations at Benghazi on the Libyan coast, and it explores the social effects of the economic development of the city's hinterland. The gradual extension of settled agriculture encouraged by the city's market and port disrupted traditional pastoralism, and culminated in the need to fortify farms against raids by the dispossessed pastoralists. This kind of modelling is independent of historical documents, and the changes which are deduced from archaeological evidence can be compared with any relevant historical information. (Based on Barker 1983b, 35, fig. 9)

The potential of further combined archaeological excavation and zoological study for the understanding of the place of animals in Roman agriculture is immense. If it is to be properly used, archaeologists and historians must appreciate the full complexities involved in the interpretation of animal remains, as Luff has outlined recently (1982, 1–25). For instance, the bones which are found around a Roman villa will probably reflect the cuts of meat which were popular on its dinner table, and have little relevance to its stock-raising economy. Excavation must make the context of any sample of bones clear, and determine if it formed rapidly or over a long period, and whether it was subject to disturbance after deposition; quite large bones can easily be removed and buried elsewhere by dogs.

Fish and molluscs were also exploited and farmed in Roman times, and their bones and shells deserve careful study. The fish bones from Benghazi shed light upon the forms of coastal fishing that were practised (Barker G. 1983, 25–30; 28, fig. 8). Bones found inside amphorae can indicate whether they contained salted fish (complete skeletons) or fish sauce (fragments only), rather than wine or oil. The sizes of the bones can indicate the season and location of fishing, thanks to the known habitats of fish at different stages in their life-cycles (Wheeler and Locker 1985). Impressive systems of tanks, dams and channels were used for fish farming on the Mediterranean coast (Schmiedt 1981; Davaras 1974), whilst many remains of fish-salting and sauce manufacturing centres have been recorded on the Atlantic coasts of Morocco, Spain and Brittany (Ponsich and Tarradell 1965; Curtis 1978; Sanquer and Galliou 1972). Oyster shells are found in great quantities on inland sites, and emphasise the ability of the transport system to deliver them in fresh condition. Products of the sea and shore must have provided return cargoes for river boats transporting inland goods to ports; Amand has suggested that this was a factor in the supply of building stone from Tournai in Belgium to coastal sites (1984, 217).

Animals provide many useful by-products, such as wool and leather, which only survive in exceptionally wet or dry conditions of preservation. Each has its own industry, from fleece and hide preparation through to woven textiles and leather goods, whilst bone and horn are themselves raw-materials for small items ranging from tools to furniture inlays. Careful scientific study is necessary to establish the species from which these materials were derived, and the study of wool in particular has allowed the evolution and spread through Europe of different colours and qualities of fleeces to be charted (Ryder 1983). Sheep-rearing has been studied in detail by Frayn (1984), whilst textiles are the speciality of Wild, who has written many specialist reports on fragments retrieved from excavations, as well as a monograph (1970). Fascinating details can emerge from textiles; some fragments from London indicate a mixture of Mediterranean and northern yarns and techniques (Wild 1975). The wool trade of the town of Pompeii is the subject of a comprehensive study by Moeller (1976).

Unlike meat, milk products are most unlikely to leave any trace detectable by archaeologists, other than possible cheese-making equipment such as pottery strainers or presses, but it must not be forgotten that cheese can be stored for long periods and transported easily. It provides an excellent means of converting milk surpluses into a marketable commodity, in an economic system which operated above self-sufficiency. In the course of his survey of the Lasithi plain in eastern Crete, Watrous recorded many milk-boiling sheds on the surrounding hills where shepherds manufactured cheese while their flocks grazed on the summer pastures (1982, pl. 9b).

Soil science

The layers of soil encountered during the excavation of archaeological sites are not only sources of artefacts, bones and plant remains; they can themselves have important implications (Limbrey 1975; Greene 1983, 145–6). For a number of years, a layer of 'dark earth' has been recorded in the course of many urban excavations in Britain, usually in the late Roman to medieval phases (fig. 29; Macphail 1981). Some of these have recently been subjected to proper scientific analysis by soil scientists and botanists, which established that the 'dark earth' is an accretion of rubbish, frequently disturbed by human and animal activity, which could also be characteristic of a market garden soil. Combining the evidence of soil science with the results of archaeological excavations in London, Macphail concluded:

> The possible implications are that late Roman London had a sparser population, with farming within the walls, and there had been a dramatic change from the early commercial expanding town

with its entrepreneurial class. Seemingly, built-up areas had been dismantled and now were possibly used for agriculture based on dumped 'dark earth', while the legal, government and military functions of the city continued. (ibid. 327)

It has long been accepted that, by the early medieval period, Roman towns in the Rhineland consisted of little more than disjointed manors with a primarily agricultural basis, apart from royal and ecclesiastical structures (Böhner 1977). The observation that the towns of Roman Britain may have contained extensive cultivated areas well before this date has interesting implications for the understanding of the changes in the character of Roman civilisation during the first four centuries AD (Reece 1980); indeed, Jashemski's work at Pompeii emphasises the fact that town and country were not as easily separable as in the modern world.

Prehistoric archaeologists have made extensive use of catchment analysis in their studies of the economies of rural sites (Greene 1983, 170–171; Jarman et al. 1982). Essentially, the technique involves constructing a hypothetical territory of accessible land around a site, and then examining the potential of the soils which lie within it. Two major kinds of criticisms can be levelled at this approach. First, the hypothetical territories may have had little relevance to a site's actual landholdings; secondly, the present distribution of soil types may be very different to that which existed in the past, for agriculture and erosion may have had serious effects. Ammerman has added the further point that soils which are considered unimportant in their productivity today may have been more highly regarded in the past, because of different farming practices (1985, 37). He also stresses the fact that catchment studies make no allowance for the inter-dependence of settlements, which could balance out their surpluses and deficiencies through exchange. Such criticisms are compounded in the Roman period, when complicated patterns of land-owning are known from documentary sources, and when trade was vigorous. Nevertheless, catchment studies do at least provide a working hypothesis which can generate interesting interpretations (see the analysis of a supposed villa estate, below p. 93).

On a broader scale, soil science is a fundamental part of the geology of the world's surface deposits, particularly in geomorphology, the

29. A layer of 'black earth' exposed in excavations at Milk Street, London. It lies between the remains of Saxon timber buildings (on the same level as the drain-pipe, a recent intrusion), and Roman buildings of the second century AD, whose floor levels are visible in cross-section in the foreground. Scientific analysis of the structure of the 'dark earth' has revealed that it was produced by rubbish-dumping and cultivation in areas of the city which had evidently gone out of occupation. (Photograph by courtesy of Museum of London, Department of Urban Archaeology)

study of changes undergone by the landscape (Vita-Finzi 1969, 1978; Sevink 1985). Like plant remains, there is a fascinating debate about the extent to which the changes which have taken place in the last 10,000 years have resulted from climatic factors or human interference initiated by the spread and intensification of land-use through agriculture. A challenging paper by Waateringe has proposed that even the soils of temperate northern Europe could be reduced to exhaustion by Roman agriculture (1983). He emphasises that the process could take up to two centuries in the areas of the Netherlands which he has considered; if he is right, the remarkable expansion and contraction of settlement in north-eastern France (below pp. 116–19) may be connected with this possibility. Barbarian invasions are usually blamed for the collapse of agriculture in this region.

ENVIRONMENTAL EVIDENCE AND THE ROMAN CLIMATE

Plant and animal remains tell us a great deal about Roman agriculture, whilst patterns of settlement reveal possible economic relationships and levels of population. Climate is, however, a parameter of even greater potential significance. The attitudes of historians and geographers towards climate and the limitations that it may have imposed upon human activities in the past vary considerably (Shaw 1981), but events in Africa in the 1970s and 1980s make it impossible to forget the disastrous effects which even short-term fluctuations in climate can cause, particularly in marginal areas. However, it is equally apparent that the origins of such disasters are hotly debated – how far have recent famines been caused by political economic mismanagement rather than simply by the failure of annual rains? A central issue is the extent to which climate is altered by human actions such as deforestation or over-cultivation, rather than independent (and therefore uncontrollable) phenomena such as solar radiation or the behaviour of the earth's magnetic field.

A wide range of scientific approaches to past climate exists, using botanical, geological and physical methods which produce a mosaic of fragmentary evidence from different parts of the world. Ideally, it should be possible to produce an agreed sequence of past changes in climate from which patterns of weather could be inferred; a combined estimate of both temperature and rainfall is essential to the understanding of agriculture. Using documentary evidence, supplemented by actual meteorological records for recent centuries, Lamb has worked out a convincing long-term pattern of summer and winter temperatures in England (1982, 76, fig. 30; detailed evidence in Lamb 1977). The later medieval and modern periods in other parts of Europe also provide documentary evidence of climatic conditions which can be compared with agricultural indicators such as harvest dates, yields and prices (Le Roy Ladurie 1971; Le Roy Ladurie and Baulant 1981).

It is generally agreed that there has been a 'Little Ice Age' in recent centuries, followed by comparatively rapid warming within the last 100 years; Le Roy Ladurie's pictorial evidence of the retreat of Alpine glaciers since the last century is spectacular (op. cit. 80–128, and pl. 19–22 etc.). The previous warm period centred upon AD 1200, when the mean annual temperature in England was over one degree centigrade higher than in 1750. This apparently small difference was sufficient to extend the growing seasons of crops by several weeks during the medieval period, and in highland areas, traces of arable cultivation abound at altitudes where no ploughing has taken place at any time since then. The effects on weather of these changes in temperature are summarised very clearly by Gribbin and Lamb (1978).

Unfortunately, the quality of documentary evidence for the climate of Roman times is patchy and inadequate, although it has been used extensively (and rather too trustingly) by Lamb

(e.g. 1982, 14, fig. 55; 154. fig. 59). Harding's summary of several different environmental climatic indicators in Europe – lake levels, peat bogs, the extent of glaciers, etc. – is not very encouraging (1982, 9, fig. 1); no clear pattern emerges for the early historical period. Furthermore, sources of evidence such as the rate of formation of peat bogs may reflect human interference with soil drainage rather than changing weather. It is essential that scientific conclusions about the Roman period should be derived from independent but datable sources, which are not directly influenced by human settlement or agriculture.

Temperature is one factor which has been studied by a number of different disciplines, and a world pattern has emerged which conforms remarkably well with recent historical evidence (Rotberg and Rabb 1981). Lamb's estimate of the temperature of England from medieval to modern times correlates well with oxygen isotope variations in New Zealand (Wilson 1981, 221, fig. 2), and also appears to correlate with growing-season temperatures indicated by tree species in Michigan (Webb 1981, 185, fig. 7), although doubts have been expressed about the validity of Webb's methods (Birks 1981, 123–133). The advances and retreats of glaciers in north America and Scandinavia have been studied in great detail, and dated by the radiocarbon method (Denton and Karlen 1973; Porter S. 1981). The advances of the 'Little Ice Age' centred upon AD 1600–1750 were of a similar magnitude to those which reached a peak around 1000 BC. The intervening period of retreat lasted from c.450 BC until the thirteenth century AD, but in north America there are signs of a short episode of glacial expansion from c.AD 700–900 (Denton and Karlen 1973, 196; see also Porter S. 1981, 103, fig. 3.10).

The record of glacial expansion and contraction in the Arctic has been found to be strongly correlated with information obtained from tree-rings (fig. 30). In California, the record of annual growth rings in bristle-cone pine trees extends back beyond 5000 BC, and thus comfortably includes the whole of the Roman period (La Marche 1974; Greene 1983, 108). It must be emphasised that tree-rings can be counted objectively, and do not rely on any other form of dating; conversely, pollen analysis, peat formation or sedimentation must be dated by the radiocarbon method or associated artefacts, which have inherent margins of error which

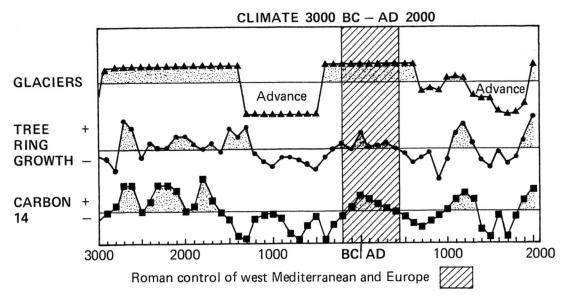

CLIMATE 3000 BC — AD 2000

30. Indicators of world climate over the last 5000 years place the Roman empire into an interesting context. The growth rate of Bristlecone Pines in California matches the phases of expansion and contraction of north American and European glaciers with some precision, whilst the fluctuating levels of carbon 14 in the atmosphere are a reflection of solar radiation. The well-documented medieval warm period and the rapid warming of the last few centuries show up clearly on all three graphs; there was evidently a similar warm phase between 200 BC and AD 400, which coincides neatly with the period of the Roman empire in the west. (Audio-Visual Centre, University of Newcastle; based on data published by Denton and Karlen 1973, La Marche 1974 and Eddy 1981)

increase with age (Greene 1983, 111–115). Tree-rings do not suffer from this problem; even in the Roman period they are accurate to a single year. Fluctuations in the levels of carbon isotopes in the atmosphere have been measured by Suess, and are generally thought to reflect variations in solar activity which also affected global temperature; Eddy has combined several indicators of temperature with Suess's measurements in a single diagram (1981, 165, fig. 4).

The width of Californian tree-rings reflects the comparative vigour of their growth, and thus, by implication, the variations of climatic conditions (La Marche 1974; Lamb 1982, 133, fig. 52). Their pattern correlates well with the known tempera-

tures of historical times, as well as the much longer record of solar radiation; the peak marking the medieval warm period is particularly apparent. It is clear that the beginning of the Roman empire coincided with a peak in temperature similar to that centred upon AD 1200. Despite the problems of converting evidence of temperature into weather and climate, it seems reasonable to accept that the known advantages for agriculture and settlement which occurred in the medieval optimum may also have operated in the early Roman empire. Indeed, Denton and Karlen concluded that: 'Extended into the future, the Holocene pattern of climatic change implies that the Little Ice Age, if it is not already over, will be succeeded by a climate regime similar to that of the Roman Empire and Middle Ages' (1973, 202).

The records of the effects of the Little Ice Age are well recorded. During the peak in temperature around AD 1200, the effects on agriculture in England were dramatic; vines grew in many parts of England, and fields extended well above the altitude reached by post-medieval cultivation (fig. 31). The population rose, and settlement extended to many marginal lands, only to be deserted in later centuries (Platt 1978, 93–96). During the Little Ice Age, the Thames froze regularly enough for fairs to be held on the ice. A study of Le Roy Ladurie's carefully collected documentary data on wine production in France has demonstrated a statistical correlation between the early date of harvests, high yields and good wine vintages (Bell B. 1981, 273, fig. 1). A period of relatively favourable results recorded by these indicators occurred between AD 1500 and 1600, at which time a small peak appears clearly in the records of both tree-ring growth (Lamb 1982, 133, fig. 52) and solar radiation (Eddy 1981, 165, fig. 4). It has sometimes been concluded that because Roman conditions were not unlike those of today, the subject does not require much attention; this attitude obscures the vital fact that our own century has been warmer than any period since the thirteenth century AD. In fact, Roman conditions implied by the long, large peak on the graphs (fig. 30) must have been especially favourable to agriculture, particularly in the north-western provinces of the empire.

Although it may be possible to establish a general outline of past climate, it should not be forgotten that an outline obscures detailed fluctuations, which can only be measured accurately in recent historical periods. The winter of 1984–5 caused severe damage to olive and citrus fruit trees around the Mediterranean and in America; one such winter in the middle of a

31. Aerial photograph of Haystack Hill, south-west of Ingram, Northumberland. A succession of earthworks of prehistoric to modern date shows up clearly in low afternoon sunshine on grassy moorland rising from c.200 to 260m above sea level on the eastern edge of the Cheviot Hills. The earliest site is a pre-Roman hill-fort with double ramparts (bottom left), and in the centre is a group of three oval stone-built farmsteads of Roman date. A medieval farmstead lies in the adjacent rectangular enclosure – it may have used the earlier remains for animal pens and haystack stands. Although the Roman sites survived, their field systems were destroyed by medieval ploughing, which formed the distinctive ridges covering much of the area. Some of the medieval fields were subdivided into narrower strips during a short period of re-use, possibly in the eighteenth century. An earthwork enclosure runs across the fields, and must therefore be of still later date; it was itself superseded by a stone-walled plantation in modern times. The three periods of cultivation – Roman, medieval and recent – reflect periods in which population pressure required this land, and when the climate allowed successful farming at this altitude (see fig. 30). (Photograph by courtesy of T. Gates; National Monuments Record, London)

generally warm phase of the Roman period would not be detectable without literary evidence, but could have had severe effects upon areas like southern Spain where olive oil was produced intensively. Furthermore, temperatures have complex effects on weather and patterns of rainfall (Lamb 1981; Magny 1981); only a few degrees difference are required to produce dramatic results.

Climate, agriculture and soil erosion

In the introduction to his synthesis of the settlement patterns of south Etruria, Potter summarised the evidence for climate in Italy derived from the evidence of pollen samples and river valley sediments (1979, 22–26). He argued that the long continuity apparent in Mediterranean crop and stock raising minimises the possibility of gross climatic changes since later prehistoric times. Pollen evidence shows a clear correlation between forest clearance in the last centuries BC and the expansion of settlement known from finds of sites. Potter claimed that there was abundant evidence of heavy deposition of sediments in river valleys from the second century AD onwards, after a period during which it had been possible to build permanent settlements on them. He equated this sedimentation with Vita-Finzi's 'Younger Fill', an episode of silting which apparently occurred all around the Mediterranean in the late classical period (1969). Unlike the pollen evidence, the 'Younger Fill' does not coincide with the phase of most intensive farming in central Italy which might otherwise have been held responsible for causing soil erosion through intensive arable farming. Since the sedimentation took place after the maximum extent of Italian settlement had been reached (in the late republic and early empire), Potter concluded that the erosion which it represents must have been caused by climatic change which resulted in increased rainfall (ibid. 24–26).

At first sight, there would seem to be a clear correspondence between rainfall and erosion, and the reduction of human settlement in central Italy. It might be tempting to extend this interpretation to other areas where a similar decline took place, and explain the failure of the Roman empire by means of environmental rather than political factors (Potter 1976). There are, of course, problems: Bell has criticised Potter's extension of the 'Younger Fill' phenomenon to explain evidence for flooding on some sites in

Roman Britain (1981, 87). Bell not only warns against extrapolating evidence from Italy to a completely different context in Britain, but also doubts that the 'Younger Fill' did in fact accumulate during a single specific period. He claims that his researches in England show that sedimentation occurred at different times in different places because of local agricultural activity rather than climatic change (1982, 131, 133, 137). Wagstaff endorses this opinion from evidence collected in Greece (1981, 260–261). This debate, and its fundamentally conflicting conclusions, highlights the dangers involved in the use of individual fragments of evidence which happen to coincide with archaeological observations in one area, and then generalising them to others.

Recent work around the Mediterranean has tended to favour human rather than climatic factors as the cause of the dramatic accumulations of sediment which took place in so many areas (fig. 32). By 1978, Vita-Finzi had virtually dismissed climate from the study of geomorphology (1978, 8, 11–13). In the area of central Italy discussed by Potter, Judson has stressed the complexity of the natural processes involved in the erosion and sedimentation patterns of streams; he points out that a change towards wetter conditions might, if anything, reduce erosion by encouraging more extensive vegetation (1983, 70–72). Judson also stresses the fact that agricultural exploitation of land can increase the rate of deposition by anything from 10 to 100 times.

Giardina (1981) has shown that reports in historical documents mentioning floods and sedimentation relate directly to the pattern of forest exploitation. Thus, a recession in agriculture, marked by the reduction in the number of settlement sites in central Italy from the late Roman period onwards, led to a decrease in major floods in Rome. However, after the end of the medieval warm period, which would have favoured the regeneration of forests, the expansion of agriculture led to a return to regular flooding, until nineteenth-century engineering works were carried out to prevent them. However, a different insight has emerged from a study of the Adige valley in northern Italy, where 'slope stability', produced by careful control of erosion by appropriate farming methods, lasted from c.300 BC–AD 600 (Coltorti and Dal Ri 1985). Pope and Andel reached a similar conclusion from their work in Greece; not even an expansion of settle-

32. Soil erosion resulting from heavy agricultural exploitation in the Greek and Roman periods has been observed in many regions around the Mediterranean. In this exposure of levels in the Ayiofarango valley in Crete (see p. 135), buildings of the fifth century BC to the early Roman period have been overlain by soil. Late Roman pottery was found at the top of the section, showing that little further erosion has taken place since then. (Photograph by courtesy of Prof. K. Branigan)

ment in the late Roman period onto steep and marginal lands caused erosion, presumably thanks to careful terracing (1984, 303).

A full review of the question of erosion and climate in Greece and around the Mediterranean has recently been included in Renfrew and Wagstaff's study of the island of Melos in the Cyclades (1983, 82–94); there is evidence for the deposition of sediment as early as 1000 BC on Melos itself, and it occurred at varying dates and rates elsewhere (ibid. 92–3). The expansion of Bronze Age population on Melos and its attendant intensification of agriculture are seen as the critical factor which removed fertile soil from large areas of sloping land and deposited it in the valleys. The question of causes is left slightly open, however: 'In conclusion, the geomorphological evolution of Melos in the late Holocene can in part be related to the changes in population, economy and settlement pattern during the

Bronze Age. Such a hypothesis does not preclude climatic change in later times having an effect on sedimentation rate' (ibid. 94).

I will summarise the only general and useful conclusions about climate which are relevant to the present chapter:

1 On the evidence of global temperature indicators, the period from c.500 BC–AD 500 included a peak in clement conditions similar to that experienced in Britain around AD 1200.

2 The soil erosion which can be shown to have occurred during this time was induced by the expansion of population and agriculture.

3 The decline in settlement which occurred at various times in the western provinces of the empire (below, Chapter 5) may have been accelerated by the deterioration of soils through erosion.

4 The possibility of deteriorating climatic conditions in the first millennium AD may have exacerbated the effects of 2 and 3 above.

It would be a mistake to try to apply any single climatic model to the whole empire; as Bintliff has pointed out, the ill-effects of a cooler, wetter phase in the west might have been advantageous in arid areas of the east (1982, 512–518). Chapter 5 shows that rural settlement did indeed continue to expand into the late Roman period in areas such as northern Syria, while it declined in Italy; is the explanation to be sought in their levels of political security, or the weather?

METHODS OF FARMING

The Roman empire at its greatest extent contained stark geographical contrasts, from the deserts of Africa to the cold mists of northern Britain. Italy itself experiences great differences in temperature and rainfall between the north and the south, and its geology and landscape also vary considerably from the Alps to Sicily (Cornell and Matthews 1982, 12–13, 16). It would therefore be false to expect any uniform system of agriculture to have existed in Italy, let alone in the rest of the empire.

Nevertheless, the Mediterranean climate does have sufficient uniformity to make its coastal lands capable of supporting generally similar crops. The warm wet winters and hot dry summers of the Mediterranean region have conditioned agricultural practices for thousands of years. A combination of crops including cereals, grapes and olives is grown by means of 'dry farming' techniques which still dominate Mediterranean agriculture (fig. 33), for which conservation of moisture is the guiding principle. Thus, whilst farmers in northern Gaul or Britain might plough their land once, to break up the surface and bury its grass and weeds before sowing a crop, a Mediterranean farmer would subject it to repeated ploughings with simple wooden ploughs, in order to break the soil down finely and to keep weeds at bay, lest they remove vital moisture.

Corn might be grown in the shade of large olive trees or between rows of vines around the Mediterranean; large cornfields of the kind which seem to have generated attempts at mechanised harvesting in Roman Gaul (White 1967b) would have been inconceivable in the dry hilly terrain of central Italy.

The importance of woodlands as a source of raw materials, fuel and fodder has been underestimated in modern accounts of agriculture. The active 'farming' of woodlands by coppicing and fencing to ensure supplies of small and large timbers has been emphasised by Rackham (1976), and such practices must have operated in

---

33. Anthropological and ethnographic studies contribute important comparative information for many aspects of archaeology. A study of modern farmers on the island of Melos in the Aegean shows how the labour involved in the cultivation of the 'Mediterranean triad' of olives, grapes and cereals is distributed through the year. Much of the work involved in olives and grapes takes place in the winter months, leaving the cereal harvest uninterrupted. The increased productivity which resulted from the introduction of this pattern of farming is considered to have been an important factor in the development of civilisation around the Mediterranean. (Audio-Visual Centre, University of Newcastle; based on data from Renfrew and Wagstaff 1981, 121, fig. 10.7)

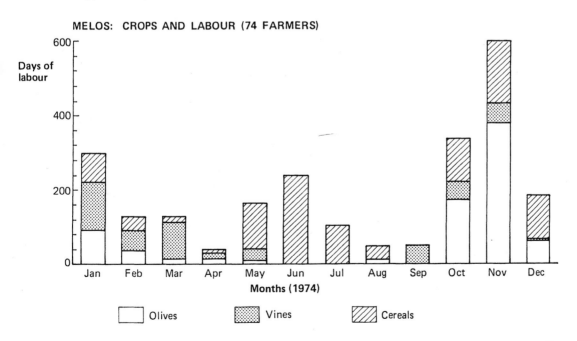

MELOS: CROPS AND LABOUR (74 FARMERS)

Days of labour

Months (1974)

☐ Olives   ▦ Vines   ▨ Cereals

the Roman period in areas such as Britain where large-scale forest clearance had already been completed in prehistoric times. Fulford has suggested that the major pottery industries of later Roman Britain were located away from towns because the demand for fuel was more important than the proximity of an urban market (1977b, 307–308). In Italy, the mountainous central areas continued to supply ample timbers for architects and shipbuilders throughout the Roman period, and deforestation does not seem to have been a problem even in metal-working areas (Meiggs 1982, 377–380). Timber was a regular trade item involving major transport organisation and appears in a number of species and sizes on Diocletian's price *Edict* of AD 301 (ibid. 333–346, 365–9). The history of Mediterranean forests has not been a happy one; it has recently featured in a study of ancient and modern 'resource depletion' by Thirgood (1981).

Organisation and landholding

An important key to the understanding of agriculture is the form and extent of rural settlement. A detailed knowledge of the nature and number of settlements of all kinds from cities to shepherds' huts is vitally important if their implications for population and marketing systems are to be properly understood. Archaeology is of major significance in this context, but historical evidence can be more important in assessing the manner in which land was owned, managed and exploited; productivity is not an automatic reflection of potential. An interpretation of the workings of the Roman agricultural economy is very dependent upon accurate information about the size of farms or estates, the demand for their produce, and the availability of labour. A good example of the integration of archaeological and documentary evidence is provided by Peyras' reconstruction of an estate in north Africa from the owner's burial inscription, Roman law, and surviving traces on the ground (1975). Unfortunately, Roman archaeology has tended to lag behind its prehistoric and medieval counterparts in conducting detailed analyses of settlement patterns and their environment, but sufficient advances have been achieved in recent years to allow some interesting conclusions to be drawn. The results of some of these are summarised in Chapter 5.

Each newly-conquered province had its own individual background of native agricultural traditions, which may have continued to exist with very little disturbance after their occupation (e.g. Mitchell 1980). The major form of disturbance came in the form of colonies of Roman citizens, which possessed substantial tracts of farmland to provide farmsteads for their settlers in addition to the cities themselves (Keppie 1983; Modena 1984). Colonisation was a feature of the expansion which took place during the republic rather than the empire, but it left visible traces in the form of regular land divisions, known as centuriation (fig. 50), which have determined the layout of fields and roads to the present day in many areas (Bradford 1957, 145–216). The field survey of the territory of the colony at Cosa in Italy has indicated that the small pioneer landholdings became absorbed into larger estates quite rapidly (Dyson 1978; below p. 107).

Most changes in native agricultural practices probably came about through the impact of military exactions, urban markets, and the monetisation of transactions, rather than from official attempts to increase output. It would be wrong to look for major technical improvements unless it could be demonstrated that output was already nearing its maximum, and that there was no spare capacity for increased production. The appearance of distinctively Roman buildings in the countryside, notably masonry villas with mosaic floors, painted wall plaster, heated rooms and bath suites, need not indicate 'Roman' owners, or a new system of landholding. There is plenty of evidence to show that the estate-owners and town councillors of Roman times were descendants of the pre-Roman aristocracy, whose status was enhanced by the adoption of the manners of upper-class Italy. However, it is apparent from the regional surveys discussed in Chapter 5 that the Roman villa estate was the principal instrument of agricultural exploitation in most parts of the Roman empire.

THE ROMAN VILLA

The most distinctive feature of rural settlement in the northern and western provinces of the Roman empire is the phenomenon of villas (figs. 23–24; 34). No comparable number of large masonry buildings in the countryside had ever been achieved before the late republic and early empire; it would not be equalled again until the post-medieval period. Unfortunately, there is extensive disagreement about the definition of villas amongst modern archaeologists and historians, which actually reflects the imprecision of the term in Roman literature (Percival 1976, 13–15): 'There is a suspicion that it is a townsman's word: that is, a villa is not simply a place in the country, but a place in the country from the point of view of someone living in a town' (ibid. 14).

Most British archaeologists would agree about the definition of perhaps 80 per cent of supposed villa sites in Britain, and will entertain no doubts about those endowed with fine mosaic floors and bath-houses. The problem arises over borderline cases – when does a farm become a villa? Excavation in Italy, Germany and Britain has demonstrated that many indisputable villas had humble origins, and developed gradually over several centuries from pre-Roman 'native' houses to rectangular buildings, first in timber and then in masonry or half-timbering (e.g. RCHM 1983, fig. 2). These modest Romanised structures might then survive as the core of a building of architectural distinction which flourished in the later empire (Percival 1976, 96–103, figs. 27–31). At what point did they become villas rather than Romanised farmhouses? A further problem is the disparity between the definitions which have been used in different areas of the empire. In the American survey of the *ager cosanus*, only the most elaborate buildings were classed as villas (Dyson 1981, and below p. 107); on Dyson's definition, many British sites would have been considered as mere farms. In Syria, Tchalenko applied the term 'villa' to buildings which undoubtedly parallel those in the western provinces, but which have no distinctly 'Roman' architectural features.

Potter's comments on the state of villa studies and the need for comprehensive excavation (above p. 67) make it important to avoid being side-tracked into problems of definition which can obscure their real interest for the study of the economy. Taken together, their distribution must be a reflection of general patterns of landholding and agricultural exploitation, and is best studied by means of regional fieldwork programmes. Individual villas might reflect the fortunes of their owners, and the lands from which they derived profits which were at least partly spent on the construction and decoration of a villa. Unfortunately, Roman literature makes it quite clear that large landowners could own many estates, not all of which would be used as residences for any length of time. Thus, a sumptuous building might be erected upon one particular estate because the owner considered it to be a pleasant place to spend time, not because it was the most profitable in terms of agriculture. Ancient historians such as Finley have often emphasised the point that fortunes made in commercial activity were not re-invested 'productively' (i.e. in manufacturing), but were spent on land and other 'respectable' pursuits. Thus, a large villa might have even less connection with agricultural productivity, and be built from earnings made in a different activity; Gorges has suggested that the extraordinary density of villas in southern Spain was initiated by profits from metal extraction (fig. 47; 1979, 29), although it is quite clear that their owners were actively engaged in intensive agriculture (Ponsich 1974, 1979; below p. 111).

Two excavated sites will be examined here in order to explore the way in which archaeology can approach the study of villas – Sette Finestre in central Italy, and Gatcombe in south-west England. Sette Finestre has impressive architectural remains, and provides an example of the potential of an integrated programme of fieldwork and excavation, linked to historical information and broader archaeological research. It helps to give a physical dimension to historical debates about the changing patterns of land management, and the extent to which 'respectable' Roman senators could be involved in commerce. This activity was universally frowned upon in the literary sources which reflect the anti-commercial ethos of the Roman aristocracy, but was obviously practised on a considerable scale (D'Arms 1981). A complete contrast is provided by the report on a site at Gatcombe in Somerset (Branigan 1977), where a paucity rather than an abundance of evidence forced the excavator to adopt a purely archaeological approach to the site, and to frame its interpretation in the form of possibilities of different levels of credibility. The manner of its publication is almost as instructive as the site itself.

Sette Finestre

The Roman colony of Cosa and its hinterland have been studied by the American Academy in Rome (Brown 1980; Dyson 1978 and 1981c). The villa at Sette Finestre has been excavated by an Anglo-Italian team, not in isolation, but together with further fieldwork up to 1984; good summaries of the villa excavation are available (Carandini and Settis 1979, Carandini and Tatton-Brown 1980). The book by Carandini and Settis 1979 has a title (*Schiavi e padroni nell'Etruria Romana* – slaves and masters/landlords

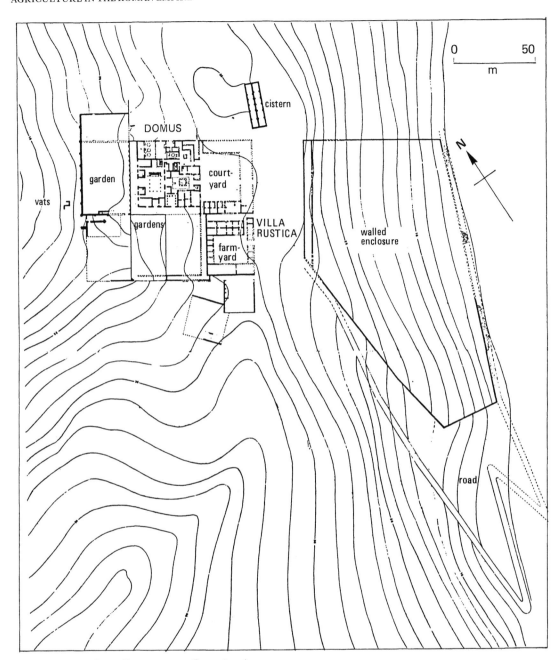

34. The villa at Sette Finestre, near Cosa, has been the subject of detailed excavations which have revealed an establishment with lavish residential accommodation (*domus*) as well as facilities for intensive farming (*villa rustica*). It may have belonged to the aristocratic family of the Sestii, who are well known from literature of the first century BC. (Audio-Visual Centre, University of Newcastle; based on Carandini and Tatton Brown 1980, fig. 7)

in Roman Etruria) which underlines the keen interest in the political implications of archaeology found amongst Italian Marxist historians (Dyson 1981b). This is also characteristic of the three-volume survey of Roman socio-economic archaeology edited by Giardina and Schiavone (1981).

The villa lies just over 3km (1¾ miles) from Cosa on a small hill in the fertile Valle d'Oro (fig. 45), which had originally been divided into small plots for colonists in the third century BC. The small farms of the colonists disappeared and were replaced by a number of villas by the end of the first century BC, most of which had in their turn disappeared by the third century AD (Carandini and Settis 1979, pann. 5–8). The complex of buildings on the hill at Sette Finestre has a compact rectangular plan, and includes a house (*villa urbana*) and farmyard (*villa rustica*), with walled or colonnaded gardens and a courtyard. On the lower slopes beside the terraced access road lay a very large polygonal walled enclosure (fig. 34).

It is clear that Sette Finestre was not simply a recreational dwelling, for attached to the residential section is a series of processing rooms for agricultural produce, with olive and grape presses and a mill (fig. 35; Carandini and Settis 1979, pann. 18–20 include further explanation and interpretation). Beneath the villa were cellars into which the grape juice could drain from the presses for wine-making; they would also provide

useful cool storage for other produce. The house and processing rooms opened onto a courtyard surrounded by small rooms interpreted as accommodation for slaves (Carandini and Settis 1979, pann. 14). The *villa rustica* consisted of a farmyard surrounded by small rooms and a granary/store building (Carandini and Tatton-Brown 1980, fig. 11). Thus, the excavated remains imply the cultivation of grapes and olives for wine and oil production, grain growing and milling, and, if the polygonal walled enclosure held animals, stock raising.

What makes the villa at Sette Finestre particularly interesting is its possible association with a Roman senatorial family, the Sestii. Lucius Sestius was a consul in 23 BC, and his name is found

35. The villa complex at Sette Finestre included a range of rooms along the north side of the *domus* equipped for milling cereals, and processing grapes and olives into wine and oil. Grape juice was fed through a drain into cellars where fermentation could take place. Wine-jars bearing the name-stamp of the Sestii, who may have owned the villa, have been found around the western Mediterranean and in France. (Audio-Visual Centre, University of Newcastle; based on Carandini and Tatton-Brown 1980, fig. 8)

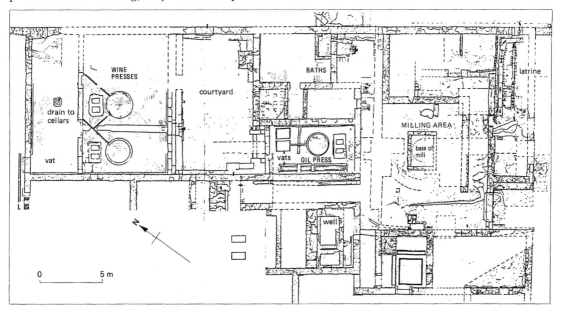

on brick stamps in Rome; his father Publius is known to have owned estates at Cosa in the first century BC. The initials LS have been found stamped on a few tiles at Sette Finestre, but the abbreviation SES occurs on wine amphorae which have been found in such quantities near the port of Cosa that it seems likely that they were made there. The same stamp occurs on amphorae found on sites and in shipwrecks in an area stretching from Cosa around the coast of Gaul and inland as far as the Rhône and Loire (Manacorda 1981, 6, tav. 1). If Sette Finestre itself was not the residence of the Sestii, it must represent the kind of estate-centre appropriate to a family of high status involved in commercial exploitation of intensive agriculture (Carandini and Settis 1979, pann. 35–37; Carandini and Tatton-Brown 1980, 20–21; Manacorda 1978, 1981). The production and export of wine amphorae came to an end in the first century BC, but Lucius's brick stamps and the occurrence of SES on arretine terra sigillata of the Augustan period suggest that brick and pottery production centred elsewhere in Italy followed the demise of the wine business (Will 1984). It should not be assumed that the Sestius amphorae were actually traded by the family; amphora manufacture was not specifically related to the needs of individual estates.

Gatcombe

This site lies less than 10km (6¼ miles) from the centre of Bristol, beside a small river which runs parallel to the Avon into the Bristol Channel (fig. 37), and comprises a walled enclosure 200m wide and at least 300m long containing many building (fig. 36). The villa itself is assumed to have lain at the south end of the enclosure, where nineteenth-century writers recorded finds of building materials, and to have been buried or destroyed in the course of railway construction. Small-scale occupation of the site lasted from the later first century AD until the late third, when the wall and the buildings it enclosed were constructed (ibid. 8, fig. 2). Their occupation lasted around a century, and was followed by a brief reoccupation in the late fourth century. The enclosure was divided into zones of buildings with specific functions, separated by open ground which was presumably cultivated (185, fig. 33). Finds indicated the use of one group of buildings for grain storage, milling and baking; another group was associated with the smelting and working of iron and pewter; a third group suggested storage, next to a slaughter-house (Branigan 1977, 182–186). Finds of domestic items and trinkets suggest that the workers may well have lived in the buildings (ibid. 186). No buildings connected with animals were found, but they may have lain in unexcavated areas, or outside the enclosure.

The walled enclosure was originally thought to enclose a small town, but the location of the site, the sudden appearance of the enclosure and its buildings, and the lack of any streets or planning make this unlikely. A rôle as a military arms factory or as the official centre of an imperially-owned estate is also considered unlikely from the finds (Branigan 1977, 187–188). The enclosure, its ranges of buildings, and the probability that a villa building formerly existed at its southern end recalls the plans of villas known in Gaul (ibid. 191). This layout is unique in Britain, however, and Branigan proposes that it may have been established by an immigrant Gallic landowner who had fled from the uncertainties of life in the areas of Gaul which came under barbarian attack in the third century AD – precisely the period of Gatcombe's comprehensive construction. The contrast between these tentative conclusions, and the strong literary link between Sette Finestre and the Sestii could not be more stark:

> It seems that we may assert that a building with architecture of considerable quality and sophistication, fitting to be called a villa, was located at Gatcombe . . . The evidence firmly supports the construction of the whole complex at Gatcombe, villa building included, in the late 3rd century AD . . . Neither the layout nor the scale of Main Phase Gatcombe prove that it was built by an immigrant Gaul, but they certainly make the suggestion a plausible one. (Branigan 1977, 191–2)

Any historian unused to the technicalities of excavation reports should remember that such tiers of fragile assumptions and suggestions can lose their essential note of caution when quoted in a secondary source. The kinds of deduction involved in the interpretation of Sette Finestre and Gatcombe must be measured on altogether different scales of judgement.

The concluding sections of the report on Gatcombe are concerned with the economy of the villa's estate, which is reconstructed (entirely hypothetically) according to local topography, and limits implied by the existence of other villas in the neighbourhood (fig. 37). Branigan arrives

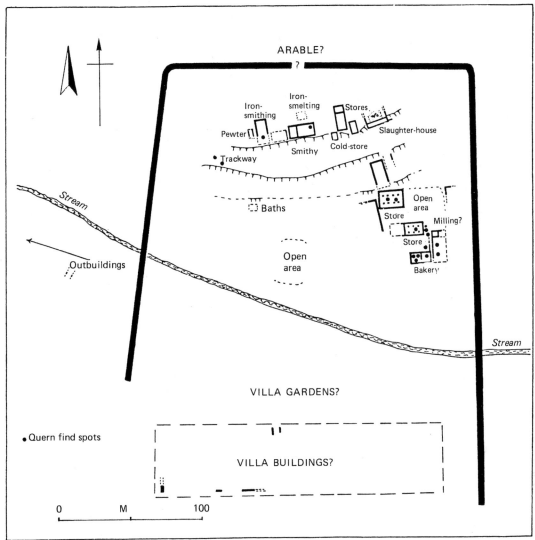

36. Buildings associated with the supposed Roman villa at Gatcombe, contained within a large enclosure wall; their functions were suggested by associated finds. The structure which the excavator presumed to have been a villa was destroyed in the nineteenth century; if it was indeed a villa, the site is unusual in the extent to which the important subsidiary buildings have been studied. (Audio-Visual Centre, University of Newcastle; based on Branigan 1977, 184, fig. 33)

at a total of 6000 ha (15,000 acres), divided between arable, pasture (upland, low lying, and summer), sheep grazing and woodland (op. cit. 196); the 'estate' also included at least eight 'native' settlements. On the basis of these factors, Branigan proceeds to 'discuss the way in which this land-use potential could have been integrated into a viable and profitable economy' (ibid. 197) using calculations of yields and stock capacity made by Graeme Barker and Derek Webley (ibid. 198–200). Medieval analogies and modern soil science enable 1000 head of cattle and 3000 sheep to be envisaged, and a workforce of 50–60 families (with additional labour during hay-making). Wheat and barley grown in a rotation system on the arable could have supported 1000–1100

people – far more than adequate for the supposed population, and therefore leaving perhaps 76,200kg (1500 cwt) as a surplus for export.

From these entirely hypothetical figures of

93

production from the supposed estate of the possible villa, Branigan proceeds to examine the archaeological evidence for the economy. He proposes a processing and organising rôle for the villa, through which products were channelled to the local markets. The native settlements are seen as belonging to dependent labourers or slaves rather than tenants – 'the potential of the Gatcombe estate could only be fully realised if it was organised as a single entity' (op. cit. 206). Inward trade is represented by commodities such as pottery, 60 per cent of which came by road from more than 100km (62 miles) away from the site. Coal and iron ore were used, and Bath stone was required for building; specialised foodstuffs such as salt and wine also came from beyond the estate. They were most probably acquired through town markets, where the estate's beef, grain, and other animal and plant products could be sold; official levies were probably transported to the army in Wales by way of the Avon and the Bristol Channel.

The main discussion of the Gatcombe report has been outlined in some detail because of its importance in illustrating one possible approach to fragmentary evidence, which presses the limits of inference as far as they will go – and further, in the eyes of more cautious critics. It is interesting to note a parallel between Branigan's approach to archaeology and Hopkins' to ancient history; the statement of hypotheses, and the cumulative weight of assumptions may not achieve concrete results, but can stimulate new ideas, and point out areas where new research is most urgently required. Branigan terminates his speculations with an orderly list of conclusions, ranked in order of likelihood: 'The mixing of fact and theory, of the certain, the probable and the possible, throws the writer wide open to charges of fantasy-building and at the same time may confuse or mislead the reader who may not be clear at the end of the exercise what is fact and what is hypothesis' (op. cit. 211).

THE GARDENS OF POMPEII

The comparatively recent revelation that precise details of plants and produce could be gained from excavation at such well known and much explored sites as Pompeii and Herculaneum is an important reminder that archaeological techniques may have much new and unsuspected information to offer. The countryside around Pompeii is famous for its large number of villas,

and a part of their economic function has always been assumed to be the supply of food to the town, normally envisaged as densely occupied by houses, workshops and businesses. An extensive study of Pompeii by Wilhelmina Jashemski has necessitated a revision of this image, for as well as the expected ornamental gardens belonging to houses, temples and public buildings, she has revealed important commercial gardens, orchards and vineyards. In exact terms, while ornamental gardens occupied 8 per cent of the excavated area, large food-producing areas occupied 9.7 per cent. As Jashemski points out:

> A study of land use within the city, and of the relative density of buildings in proportion to the amount of open space, is of considerable importance in making any estimate of the size of the population. The amount of open space and the amount of land under cultivation tell us a great deal about the quality of life in this ancient city. Ancient Pompeii, with its many open areas of green gardens, parks, vineyards, orchards, and vegetable plots – must have been very beautiful indeed, and very different from the crowded, overbuilt city sometimes described by modern scholars. (Jashemski 1979, 24)

The detailed understanding of the gardens of Pompeii is possible only because of the destruction of the city by the eruption of Vesuvius in AD 79, which buried it under a thick layer of hot ashes. Unless disturbed by subsequent clearance, the soil surface of that date lies immediately below the ashes; any plants, shrubs or trees growing at the time would have been covered, and were either charred by the heat or gradually decayed away. For archaeological purposes, the decay of the roots was important, for small roots left empty cavities, and larger root holes became filled with ashes. If the overlying ashes are carefully removed to expose the Roman ground surface, these cavities can be revealed, measured and planned. Furthermore, Jashemski demonstrated that the cavities could be used as moulds after excavation and emptying; after being filled with cement and reinforced by wires, the surrounding earth could be removed to expose the form of the root system. This allowed many species of large plants and trees to be identified, and thus assisted in determining the produce of individual gardens (Jashemski 1979, 23, fig. 31). Fortunately for archaeology, Vesuvius erupted in August, when many plants were bearing fruits and other crops, from which remains of seeds, beans, pips, nuts and stones survived, allowing further precision in the

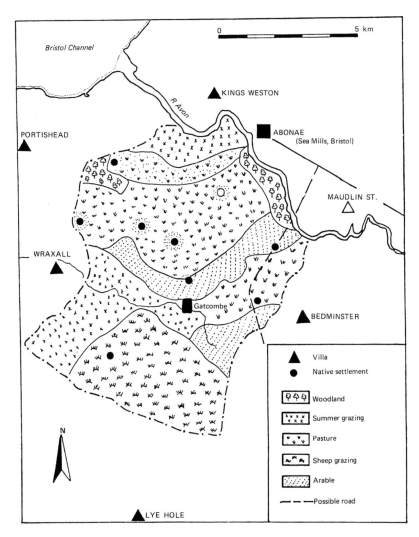

identification of species (op. cit. 211, figs. 307–8; 241, figs. 352–7; 290, fig. 437).

A large vineyard

A striking example of the revision of concepts demanded by Jashemski's work is provided by the open area (*c.*75 × 85m [246ft × 279ft]) immediately north of the city's amphitheatre, which had been named the *forum boarium* because it was thought by early excavators to have been a cattle market (op. cit. 202–218). Excavation and root-cavity casting revealed that it was filled by orderly rows of vines, each plant placed 4m (13ft 2in) apart and supported by a wooden stake. In addition, numerous trees were found, many between the second and third rows of vines away from the vineyard wall. Some were demonstrably

37. A possible 'villa estate' at Gatcombe, near Bristol. The boundaries are suggested by geographical features and the location of other villas, and the land-use is reconstructed from surface geology. It must be emphasised that this is an entirely hypothetical exercise; the value of such 'model-building' exercises is to draw attention to environmental factors which might have influenced the actual territories and economy of a villa. (Audio-Visual Centre, University of Newcastle; based on Branigan 1977, 194, fig. 34)

olive trees, and it seems likely that the remainder would have provided a range of fruits; vines could, of course, have grown up these trees as well as their supporting stakes. The vineyard also contained two outdoor dining areas with reclining benches (*triclinia*). The presence of many animal bones, often bearing signs of butchering, suggests that meals were served commercially in the leafy shade of the vines; the vineyard was located in a prime position in relation to the amphitheatre, ideally placed to attract high-class diners.

Adjacent to the owner's house in one corner of the vineyard were a wine-pressing room and a shed containing ten huge earthenware jars (*dolia*) set into the ground, in which grape juice would have been fermented (Jashemski 1979, 226). It would have been possible to produce up to 12,500 litres (2750 gals) of wine. To complete the establishment, a shop front with a counter under a colonnade opened out onto the adjacent street now known as the Via dell'Abbondanza. Jashemski concludes that:

> A vineyard required more intensive care than any other Mediterranean crop but, if properly culti-vated, it yielded large returns. The precision with which this vineyard had been planted and the care with which it had been cultivated suggest that the ancient vintner was a careful husbandman who enjoyed a good revenue from his vineyard which, judging from its prominent location, was a show-place much enjoyed' (op. cit. 214–15).

One might add that additional income from his (or her) rôle as *restaurateur* would have been useful, particularly as house wines and home-grown olives, nuts and soft fruits would have been available at the right seasons.

A market-garden orchard

The 'cattle market' area was by no means the only commercial vineyard in Pompeii (Jashemski 1979, 219–232), and wine was not the only marketable product. In region I of the city, there is a building known as the 'House of the ship *Europa*', named after a drawing of the ship scratched onto one of its walls (fig. 8). Two houses assumed to be in single ownership front onto a street, and behind them lies an open area, 55m (180ft 5in) long and 31m (101ft 8in) wide (fig. 38). Approximately one third of this area nearest to the house formed a raised terrace which had been planted with young trees; larger trees were found all around the garden's enclosing wall. The lower terrace contained areas of vines, and paral-lel sets of beds of soil, with small tree roots along them. On the evidence of the plant remains which were found, these plots seem to have been for growing vegetables, sheltered from direct sun by nut bushes – a classic example of intercultivation.

Altogether, 240 trees were recorded, most of them young and closely spaced. Several had been planted in earthenware pots with large holes, and these have been interpreted as an indication of grafted species, probably soft fruits, cultivated in a manner described by Pliny the Elder (Jashemski 1979, 239–240).

Other specialised gardens studied by Jashemski at Pompeii include a large orchard (1979, 251–265), and an establishment where flowers may have been grown in well-watered beds shaded by large trees, probably for the production of perfumes as well as the flowers themselves (ibid. 279–288). The obvious implication of so much commercial rather than purely ornamental gardening, in the final years of Pompeii at least, is that the kind of agricultural production hitherto assumed to have taken place on farms and villas near to towns could in fact exist within them as well. The distinction between town and country is therefore truly blurred.

FURTHER READING

The starting point of Roman agriculture must be White's *Roman farming* (1970), and his more specialised works such as *Farm equipment of the Roman world* (1975); agriculture is also included to an extent in his *Greek and Roman technology* (1984). The villa system is discussed by Percival in *The Roman villa* (1976); the contribution of aerial photography is evident in articles by Wilson in *Britannia* 1974, and Agache in *Antiquity* 1972. Our growing knowledge of villas and their associated structures is reflected in two books, Rossiter's *Roman farm buildings in Italy* (1978) and Morris's *Agricultural buildings in Roman Britain* (1979). Carandini's final report on the villa at Sette Finestre should be available by the time this book is published.

Land-holding and tenancy is the subject of *Terres et paysans dépendants dans les societés antiques* (Besançon 1979); the political issue of tenancy figures prominently in the writings of Kolendo, who has also written a general book, *L'agricoltura dell'Italia antica* (1980). Archaeological aspects of land-holding are featured in a collection of papers edited by Bowen and Fowler, *Early land allotment in the British Isles* (1978). Agricultural products have been the subject of numerous monographs, art-icles and conference proceedings. For wine, see Hagenow's *Aus der Weingarten der Antike* (1982); for oil, *Produccion y comercio del aceite en la antigüedad*, edited by Blazquez (1980); for grain, Rickman's

The *corn supply of ancient Rome* (1980) and Tengström's *Bread for the people* (1974). The important resource of wood has been studied by Meiggs, *Trees and timber in the ancient Mediterranean world* (1982).

The exploitation of animals in farming, as reflected by their bones found on archaeological sites, has been surveyed by Luff, *A zooarchaeological study of the Roman north-western provinces* (1982). Frayn has produced a monograph on *Sheep rearing and the wool trade in Italy during the Roman period* (1984), and Wild has considered woven materials in *Textile manufacture in the northern Roman provinces* (1970). Fish and their products are the subject of Ponsich and Tarradell's *Garum et industries de salaison* (1965).

The use of archaeology in investigating agriculture is central to Shackley's *Using environmental archaeology* (1985), and *Early European agriculture* by Jarman *et al.* (1982). The climatic setting involves complex research and hypotheses, which are very well set out in Flohn and Fantechi's *The climate of Europe: past, present and future* (1984); their implications are discussed by papers included in *Climate and history*, edited by Wigley *et al.* (1981). The physical context and potential of agriculture is dependent on surface geology, from the location of sites to their local soils. These themes are covered by Vita-Finzi in *Archaeological sites in their setting* (1978), and *Soil science and archaeology* by Limbrey (1975).

The post-Roman history of agriculture is a complex subject, full of far-reaching political and social implications. As usual, Braudel provides fascinating insights into food, diet, social status and economics (*The structures of everyday life*, 1981). Postan's *Essays on medieval agriculture* (1973) considers its relationship with other aspects of the economy, whilst Abel charts the ups and downs of agriculture and their effects (*Agricultural fluctuations in Europe*, 1980). A different perspective, written in a provocative manner, can be derived from Watson's *Agricultural innovation in the early Islamic world* (1983). An attempt to lay down general parameters for the study of agriculture as a whole has been made by Green's chapter 'Towards a general model of agricultural systems' in volume 3 of Schiffer's *Advances in archaeological method and theory* (1980).

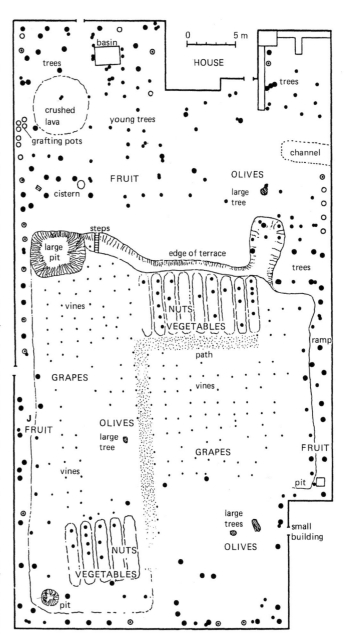

38. The garden of the House of the Ship *Europa*, Pompeii. Each black dot represents the position and size of a root cavity discovered by excavation; lower-case labels indicate plant species, capitals indicate crops, many of which were represented by preserved plant remains. It seems that the potential of the garden's production would have exceeded the requirements of the household, and that the garden may therefore have had a commercial function. (Audio-Visual Centre, University of Newcastle; based on Jashemski 1979, 236, fig.346)

FIVE

Regional surveys of Roman settlement and agriculture

SURVEYS, STRATEGIES AND SAMPLING

Current interest in social and economic aspects of the archaeology of all periods, combined with the use of more scientific theoretical approaches, has proved very profitable for Roman archaeology. Social evolution can be examined through the study of settlement patterns and the manner in which resources of the land were exploited; as a result, an enormous number of multi-period field survey projects have been generated all around the Mediterranean and other parts of the former Roman empire (fig. 39). Few have been initiated with Roman archaeology as their prime objective, but their results allow the Roman period to be set into the wider perspective of prehistoric and medieval times. The impressive extent of recent and current work around the Mediterranean can be measured by examining the papers included in Keller and Rupp's publication devoted to field surveys. Their maps include 97 projects from Spain to the Levant, with particular concentrations in Italy and Greece (1983, 8–15, figs. 1–4).

Field survey projects are filled with methodological problems in their design and execution. Political and agricultural circumstances can impose limitations on the accessibility of survey areas, whilst statistical difficulties arise from attempts to draw comparisons or generalisations from their results. Cherry has written an interesting exploration of field survey as a conclusion to Keller and Rupp's volume (1983, 375–416); he emphasises the difficulty of finding direct matches between the kind of information that fieldwork can recover and specific questions which may be posed by historians (388). It is hoped that the results of surveys outlined below will help to demonstrate their unique strength, which is the way in which they can provide large quantities of information unobtainable in any other way, whose importance therefore increases in areas where historical sources are lacking. The urban bias of most Graeco-Roman writers is to some extent balanced by the newly revealed distribution maps of farms, villas and rural industries. Virtually every region that has been explored has produced results which demand the revision or review of existing ideas: 'It would be an obdurate historian indeed who could reject the fruits of this sort of rural archaeology on the grounds that it is somehow "unreliable" or "non-historical"' (Cherry 1983, 389). Snodgrass has also preached the virtues of field survey to historians in the French periodical *Annales* (1982).

Modern geography uses many statistical techniques which have been applied to human settlement patterns of the past (Hodder and Orton 1976). The distribution of Romano-British towns has been related to theoretical market territories (Hodder and Hassall 1971), and their spatial relation to villas in the surrounding countryside has also been examined (Hodder and Millet 1980). However, if such data is going to be used in statistical tests, it is important that an awareness of the 'fruits' of field surveys should be accompanied by a critical perception of their limitations; research strategies should be examined with care. In some areas (such as the Libyan valleys, northern Syria or the Cheviot hills in England) sites still exist on the surface as visible monuments and field systems. In central Italy, most information has been recovered in the form of postsherds and building debris uncovered by new intensive arable cultivation of land which had been disturbed very little since the Roman period. In the Somme valley and Northamptonshire, most sites are known from aerial photographs showing faint

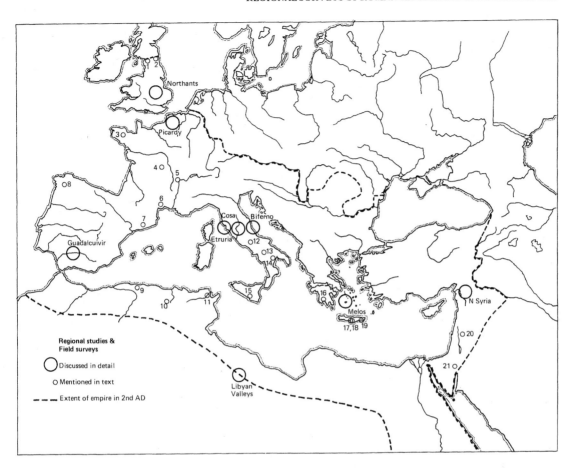

traces of sites which have been under plough for centuries, but are now subjected to more intensive cultivation than ever before. Each of these types of information has its own problems of survival and interpretation, and each field project will have approached the recovery and recording of evidence in a different way; the question of sampling is therefore fundamental.

Sampling

It must always be determined whether an area has been surveyed totally or selectively. Even 'total' survey is restricted by problems of accessibility for teams of field-walkers, and the nature of ground cover by plants (figs. 40, 42). Random sampling tries to remove subjective biases by selecting parts of a survey area according to a statistical random-number table, whilst a structured sample aims to maximise information by exploring specific areas, in order to ensure, for instance, that any major differences in terrain or

39. Regional fieldwork studies with important implications for the Roman period have been undertaken in many parts of the empire, and many more are currently under way; the decade to 1985 has seen a dramatic expansion of this kind of research. A selection of published examples is considered in Chapter 5. They vary from intensive multi-period studies involving new fieldwork, to single-period summaries of known sites. The numbered areas are: 1, Solway; 2, Cheviots; 3, Armorica; 4, Berry; 5, Lyon; 6, Beziers; 7, Tarragona; 8, Galicia; 9, Cherchel; 10, Diana Veteranorum; 11, Carthage; 12, Liri valley; 13, Buccino; 14, Metaponto; 15, Heraclea Minor; 16, Nichoria; 17, Mesara; 18, Ayiofarango; 19, Lasithi; 20, Golan Heights; 21, Negev. (Audio-Visual Centre, University of Newcastle)

soil-types are encompassed. The purpose of careful sampling is to allow further deductions to be made by generalising from a known base of information. The objectives of the survey should

determine the strategy of its design. Thus, if the main interest is in the extent to which different soils were exploited in different periods, a structured sample of equal areas of different soils should be investigated; if, however, it is the relationships between sites of different kinds that is of most interest, a continuous area of the largest manageable size will yield better results than a scatter of smaller samples.

These objectives are rarely separable in practice, of course; the available resources of money, time and labour will limit the extent to which a satisfactory compromise can be reached. Not all surveys are published in a manner which allows the problems of information recovery and sampling to be assessed; however, a good explanation of the research design involved in a specific multiperiod survey on the coast of Yugoslavia has been expounded in welcome detail by Batović and Chapman (1985). They specifically cited the four basic questions which Cherry and Shennan (1978, 22) outlined as most suitable for elucidation by a field survey:

1 The number of sites in the area.

2 The number of sites by period and function.

3 The relationship between archaeological sites and environmental variables.

4 The interrelationships between archaeological sites.

40. Field survey needs careful planning and meticulous execution. In areas such as the Libyan desert, the problems of recording are rather different from those encountered where modern agriculture has destroyed surface structures (fig. 42). In both cases, chronological information must be recovered by examining any datable artefacts which occur on the surface. Selective excavation may be needed in order to clarify surface remains. Each survey has its individual problems, which must be taken into account in the interpretation of the results. (Photograph by R. Burns)

The skills of survey directors and their assistants are critical, and it is the duty of all archaeologists who publish fieldwork projects to explain their objectives and strategies as fully as possible, and to discuss all of the practical matters which may influence the validity of their results. Readers of the results should take careful note of these factors, as well as the date and size of the survey. Cherry has made it abundantly clear that recent surveys in Greece have been around ten times more productive in site discovery than those conducted before 1970; the major difference is that the more recent surveys have tended to examine smaller areas in greater detail (Cherry 1983, 410, fig. 1). Compromises need to be made not only between sampling strategies, but also with the scale of survey; will an intense survey of a small area be more informative than a less detailed survey of a region? The former will probably reveal more sites, but the latter may allow greater insights into general trends, even though site density is likely to be underestimated.

A good example of a recent full publication of a survey project is the study of Melos (fig. 41) edited by Renfrew and Wagstaff (1982). The maximum scope of the survey was defined by the fact that Melos was an island a little over 150km² (58 sq. miles) in area lying 100km (62 miles) south-west from the mainland of Greece. The research goals and survey strategy have been summarised by Cherry (in Keller and Rupp 1983, 279–280):

> Our goal, in short, was the diachronic investigation of human settlement on Melos in relation to the changing island environment, focusing in particular on those internal and external factors which might

have affected the major episodes of change and stability in the island's history . . . In order to cancel the biases in previously collected data and to ensure that our efforts were spread over all parts of the island, a 20 per cent stratified, systematic random transect sample was selected – 2 sets of 1km wide strips at 5km intervals running N-S across the landscape . . . Survey tracts were fieldwalked by a group of 10–12 people, organised in one or two teams and walking in the parallel lines *c.*15–25m apart (depending on the nature of the terrain) . . . The team worked in close collaboration with a geologist, 3 geomorphologists and 2 historical geographers . . . Baldly, the total number of sites of all periods on the island has been raised from 47 to 130 . . . and overall site density is now seen to be 6 times greater than formerly supposed . . . (op. cit. 279–280)

Cherry's list of difficulties encountered in the survey ends on an ironic note: '(8) Problems of convincing colleagues that intensive, probabilistic sample survey is a legitimate and tested technique' (ibid. 281)! The Melos publication deserves detailed study for its comprehensive treatment of the advantages and drawbacks of fieldwork projects; the results achieved in understanding the Roman period are outlined in their appropriate place below (p. 135).

---

41. The island of Melos in the Aegean has been surveyed using carefully designed strips at regular intervals. The number of sites discovered in these samples forms the basis of projections of the original site-densities over the whole island. (Renfrew and Wagstaff 1982)

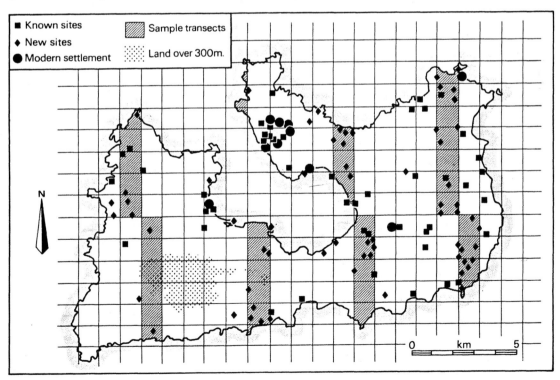

- ■ Known sites
- ◆ New sites
- ● Modern settlement
- ▨ Sample transects
- ⬚ Land over 300m.

N

0   km   5

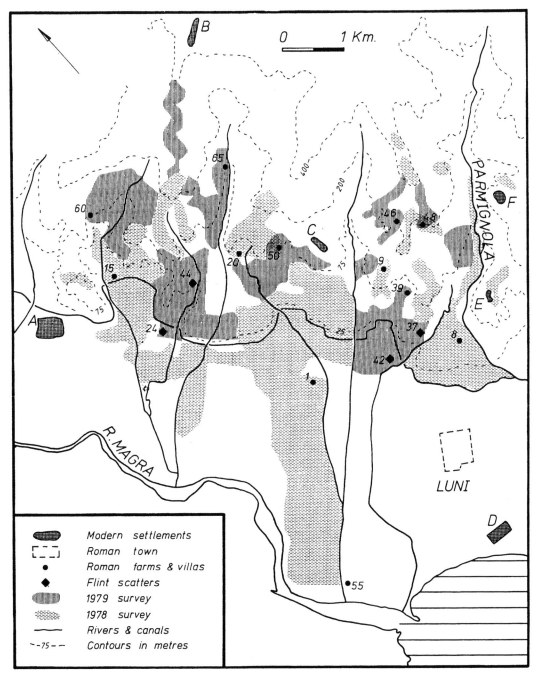

42. Even the best planned survey projects cannot hope to apply their examination evenly over large areas where modern settlement and agriculture exist. This plan of a field survey in the vicinity of Luni (a Roman town on the east coast of the Gulf of Genoa) is important because it shows the actual extent of inspection in detail, rather than simply recording the resulting sites. The project was designed to answer a specific question: did the city's brief prosperity result from specialised trade (in wine and marble), or did it reflect successful agriculture in its rural hinterland? The comparative poverty of the latter suggests that the first answer is correct. (Mills 1981, 262, fig. 21.1; see also Ward-Perkins *et al.* 1986)

The archaeological studies presented here provide an opportunity to examine rural settlement and agriculture in a variety of different geographical and cultural settings. In order to arrive at a perception of a system which may be compared and contrasted with those found elsewhere, it seems logical to begin with Italy, the province at the centre of the Roman empire in both the geographical and political sense. Parts of several western provinces will be examined, in Spain, France and England, before attention is turned to north Africa, Greece, the eastern Mediterranean islands and the Near East.

RURAL SETTLEMENT IN ITALY

Some Roman authors wrote specifically about settlement and agriculture, others mentioned these topics less directly in the course of their historical or political works. Much of the history of the expansion of Roman power in Italy, and the Civil Wars which brought the republic to an end, involved colonisation by means of new towns and divisions of farmland (Keppie 1983). The displacement of small-scale farmers by large estates worked by teams of slaves is another theme of the historical sources of the Roman period. Attempts to integrate the historical information with physical evidence began long ago, and a good example is Day's study of the villas around Pompeii (1932). Unlike the historical documents, archaeological evidence relevant to these agrarian issues can be expanded by survey and excavation, but it is important that the opportunity of continuing the integration of history and archaeology is not lost where good documents exist. For example, D'Arms' study of villas around the Bay of Naples emphasises the cultural dimension of a settlement pattern which could not be gained from archaeology alone (1970), whilst the analysis of the agrarian history of the Cosa region is inseparable from an understanding of the activities of local senatorial landowners (Manacorda 1981; Rathbone 1981).

THE ETRURIA SURVEY

The first and still one of the largest survey projects carried out in Italy was initiated by the British School at Rome soon after the end of the Second World War, when changes in land ownership and exploitation led to the ploughing and cultivation of large areas of hitherto neglected land, thereby permitting the collection and recording of artefacts and architectural debris from the surface. A series of publications covering parts of the region appeared over the years, but these have been updated and synthesised in articles and a book by Potter (1978; 1979; 1980 – see also Dyson 1981b). Potter's book (1979) embraces an extremely long span of time from the Stone Age to c.AD 1300; we are thus able to place the observations about the period of the Roman empire into a broad chronological perspective.

From Etruscans to the Roman empire

The southernmost part of the area included in the south Etruria survey lies only c.10km (6¼ miles) north of Rome; it extends roughly in a diamond shape for a further 40km (25 miles). By the time that control had passed from the Etruscans to Rome (before 300 BC), the landscape had already undergone a considerable degree of development away from the thinly scattered settlements of the Bronze Age. Sites were widely dispersed throughout the area, with some larger centres linked by tracks and roads. The land improvements had been made by means of large-scale drainage schemes, whilst sites with imported pottery and monumental architecture indicate growing trade and wealth. Potter sees the Etruscan pattern as '. . . the culmination of a long phase of population growth during the first millennium, combined with a sustained and ever increasing pressure upon land . . . It was a transformation whose scale and speed can only impress' (op. cit. 92).

The period after 300 BC saw the decline of the Etruscan towns, further dispersal of settlements into the countryside, and the construction of major arterial roads through the area. This new pattern was not a break from the old, however, as nearly 70 per cent of pre-existing sites continued in occupation. The new settlements doubtless included land allotments made to Roman citizens, and occupation extended to include even marginal land. Expansion and clearance at this stage is clearly reflected in the decline of woodland species present in samples of pollen from the area, and a 'drastic and sudden' increase in sedimentation in the lake from which the pollen came, resulting from agricultural activity (Bonatti 1970, 30–31). The construction of roads stimulated the growth of new towns and road stations exploiting the traffic which they carried to and from the north of the peninsula. The new pattern established during the republican period set the scene for the early empire, and reached its peak in the first and second centuries AD (fig. 43).

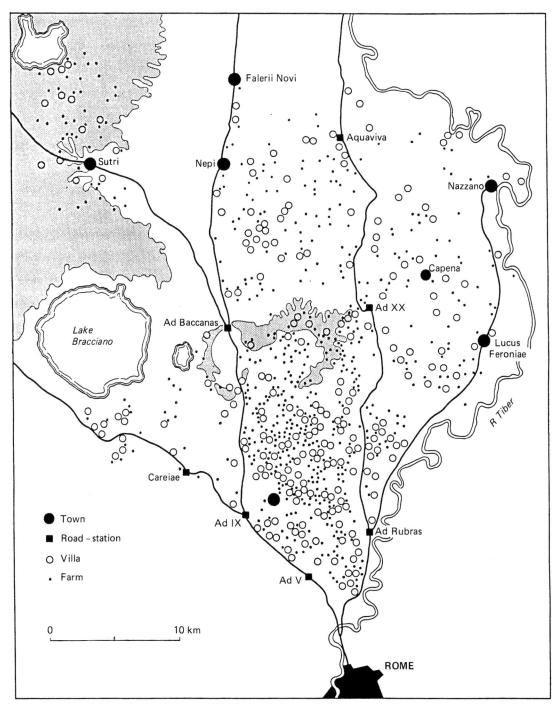

43. Settlement in southern Etruria reached its greatest intensity in the early imperial period before entering a decline. Marginal lands were fully exploited, to an extent not matched again until the twentieth century; in fact, it was the expansion of modern agriculture that gave rise to the opportunity to record these sites as they were revealed by ploughing. There is a noticeable increase in the concentration of villas and smaller farms towards Rome, which provided a large market for their products. (Audio-Visual Centre, University of Newcastle; based on Potter 1980, 81)

The data recovered from fieldwork are sufficiently plentiful to allow an assessment of the distribution and ranking of sites of different sizes and characters. In the northern part of the survey area (*Ager Faliscus*), 35 per cent of the sites seem to be the remains of small buildings such as shepherds' huts, whilst 43 per cent were classed as small farms, of sufficient architectural distinction to possess masonry walls, floor mosaics and painted wall-plaster. The remaining 22 per cent comprised villas with such additional features as baths and colonnaded courtyards. Many of these may well have developed from more humble structures of the preceding category, like that revealed by excavations at Monte Forco (Jones G. 1963, 148–149, figs. 17–18). The larger villas occurred more frequently in the southern part of the overall survey area, which was nearer to Rome, and have an average density of around one to every 2km^2 (494 acres). To the villas, farms and huts must be added a range of religious sanctuaries and cemeteries, as well as quarries, and industrial sites such as tile and pottery kilns. In summary, the area presents an impressive picture of a densely occupied and fully exploited landscape, no doubt enhanced by the influence of Rome, which was accessible by good roads to the south.

Late Roman decline

Whereas the period up to the early empire was characterised by expansion, after the second century AD there was continuous decline. By AD 500, between 50 per cent and 80 per cent of rural sites in various parts of the survey area had come to an end, and the cultivation of marginal land was abandoned until the present century. The decline of larger sites was less marked than that of smaller ones, although large villas never totally dominated the landscape at the expense of smaller farms. Many smaller sites may have been abandoned because of growing insecurity, and their populations absorbed by their neighbours; there is certainly no evidence that they simply moved into towns, for these show a parallel decline. Eventually, as insecurity increased, defended hilltop sites, characteristic of the medieval period, replaced the dispersed pattern of Roman sites. If the early imperial pattern is interpreted as the culmination of a long period of population increase, the reverse is presumably true after AD 300.

The decline of rural settlement in late-Roman central Italy is put into perspective by a recent paper by Whitehouse (1985), who detects no further changes from the fifth to ninth centuries AD in the Campagna, an area to the south of Rome, despite a number of invasions and military episodes. The possibility that climatic deterioration caused flooding on valley sites has already been discussed; if it did in fact occur, the wetter conditions might also have increased the dangers of disease. Higher rainfall could have caused serious erosion of the countryside and its ploughsoils, which had been largely cleared of woodlands in the late Etruscan and early Roman periods. However, Giardina has argued that the clearances alone could account for erosion and sedimentation without any necessary increase in rainfall (1981, 108).

OTHER SURVEYS IN ITALY

A very clear pattern of expansion and contraction has emerged from the Etruria survey, although Potter repeatedly points out that there are local variations within the area. The scale of Roman settlement expansion may have been exaggerated by the fact that Roman pottery, other artefacts and architectural materials are very distinctive, and therefore more easily recovered during surface collection than prehistoric potsherds and flints. Gennaro and Stoddart have recently shown that there has been a dramatic increase in the rate of discovery of prehistoric sites since the British School's original surveys were completed (1982, 12–17). However, taking the Roman period itself, is Etruria typical of Italy, and, in general terms, of the empire? Further surveys elsewhere in Italy allow us to begin to answer the first question at least.

The Molise survey

The Biferno valley runs from the Appenines into the Adriatic on the eastern side of the Italian peninsula on approximately the same latitude as south Etruria. A large-scale survey of samples of the many different local environments and landscapes within the valley has been conducted under the direction of Graeme Barker (fig. 44; Barker G. *et al.* 1978; Lloyd and Barker 1981). A hierarchy of sites was recorded: towns, 'villas' and 'farmsteads' (i.e. larger and smaller rural sites). Although their density is similar to that of sites in southern Etruria, their chronological distribution differs markedly, for less than half of the sites occupied in the republican period continued into the early centuries AD. However, those which did

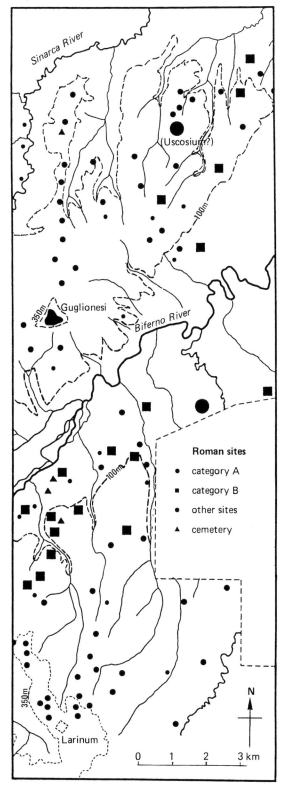

Roman sites

• category A

■ category B

• other sites

▲ cemetery

survive remained in occupation until the fifth century. Unlike Etruria, the initial reduction in sites is not seen to be the result of population decline, but rather an increase in nucleation for agricultural reasons. There are problems in comparing the categories of sites with those of Etruria, for the term 'villa' obscures the fact that these large settlements do not match those of Etruria in their architectural appointments. Lloyd has suggested (1981, 303) that such sites may have represented the centres of estates whose owners lived in the nearby towns; the absence of elegance need not necessarily denote a lack of agricultural success.

The *ager cosanus*

Cosa lies on the coast of Italy 140km (87 miles) north-west of Rome, on a promontory with good harbours. The Roman colony was established in 273 BC, and the considerable amount of excavation which has taken place in the city indicates that its principal period of prosperity was the last two centuries BC. Its landward territory (the *ager cosanus*) is *c.* 100km (62 miles) long, and extends up to 80km (50 miles) inland, and contains several different kinds of environment, notably the coastal plain, the main river-valleys, and a large upland area. Fieldwork was conducted after the instigation of land reforms similar to those affecting Etruria, and datable sherds of pottery and architectural fragments were likewise recorded from surface scatters (fig. 45; Dyson 1978, 251–256; 1981c). Since the methods of data collection were similar, the results from the Etruria and Cosa surveys should provide a valid basis for comparison.

There are differences between the areas, however. Although the Cosa survey area lay in the vicinity of an ancient town, the importance of Cosa was in no way comparable to that of Rome.

44. This section across the Biferno valley in eastern Italy reveals a varied pattern of rural settlement. Villa sites (category B) are common near the 100m contour south of the river, but scarcer to the north. It is possible that the estate owners in the latter area lived in urban surroundings, and left the running of their land to bailiffs, whilst those to the south used their villas to a greater extent, and built them in an accordingly comfortable style. (Audio-Visual Centre, University of Newcastle; based on Lloyd and Barker 1981, 297, fig. 24.2)

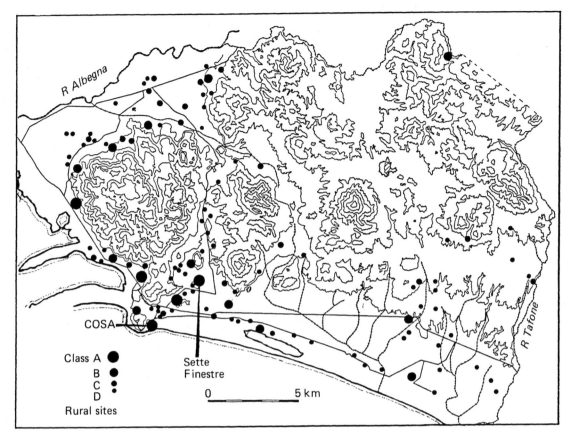

45. The *ager cosanus*, Italy. The valleys inland from the city of Cosa were densely occupied in the Roman period, and contained most of the richer villas (classes A–B), including the important excavated site at Sette Finestre (figs. 34 and 35). Few of the small farms of republican date survived into the empire, however. (Based on Dyson 1978, 262, fig. 6)

Furthermore, the Etruscan city of Veii had already provided an urban focus in south Etruria, and no such pre-Roman centre existed near Cosa. The sites recorded in the *ager cosanus* ranged from palatial villas (classified by Dyson as category A), through more modest villas (B and C) to small houses or villas without any architectural pretensions (category D; Dyson 1978, 257). Few traces were found of sites belonging to families of early colonists, but their settlements may well have been small and short-lived, as individual smallholdings became consolidated into larger properties. The pattern of settlement in the republican period consisted of a few large villas and a mixture of the three smaller size-categories, giving an impression of a well-populated landscape. During the early empire, the number of the smallest sites of category D declined sharply whilst that of A and C increased. In the later empire, the number of category C sites declined as well, whilst A and B were less prosperous than before.

Thus, a similarity between the Cosa and Molise areas is that the density of sites had diminished by the imperial period; it seems that this was the result of consolidation rather than depopulation. However, the palatial category of villas found near Cosa or on the coast is absent from both Etruria and the Biferno valley. Dyson suggests that these buildings were not *latifundia* (the centres of vast agricultural estates), but *villae maritimae*, luxurious country residences belonging to very rich owners who perhaps sailed to them from Rome (1978, 261). The distribution of the smaller categories of sites is fairly uniform in relation to available farmland, and seems incompatible with an image of a landscape dominated by *latifundia*, despite the existence of literary sources which say that it was (ibid. 260; Rathbone 1981).

Dyson draws interesting parallels between the colonisation of the *ager cosanus* in the third century BC and the land reforms of 1951, which broke up large estates and increased the number of farms from 130 to *c*.800. Around 100 Roman sites have been discovered by fieldwork, and it is, of course, extremely unlikely that all of the sites which once existed have been found. 'If we use a recovery rate of 1:4, we find a sustaining level of ca. 400 farms in the Ager Cosanus and can place the level of agricultural activity in the ager during the Late Republic and the Early Empire at somewhere between that of the current highly mechanised Ente Maremma and the depressed pre-reform situation' (op. cit. 264).

The American survey of the Cosa region has been enlarged upon by Anglo-Italian work conducted in association with the excavation of the villa at Sette Finestre (Carandini and Settis 1979). Structured surveys of the Valle d'Oro and the Albegna valley have demonstrated that the *ager cosanus* is by no means uniform in the history of its occupation. For instance, the density of sites remains similar from the coast to the hills, but further up the valleys, the smaller sites survive longer into the imperial period, and villas go on into the late Roman period. On hilly ground, villas did not develop, but smaller sites continued into the imperial period. Around Heba, an inland colonial city, it is evident that some villas were sited to take advantage of the town rather than being built in relation to the nearest road or river. Full publication of the remainder of the excavations at Sette Finestre as well as these field surveys will make the *ager cosanus* still more interesting for the study of the interaction between town and country, rural settlement and agriculture.

Surveys south of Rome

The neat uniformity of the pattern of growth, stability and decline charted in south Etruria is not repeated in exactly the same way in either the *ager cosanus* or the Biferno valley; indeed, it would be surprising if the proximity of Rome had not distorted this region in some way. How do other parts of Italy compare?

In the Liri valley (*c*.100km [62 miles] southeast of Rome), settlement of Roman colonists took place from the fourth century BC in an area which had hitherto been comparatively empty. The settlement pattern remained static into the imperial period, but increased briefly in the second to third centuries AD before declining again

(Wightman 1981). In an area 50km (31 miles) east of Salerno, Dyson has investigated an area without the obvious attractions of the *ager cosanus*, which nevertheless proved to have been densely occupied: 'virtually every suitable ecological niche around Buccino had a villa in it during the Roman period' (1983, 188). Unlike the *ager cosanus*, farms of modest size survived from the republican period through the empire and on to the fourth century AD; no real break occurred until the sixth century, when war raged between the Ostrogoths and a Byzantine army intent upon reconquest (ibid. 190). In a high valley in the province of Potenza, a similarly dense pattern of Roman sites has been revealed, many of which appear to have been reoccupied in the fourth century AD after a hiatus in the third; no occupation is then evident from the seventh to the eleventh centuries (Keller and Rupp 1983, 187).

Results are also becoming available for coastal areas of southern Italy, where it must not be forgotten that several Greek cities had been in existence since the seventh century BC. Perhaps the most impressive survey is that of the hinterland of the Greek colony of Metaponto (founded *c*.650 BC), where dense settlement belonging to the archaic and classical Greek as well as the Roman periods has been found on river terraces, plains and higher plateaus, with a high degree of continuity (Keller and Rupp 1983, 191–192). D'Arms has traced the origins of villas near the city of Naples (a former Greek colony), and has emphasised the Greek notions of artistic and literary culture which were incorporated into these private country houses, although they were themselves a distinctly Roman invention (1970, 167).

On the island of Sicily, Wilson has charted the spread of farms in the vicinity of Heraclea Minor in the last three centuries BC, which were replaced by a small number of very large villas which lasted throughout the Roman empire; some new farms which appeared between AD 400 and 700 may have belonged to tenants on large estates (1981, 253–257, figs. 20.2–4). More recently, Wilson has demonstrated the way in which the Roman imperial period was an interlude of dispersed settlement, between phases characterised by nucleated hill-top centres. The spread of the population into the countryside also stimulated the growth of new market centres and villages, away from the traditional urban sites (1985, 323–5). On another island, Sardinia, Rowland has detected the now familiar pattern of dense rural settlement, which was far from being dominated by large estates (1984, 298).

CONCLUSIONS: ROMAN SETTLEMENT IN ITALY

The late republican period seems to show the greatest degree of settlement expansion in central Italy, followed by consolidation and/or decline. However, the spread of very large estates which absorbed their neighbours may well have been limited to the prime coastal and river valley areas, as the pattern of inland sites shows a much stronger survival of smaller sites. In the south, the Greek background is important, but there is not yet much basis for studying the evolution of settlement. In a recent summary of further work near Cosa, Dyson remarked that:

> . . . settlement history in the Albegna river valley is highly varied and localised, a reflection of the complex interacting forces of ecology, past history, and access to the larger world of Rome. It shows again how little we know about Roman settlement and how inadequate will be the preconceived generalisations about settlement forms that we have tended to adopt in the past, especially from historical sources. Much hard archaeological work lies ahead of us before we have a really accurate notion of the social and economic history of this or any other section of Roman Italy. (1981, 274)

One observation that can be made about the economy of Roman Italy will be echoed in the discussion of areas such as north-eastern France and northern Syria: the density of rural settlement is so great that the significance of towns (or even villages) is proportionately reduced. Local markets, and craft activities independent of towns, must have been of considerable importance, and must be taken into account in an analysis of the economy in general. The extent to which various categories of fine pottery penetrated the countryside is also impressive, and denies the notion of self-sufficient estates producing all their own essentials. The phenomenon is repeated on a smaller scale by local coarse pottery; Dyson concluded from pottery excavated on villa sites around Buccino that: 'the great variety of forms shows local commercial potters responding to large and complicated local market demands', a situation which contrasted sharply with that found on nearby sites in medieval times.

Field survey in Italy still remains patchy in its geographical cover, and inconsistent in its conclusions; when it is combined with programmes of excavation (as in the *ager cosanus*), we may begin to gain a concrete perspective on the writings of argronomists such as Varro or Columella. Broader issues of landholding such as the importance of *latifundia* run with slave labour or estates occupied by free tenant farmers are more difficult to approach through archaeology, but there is no other source which can provide such a large amount of new information.

Further detailed chronological analyses must await full publication of these and other Italian surveys, including those related to political themes in Giardina and Schiavone's volume of studies (1981). A considerable amount of work needs to be done before any valid synthesis can be made which compares the results of all these surveys, but takes into account all of the relevant technical factors involved in the recovery of the information. Ancient historians are ready for this information, and are reviewing their texts in order to incorporate the implications; a good example is Garnsey's exploration of the problem, 'Where did Italian peasants live?' (1979), whose title is an impressively direct statement about our continuing ignorance of fundamental issues.

RURAL SETTLEMENT AND AGRICULTURE IN THE PROVINCES OF THE ROMAN EMPIRE

Surveys of settlement carried out in Italy indicate that population expansion reached its peak in the late republic or around the beginning of the imperial period. The pattern then shows signs of consolidation, with the possibility of landholdings being increased in size at the expense of their neighbours. Even allowing for further nucleation of scattered settlements, the reduction of their overall numbers implies a decrease in population after the second century AD. In general, these findings are in agreement with the historical pattern of Italian agriculture derived from the contemporary writers, although there are important modifications, notably the fact that *latifundia* do not appear to have dominated the landscape. The intricate details of the date and density of settlement in Italy and its regional variations could not, however, have been determined without archaeological fieldwork.

Ancient authors tell us little about the agriculture of the provinces of the Roman empire, least of all those on the periphery like Britain, yet it is in areas like this that the influence of Rome may have been most marked. In Greece and Egypt, agriculture had been orientated towards the needs of a complex monetised urban economy for centuries before they became provinces of the Roman empire, but the occupation of areas such as Britain, Gaul, Spain and north Africa introduced a system of government entirely different from that of the pre-Roman period.

SPAIN

The valley of the Guadalcuivir

The Roman province of Baetica occupies an area at the southern end of the Iberian peninsula; one of its most important geographical features is the river Gaudalcuivir, which flows from deep inside the province to the Atlantic near the Straits of Gibraltar. It winds a meandering but navigable course, and provided an outlet for agricultural produce which could be shipped either into the Mediterranean or northwards to Gaul and Britain. Writers such as Pliny and Strabo celebrated the fertility of Baetica, as well as its important mineral resources.

The results of archaeological fieldwork carried out in the valley of the Gaudalcuivir by a French archaeologist, Michel Ponsich, have been published in detail (1974; 1979). Ponsich had the benefit of a programme of fieldwork which had already been carried out by French geographers, and his reports take full account of the region's geology and present forms of settlement and land-use. The area selected for study lay between Seville and Cordoba, and included around 100km (62 miles) of the course of the Guadalcuivir. The total area of the survey was over 3000km² (1158 sq. miles), and was based upon seven sheets of Spain's 1:50,000 scale maps, rather than any ancient or modern political or physical territories. No conscious sampling strategy was involved, but the separate treatment of each of the map sheets in Ponsich's publication does, in fact, allow attention to focus on different balances of soil-types and terrains both along the river itself and at some distance from it. It would be interesting to compare the results of this general approach with a more scientifically designed fieldwork programme which allowed more intensive study of a smaller total area. However, the landscape is changing rapidly as a result of the mechanisation of agriculture, and, as in Etruria or the Somme valley, the pace of destruction of archaeological remains may never allow the luxury of comparisons.

Ponsich's work has revealed a pattern of settlement of an intensity which conforms with the results of fieldwork in Italy and the provinces, and he has outlined a hierarchy of sites according to the following criteria (1974, 16):

1 As well as the Roman towns which were already known to exist, some agglomerations of settlement were recorded, presumably *minor towns* and *large villages*.

2 *Villas* were defined by the presence of substantial architectural remains, baths, marble, mosaics and imported pottery; many were associated with olive presses and tile kilns.

3 Less sophisticated remains of substantial buildings without the signs of luxury or ornamentation found in villas were defined as *farms*.

4 Small scatters of masonry and roof tiles were taken to be remains of *buildings or sheds* used for storage of farming equipment, etc.

5 Very slight traces of buildings were considered to be possible sites of *shelters*.

Most villas had access to land suitable for intensive olive cultivation and for cereals, as well as the possibility of grazing livestock on higher ground. The greatest density of farms was associated with cereal-growing areas, and most of the sheds occurred on arable land (Ponsich 1974, 17). It should be noted that the ploughing of this kind of land would have increased the likelihood of discovery of such sites, whilst substantial remains of villas had a high chance of detection throughout the area. This is something which can only be understood fully if a carefully designed sampling strategy is employed, taking very detailed account of ancient and modern land-use and any other factors which might distort the survival and recognition of Roman sites; the Italian and British surveys in the Cosa region make this kind of allowance.

The general conclusions of the Guadalcuivir survey underline the intensity of rural settlement, and the rôle of towns, which Ponsich sees as intermediaries for the concentration of produce for shipping, thus facilitating agricultural exploitation (op. cit. 285). As the countryside was the source of their wealth, it should be the primary source of information about the towns; thus, Ponsich's conclusion suggests that the approach of many classical archaeologists, centred upon town planning, public buildings and civic architecture, is misguided. Finley's emphasis on the reliance of ancient towns upon their hinterlands adds emphasis to Ponsich's views, and by implication underlines the importance of archaeological fieldwork.

One particular area of Ponsich's study deserves attention, for it is an interesting case of the interplay of geology, soils and settlement (fig. 46). Area 4 lies due west of Seville, and does not include any part of the river Guadalcuivir. It is divided diagonally by a steep escarpment to the north-west of which is a high terrace with well-drained soils, and to the south-west a lower area of thin but fertile soil (Ponsich 1974, 215–217, and fig. 84). The escarpment has many springs, but the south-west area is devoid of fresh water. The map of Roman sites shows an even scatter of villas and farms over the higher ground, which would have favoured intensive olive cultivation supplemented by cereals (ibid. fig. 85 facing p. 216). The escarpment has a string of villas and several large settlements (villages), as well as the city of Carmo. The lower plain was divided into regular square plots by the widespread Roman practice of land division – *centuriation*. It was devoid of villas, but had remains of numerous sheds.

Three systems of agriculture seem to have been practised, with different forms of site location. The fertile terrace supported large estates and farms suited to intensive production, and the escarpment was suitable for villas exploiting both olives and cereals. The lower plain was used for cereal production, but not settled; the labourers and landowners lived in Carmo or the adjacent villas and villages along the escarpment where fresh springs existed, leaving their equipment in the many sheds. When the cereal harvest was over, plenty of spare labour would have been available to the large estate owners on the high terrace for the later olive harvest and oil processing (Ponsich 1974, 280–282).

The date range of the intensive agricultural exploitation of Baetica lies entirely within the first four centuries AD, and, like that of north-eastern France, overlaps and succeeds the peak of settlement revealed by surveys in Italy. An important aspect of Ponsich's survey is the light which it sheds upon olive oil production, for Baetica has long been acknowledged as the principal source of the oil which reached Rome under the empire (fig. 4). The Monte Testaccio in Rome has been estimated to include the broken remains of 40 million amphorae which accumulated over three

centuries, of which 130,000 may have come from Baetica each year (Ponsich 1979, 19). Their name-stamps and inscriptions have been studied for decades, and can be dated quite accurately because of references to emperors and consuls.

Ponsich's fieldwork has located the sites of numerous kilns where the huge globular amphorae were made and fired, and broken fragments with name-stamps now allow amphorae found in Rome to be related to specific sites in Baetica. The apogee of production and export to Rome was reached in the decade 150–160 AD (Ponsich 1974, 293), after which there was a steep decline. Ponsich suggests that the stimulus to intensive production was provided by the requirements of the city of Rome, where oil was included in the free provisions to which thousands of Romans were entitled, and the expanding military and civilian markets of Gaul, Germany and Britain. He suggests that a fall in prices resulting from over-production was the reason for decline, rather than Moorish raids in the later second century (ibid 289), although Jones has come to the opposite conclusion in the case of the region's mines (Jones G. 1980).

The density of sites in rural Baetica underlines the complexity of rural settlement, and the importance of understanding geology and physical geography. A similar complexity in the farming economy is exemplified by the kilns where the large globular Dressel 20 amphorae were made as

---

46. In this area of Ponsich's survey of the Guadalcuivir valley, a scarp divides low-lying flat land from a plateau. Along the scarp lies a string of villas whose estates probably took in a mixture of plateau and lowland. The plateau has a scatter of well-spaced villas and farms, whilst on the low ground there are only small farms and store buildings amongst possible centuriated land boundaries. It is likely that the low ground was farmed by inhabitants of the town of Carmona who travelled out to their fields, which were particularly suited to cereals. The higher plateau was more suitable for olives and vines, so intensive farming by means of villa estates was more appropriate there. The map of this small area of a very large survey demonstrates the importance of local soils and geology in the understanding of settlement patterns. (From Ponsich 1974, fig. 85 opposite p. 216; grid in kilometres)

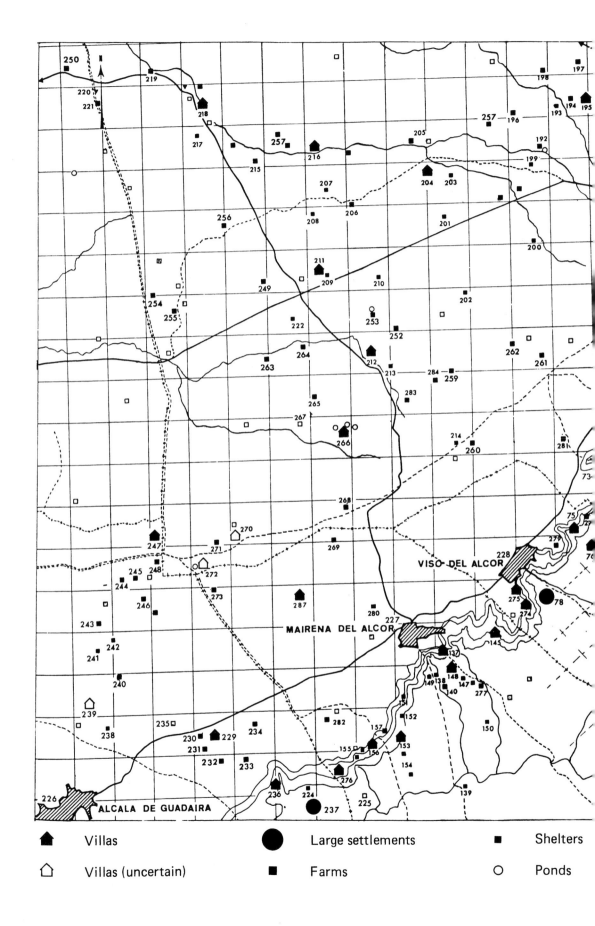

Villas	Large settlements	Shelters
Villas (uncertain)	Farms	Ponds

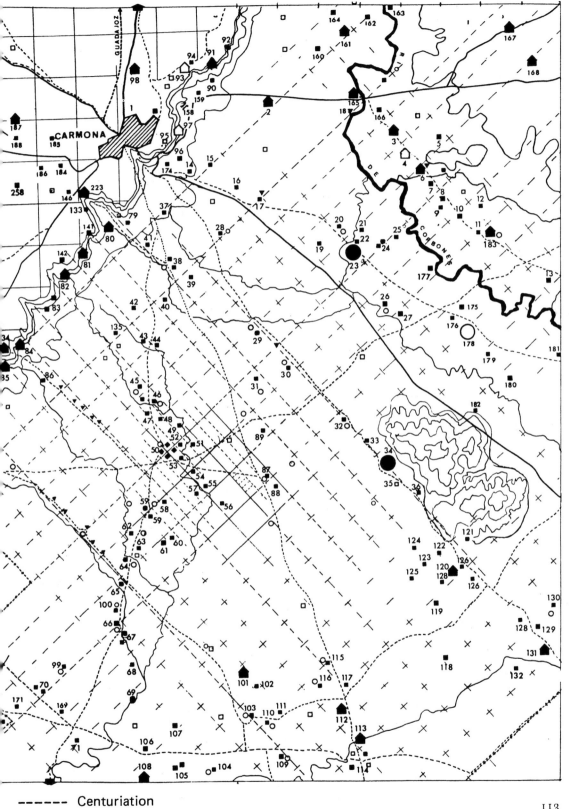

------- Centuriation

containers for the export of olive oil. The name-stamps impressed into their handles add a further level of information lacking from other forms of strictly agricultural evidence. It might be thought from Roman literature that olive cultivation would be carried out on vast slave-run *latifundia*, each estate possessing craft workers who could meet its own needs for equipment, including amphorae. This is demonstrably not the case, however, for whereas tile kilns are located near most of the villas, amphora kilns required better clay whose sources were more restricted. A tremendous variety of stamp forms is known, including place-names and personal names of slaves or freedmen and Roman citizens. Kiln locations suggest that some were operated for a large number of estates, others for just one estate owner (Ponsich 1974, 292–3). The amphora makers may also have produced tiles at villa sites when building work was in progress, and could indeed have worked as potters on a seasonal basis, spending some of their time as farm labourers when extra work was available at harvest times.

It may be argued that Baetica is a special case of rural settlement, in an area favoured by the demand for olive oil and metals; many more surveys of other parts of Spain will be needed before a judgement can be made. Whatever their results, the rapid development of intensive oil production in Roman Baetica is impressive, not least for the considerable impact which locally-spent profits must have had on other parts of the economy, both rural and urban. The organisation of transport on land and on the Guadalcuivir, the supply of exotic stone, mosaics and fine tableware to villa dwellers, and the dynamic cycle of harvesting, processing and exporting olives, must all have brought large numbers of individuals into the economy in the early empire, and stimulated the use of coinage and markets. However, the potential 'multiplier effect' brought no further advance or economic 'take off'. Much of Baetica went out of intensive cultivation until the twentieth century; the products of the Industrial Revolution have now become both the agents of discovery and rapid destruction of a landscape which had remained stable for centuries.

The Mediterranean coast

It is unfortunate that the date-ranges of individual sites have not been mapped in Baetica in the manner achieved in Etruria, to see whether there are equally obvious changes in the life-spans and relative proportions of villas and farms. Some kind of perspective can be gained from a study of settlement in the extreme north-eastern corner of Spain, in the area of the city of Tarragona (Roman Tarracona; Keay 1981). There, the rural hinterland of the coastal cities included many modest farming sites of a size appropriate for individual family units in the first century AD, some of which grew in size and domestic and agricultural amenities in the second century (454–5, figs. 28.2–3). It seems that the area was owned largely by prosperous absentee landlords living in the cities until the later second century. A distinct change took place in the third century, when large villas with lavish residential accommodation were constructed, presumably by similar landowners who had previously spent their time and wealth in the towns. In the third and fourth centuries, the number of small rural sites dwindled, and the towns declined as the villa estates grew (466, 467, fig. 28.8). Keay has published a further discussion of the development of the area into the post-Roman period (1984).

Settlement in Galicia

The extreme north-western corner of Spain has long been considered rather isolated from the Mediterranean culture of its southern and eastern coasts. Although military campaigns into the area began in 139 BC, it was not until the first century AD that conquest and Roman organisation were complete. Villas started late in Galicia; only 11 out of the 75 recorded by Tranoy have origins in the first or second centuries AD. Along with other sites, most of these underwent their greatest development in the third and fourth centuries (Tranoy 1981, 240–1). Meanwhile, the fortified pre-Roman hilltop *castros*, which are a distinctive element of this region, continued in occupation or were reoccupied in the late empire; there is no sign of any decline in population or economic activity in the late Roman period. Tranoy envisages the coexistence of Romanised farming and indigenous systems, in which villa-based exploitation centred upon more favourable valley and coastal locations (op. cit. 419–420).

Spanish villas in perspective

The French contribution to the study of rural archaeology in Roman Spain is not restricted to the Guadalcuivir and Galicia. Gorges has completed a major inventory and discussion of the villas of the whole Spanish peninsula (1979),

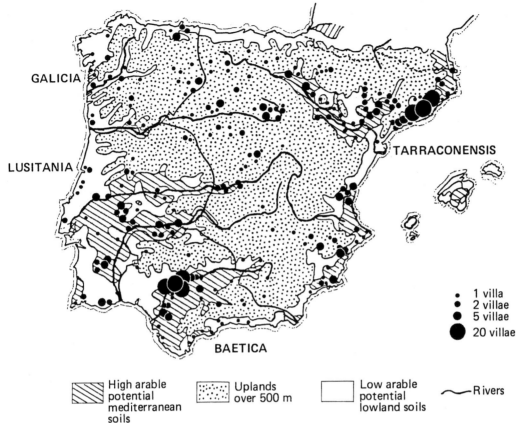

GALICIA

LUSITANIA

TARRACONENSIS

BAETICA

· 1 villa
• 2 villae
● 5 villae
⬤ 20 villae

High arable potential mediterranean soils

Uplands over 500 m

Low arable potential lowland soils

Rivers

which allows the regional studies to be seen in a wider perspective (fig. 47). The date and nature of villa development can be seen to be very uneven. In the first century BC they were almost all to be found in the north-eastern coastal district (op. cit. 28, fig. 4), but tremendous expansion took place in Baetica at the time of Augustus, which produced the dense concentration revealed by Ponsich (30, fig. 5). Gorges suggests that their growth may have been stimulated by the reinvestment of profits from the nearby mining districts (29). The pattern of settlement continued to expand throughout the first century AD, and intensified in the second, when even the high central plateaus were exploited by villa-based agriculture (35, fig. 6; 37–38). The Germanic invasions of the third century caused some damage in the north-eastern parts of Spain, before a new pattern emerged by the early fourth century AD, which Gorges describes as a period not just of renewal, but renaissance (48); the peninsula was fairly evenly covered with large sumptuous villas, whose splendour contrasted sharply with the decay of the towns. The former

47. Regional studies need to be placed into a wider context; this distribution map of villas in Spain shows that the areas examined by Ponsich (central Baetica) and Keay (the coast of Tarraconensis) are quite exceptional in their density of sites. Does the intensity of sites result from a genuine concentration in these areas, or is it a product of selective modern research? In future years, further intensive studies and aerial photography will undoubtedly change the overall pattern of our knowledge. (Audio-Visual Centre, University of Newcastle; based on Gorges 1979, figs. 9 and 16)

dense concentration of villas in Baetica had disappeared by this date (50, fig. 8).

Thus, Gorges' analysis of villas demonstrates the inseparability of local and regional surveys – the areas around Tarragona and the valley of the Guadalcuivir are very interesting, but not typical of the whole peninsula. Furthermore, villas possessed estates of significantly different sizes in different areas, from the 'minifundia' of the north-east to the *latifundia* of the south-west (op. cit.

94–99). A further factor to be considered is that the use of aerial photography is in its infancy in Spain; the present pattern of 1300 possible (or over 600 probable) villas is certain to be increased by further fieldwork (7–8, 18–19). However, the small- and large-scale surveys already completed have provided a wealth of information which must be taken into account in any study of the economy of Roman Spain, and which can be compared with the history and geography of the peninsula, and the comparatively plentiful Roman literary evidence for the exploitation of its resources.

AGRICULTURE AND SETTLEMENT IN GAUL

Roman Gaul was roughly equivalent in area to modern France, and was subdivided into a number of provinces (Drinkwater 1983). The southernmost, Narbonensis (a province since 122 BC), had much in common with Italy, as Provence does today. There, the vine and the olive could be cultivated along with other crops by means of Mediterranean 'dry' farming techniques (above p. 87). Further north, however, the traditions of Graeco-Roman civilisation were absent, although wine and luxury goods had been traded up the Rhône valley since a Greek colony was established at Marseille in the fifth century BC. The remainder of Gaul and the lands up to the Rhine were conquered by Julius Caesar in the 50s BC, and organised into provinces by the emperor Augustus 40 years later. There were some slight disturbances in the first century of Roman rule, but from then on the provinces developed peacefully until barbarian raids from across the Rhine began in earnest in the later third century AD. The areas in the north and east of Gaul suffered most, whilst the south and south-west continued in relative peace, which was not unduly disturbed when they were absorbed into the kingdoms of the Goths and Franks in the fifth and sixth centuries AD.

North-eastern France

One of the most spectacular examples of the impact of modern archaeological fieldwork on Roman archaeology has been the aerial prospecting carried out by Roger Agache in north-eastern France since the early 1960s (figs. 23, 49). Much of this region is covered by large arable fields in which variations in the growth of cereals and other crops allow traces or even complete plans of buried sites to be visible from the air (Greene

1983, 42–48). Furthermore, many Roman buildings were constructed with foundations of pale stone, and their plans show up clearly on freshly ploughed fields. In addition, Agache has provided an exemplary series of both popular and academic publications of his methods and results (1970; 1975; 1978; Agache and Bréart 1975). The dominant impression to be gained from his work is of a fully occupied rural landscape containing an impressive range of settlements ranging from 'native' farms with traditional round timber houses to spectacular complexes of villas and associated buildings, some of great architectural distinction.

Agache has discovered a remarkable number of sites. For example, to the east of Amiens along the valley of the river Somme, four Roman roads enclose a diamond-shaped block of land around 1600km² (618 sq. miles) in area (fig. 48; Agache 1978, fig. 42). After researches up to April 1976, it was known to contain ten villa complexes whose remains exceed 200m (656 ft) in length, 128 smaller villas, and 39 probable villa sites. In addition, there were seven extensive and 243 smaller sites with Roman masonry foundations, and 127 further traces of sites which were probably occupied in the Roman period. At the western end of the diamond near Amiens, and at other points close to the Somme, systems of enclosure ditches were also observed, many of which may have contained timber farmsteads of Iron Age or Roman date. The countryside also contained demonstrably non-agricultural buildings – 15 temple or religious sanctuary sites and one theatre.

The surviving traces of the former Roman landscape show that, as in Italy, the entire countryside was densely occupied by thoroughly Romanised sites. Even villas were numerous, with an average density of more than one per 10km² (247 acres) in this particular section of the Somme valley. Many more sites may still await discovery, for, like the other fieldwork programmes outlined in this chapter, the results present only a minimum estimate of the original number of sites. Agache contrasts the dispersed form of Roman settlement with the nucleated pattern which existed from medieval times until the recent mechanisation of farming (1978, 420–421, fig. 38, ph 250 bis). The dispersed Roman pattern succeeded by medieval nucleation is again reminiscent of observations made in Italy, for the same reasons of security. In fact, the density of Roman sites recorded in the Etruria survey is very similar to that found in north-eastern Gaul (Potter 1979, 121, fig. 35).

Many of the Gaulish villas were constructed on the sites of pre-Roman settlements, and therefore probably belonged to natives of the area rather than to Italian immigrants. The villas began life in the first century AD, and most seem to have flourished in the second century. The life-span of the vast majority was short, however, and the Germanic invasions of the later third century are the most frequently cited cause of their demise. If an alternative needs to be sought, Waateringe's suggestions about the exhaustion of soils in the Netherlands should be taken seriously, for he proposes that the effects of over-exploitation may have taken two centuries to be felt (1983). Whatever the exact cause of their abandonment, ruined villas remained a prominent part of the landscape until the post-medieval period, serving as occasional quarries or shelters.

In fact, not all villas perished in the third century. There seems to be sufficient evidence for the survival of a limited number, which came to be defended centres of population, now nucleated rather than dispersed. These sites became the villages of the medieval period, many of which have been occupied to this day. Inspection of Agache's maps makes it clear that most of the gaps in the distribution of Roman sites are occupied by modern villages, whose buildings do, of course, reduce the possibility of discovering buried sites from the air. If they do indeed conceal the sites of the villas which survived the third century AD, then any estimates of the number of Roman sites have to be increased. Here there is a contrast with the situation observed in Italy, for in northern France the possibility of founding new settlements on naturally fortified hill-tops was not available, because of the limitations of the open landscape.

Villas in Brittany

The contrast between the landscapes of north-eastern and north-western France is very great, but, like Galicia in north-west Spain, the remoteness of Brittany did not prevent the area from participating in a clearly Roman way of life. The Armorican peninsula continued to rely upon fishing and seaborne trade as well as agriculture; many Iron Age farmsteads developed into villas in the first two centuries AD, so that by AD 200 there were well-equipped urban and rural sites. However, insecurity began to grow from the 190s,

when the first of a series of peasant revolts occurred, which became a characteristic of western France in the later Roman period (Galliou 1981, 261). Nevertheless, many villas did expand or were embellished in the third century, perhaps because military activity on the Rhine frontiers provided a ready market for their agricultural products, as well as those of north-eastern France.

Although urban life continued, '... new relationships evolved between country and city, with the development of a landed gentry whose wealth rested upon agriculture and trade, and who had "manor houses" built in the vicinity of towns' (Galliou 1981, 270). However, this phase was brought to an end by the troubles of the late third century; as in the north-east, villas were abandoned and decayed, whilst pollen evidence shows that cultivation as a whole declined. There may well be a connection between the fate of villas in northern Gaul and the prosperity of Britain in the fourth century, as landowners took their capital to invest in a province protected from invasion by at least 30km of sea.

The south of Gaul – Lyon and Béziers

The territory surrounding Lyon, capital city of the three provinces of Gaul, suggests that decline in rural settlement was not simply a result of peasant revolts or Germanic invasions in the third century AD. Walker has studied the gradual evolution of villas and the continuation of pre-Roman native sites into the Roman period, which reached its highest degree of development in the second century AD. The villas were situated on the best valley soils near the Rhône and Saône rivers, and the concentration of rich examples near Lyon itself may indicate that they belonged to prosperous urban merchants (Walker 1981, 320–322).

48. The Somme valley to the east of Amiens is densely packed with sites discovered from the air by R. Agache. The few gaps between known sites are filled by woods or modern villages, which may well conceal further sites. Although this area has been exceptionally well studied, and consists of excellent farmland within reach of the Rhine frontier, its fully-occupied landscape seems to be the rule rather than the exception wherever settlement surveys have been carried out in the Roman empire. (Taken from the map accompanying Agache 1978)

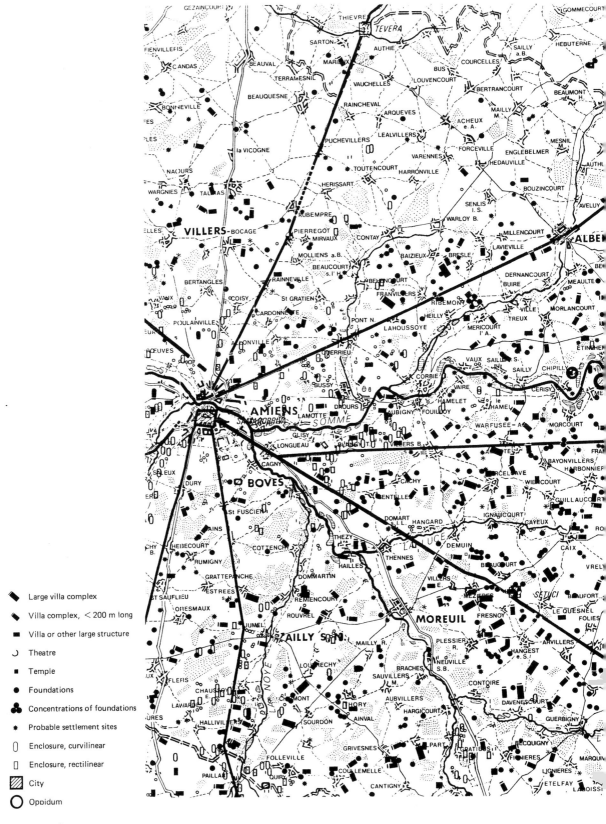

Large villa complex

Villa complex, < 200 m long

Villa or other large structure

⌣ Theatre

Temple

● Foundations

♣ Concentrations of foundations

✳ Probable settlement sites

◌ Enclosure, curvilinear

▯ Enclosure, rectilinear

▨ City

○ Oppidum

118

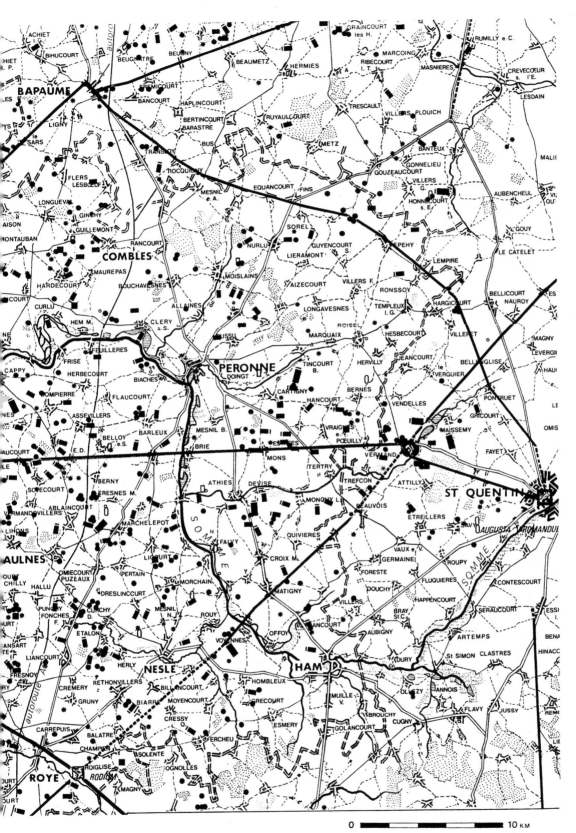

49. Aerial photograph of a further Picardy villa, Warfusée-Nord, Somme (see also fig. 23). Agache's map (fig. 48) differentiates between villa-complexes of different sizes, and many of them feature extensive courtyards and subsidiary buildings. Clearly visible furrows have been left by the plough which revealed the foundations. (Photograph by courtesy of R. Agache)

However, there was a profound decline in rural settlement from the end of the second century, and most villas were abandoned in the third. Presumably, fundamental socio-economic factors, possibly combined with climatic change, were at work. Walker suggests that the late Roman settlement pattern was more nucleated, consisting of a population grouped around surviving villas and vici which were situated in strategic positions; like Agache, he proposes that many of these centres underly present villages (op. cit. 324).

In complete contrast to the Lyon region, the territory of Béziers, a city near the Mediterranean coast of south-western France, shows a continuation of prosperity through the fourth century AD and well into the fifth, by which time it had become part of a 'barbarian' kingdom ruled by Visigoths (fig. 50; Clavel 1970, 614). The area was already well populated and acquainted with Graeco-Roman civilisation because of the flourishing Greek city of Marseilles, founded in the sixth century BC and incorporated into Roman rule in the second century BC. At Béziers, a Roman colony was founded on a pre-Roman site in 36/35 BC; surviving Celtic place-names indicate that the native population was not completely displaced by Roman settlers, even in close proximity to the city (op. cit. 307). The pre-Roman settlement pattern became more dispersed in Roman times, and Clavel has recorded 203 villas in the city territory, which (where dated) begin in the first century AD, and in many cases survive into the fourth century and later (302). The survival of a Roman way of life in much of south-western France is confirmed by James' study of stone carving, pottery manufacture and other facets of Roman life (1977). Thus, like Spain, the rural archaeology of Gaul shows that significant contrasts will be found between different areas. The contrasts make it difficult to make safe generalisations about the whole area, but are in themselves highly informative and invite closer analysis of the geography and history of each area in relation to its economy.

Towns and Romanisation

The evidence for intense Romanisation of the countryside which has been revealed in northern Gaul stands in contrast to the rather meagre nature of the region's towns. The towns might have been thought of as the best measure of 'Romanisation', if it were to be defined as a process of acculturation to Mediterranean urban civilisation. This issue has been examined very thoughtfully in another recent survey of Roman settlement in Gaul by Alain Leday (1980), who has observed a similarly impressive density of rural settlements in Berry, an area at the very centre of Gaul. His conclusions merit quotation:

> ... at every level the Bituriges assimilated the Roman culture very thoroughly; they grafted it onto the native stock of their traditional beliefs, techniques and way of life, so well that the respective

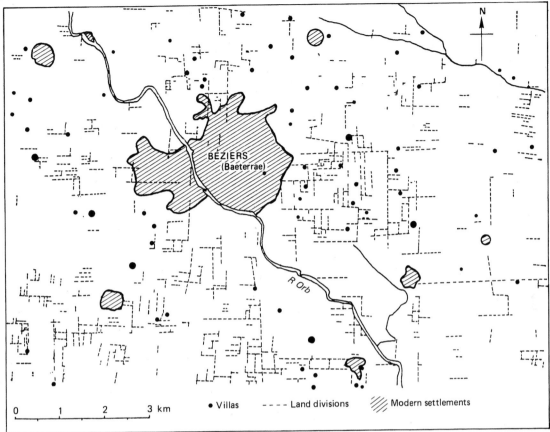

0   1   2   3 km   • Villas   - - - - Land divisions   ///// Modern settlements

50. Villas and land divisions around Béziers, in south-western France. The broken lines represent traces of centuriation, a system of land division by which regular plots of land would have been assigned to the colonists who first occupied the city. Although they were soon swallowed up into larger estates, fragments of these rectilinear boundaries are a persistent feature of the landscape around many Roman cities. There is a marked contrast between the dispersed Roman settlements and the nucleated modern centres. (Audio-Visual Centre, University of Newcastle; based on Clavel 1970, 301, carte 18)

part played by these two influences is often difficult to determine.

... Gallo-Roman civilisation ... has too often been characterised as essentially urban; the *vici* and the *conciliabula* have too often been seen as examples of urban planning with structures and functions typical of towns. The villa has too long been considered an extension of the domus, supplemented by agricultural activities which nobody today denies existed and were necessary but which have not as a rule been seen as an essential part of their structure. Our research has led us to form a totally different picture: the picture of a region that was prosperous in the time of the Romans, with a densely populated countryside with all the land in use, with small towns and villages, and a capital which was apparently itself not a very large town. ... Gallo-Roman civilisation did have its large towns, but properly speaking it was not an urban civilisation: the villa produced, and the *vicus*, which usually in no way resembled a town, manufactured and distributed: the majority of the active population lived in the countryside. This was densely occupied, wherever there was the least possibility of wresting any production from the land. (Leday 1980, 431)

It is to be hoped that regional surveys in Gaul will continue at an increasing pace, for in many ways the area is of more interest than Italy. It contains a wide range of upland and lowland environments, and climatic conditions which vary considerably from the Mediterranean coast to the Atlantic and English Channel, and its contacts with classical civilisation are well documented.

The *Carte archéologique du Cher* (1979) provides a useful model of the way in which settlement evidence can be presented and mapped in an informative and inexpensive manner.

ROMAN BRITAIN

Britain was conquered and brought into the Roman empire in AD 43 during the reign of the emperor Claudius. This was not the first time that Roman forces had entered the island; Julius Caesar had conducted exploratory campaigns in 56 and 55 BC, which met with stiff resistance. In his description of Britain, much of which was copied from Greek geographers, Caesar observes that: 'The population is innumerable; the farm-buildings are found very close together, being very like those of the Gauls; and there is a great store of cattle' (*Gallic War* 5.12). Whilst this was once interpreted as being typical of his usual exaggeration designed to disguise a lack of military success, archaeology has demonstrated that it is in fact true of the parts of south-eastern England which Caesar actually saw.

The landscape of the parts of Britain which came to be occupied by the Romans varies considerably, from the fertile downs and river valleys of the lowlands in the south-east, to the highlands of Wales and the Scottish border counties. The upland areas remained under military garrison throughout the three and a half centuries of Roman rule, whilst most of lowland England proceeded onto a course of purely civilian development within a generation of the conquest, as forts were moved progressively westwards and northwards. As in Gaul, there were rebellions in the early stages of occupation, notably that of the Iceni led by their queen Boudica in AD 60. From the early second century AD, the northern frontier was fixed across the Tyne-Solway line, except for a brief period (*c.*AD 140–165) when it was advanced to the Forth-Clyde isthmus. Pressure from the tribes who inhabited Scotland varied in intensity, but after a fairly peaceful period in the third century, attacks from the Picts became more frequent and serious, particularly when combined with Irish and Saxon piracy along the western and eastern coasts. The English Channel provided an effective barrier against the devastating onslaughts of Germanic tribes from east of the Rhine suffered by Gaul in the same period.

Thus, Roman Britain consisted of several distinct zones with different characteristics: the northern frontier; the uplands of Wales and the north with networks of garrison forts; and the greater part of lowland England, where a purely civilian life could be conducted in a manner similar to that of Gaul or even Italy. Archaeological and historical research into Roman Britain has been undertaken by eminent scholars at a national and local level for several hundred years, combined in recent years with the use of advanced techniques of excavation and scientific analysis. Furthermore, Roman sites in Britain have been carefully recorded on official maps since the late eighteenth century, and this tradition has been maintained until recent years. The rapid expansion of rescue archaeology since the 1960s has greatly increased our knowledge of Roman towns and the countryside. The results of recent research in contrasting geographical zones will be examined: Northamptonshire in the civil lowland zone, and Northumberland and the Solway Firth region in the military north.

Roman archaeology in Britain has been concerned primarily with history, and because Britain was occupied by a large garrison of soldiers, 'history' has tended to mean military history. There has been little opportunity to carry out comprehensive programmes of research approaching the scale of the Molise or south Etruria projects. The pressure of rescue archaeology is largely to blame, for archaeologists based in urban or regional excavation units must understandably concentrate on local programmes of work governed by time, money, and threats to sites from development. Each regional unit tends to have its own methods and objectives, so that comparisons between work carried out in different areas can be very difficult. With backlogs of complicated and expensive excavation reports to prepare, few units have time to publish lists of sites based upon their Sites and Monuments Records, let alone syntheses.

Northamptonshire in the Roman period

Although Northamptonshire is not a meaningful unit of land from the Roman point of view, it is presented here as a 'case-study' of an area of lowland Britain for the reasons outlined in the last paragraph. The information available results from fieldwork carried out not by a 'rescue' unit, but by the (permanent) Royal Commission on Historical Monuments. The county of Northamptonshire was selected for scrutiny by the

RCHM for a variety of reasons, stated in the foreword to the first of the four volumes of inventories (RCHM 1975; 1979; 1981; 1982) which covered the county:

> The publication of an inventory of the earthworks in Northamptonshire was considered by the Commission to be very desirable in view of the wealth of archaeological sites in the county and the lack of a co-ordinated catalogue of them. The effects of deep-ploughing, ironstone mining, gravel quarrying and urban development in the area present a threat to so many of the sites as to render the preparation of an inventory a matter of increasing urgency. Of the four hundred or so monuments which have been listed in the north-east of the county, many have not hitherto been recognized. (RCHM 1975, vii)

Thus, the principal motivation behind the Northamptonshire inventories was the recording of known sites, although the process led to many new discoveries. Unlike the work in Italy and Libya, there were no specific research objectives related to particular periods or problems; the results are therefore not directly comparable. Indeed, discussion and interpretation are kept to a minimum in the inventories; the wider implications of the fieldwork appear in other publications by the archaeologist who carried out much of the basic research, Christopher Taylor (e.g. 1975; 1983; see also his book on techniques of field archaeology, 1974).

The Northamptonshire inventories and Taylor's related articles contain extremely detailed expositions of the numerous factors which may influence the discovery (or non-discovery) of ancient sites. The reasons were far more varied than in Italy or Libya, because of the intensity of modern agriculture and settlement, and the terrain and geology are more diverse than in the Somme valley, where the conditions for aerial photography were also better. Taylor listed the following factors which strongly influenced the recovery of sites (1975, 111–112):

1 Geology and soils: the limestone and gravels of the Nene Valley provide good conditions for aerial photography, but clays and glacial deposits in the east of the county do not.

2 Vegetation: forest and permanent pasture inhibit both aerial photography and surface examination.

3 Past cultivation: medieval ridge-and-furrow fields conceal earlier sites until they are sufficiently deeply ploughed to reveal them.

4 Modern occupation: present settlements mask large areas, and urban expansion in recent decades has been considerable; however, discoveries of sites may not have been reported for fear of delaying construction work.

5 Archaeological fieldwork: despite extensive observation by both professionals and amateurs, examination is patchy. 'The blank or apparently sparsely occupied areas on the distribution map are not necessarily to be explained by simple geographical factors such as the existence of heavy soils, or the shortage of water. In almost every case, the explanation is lack of fieldwork and air photography in these particular places' (op. cit. 112).

The Roman settlement pattern in Northamptonshire

All of these factors re-emphasise the fact that our record of Roman sites is a minimum estimate, from which it is very difficult to assess their original density. Taylor has provided an interesting quantification of the progress of discovery; in part of the Nene Valley, the number of Roman sites recorded on the 1931 edition of the Ordnance Survey's *Map of Roman Britain* was 36; it rose to 130 on the 1956 edition, but by 1972 the total had reached 434. In the Northamptonshire inventories, over 600 Roman sites are recorded (fig. 51). The RCHM inventories are published in a full and widely available form, and the information was gathered in a uniform manner, largely by a single researcher. Furthermore, the *Archaeological Atlas of Northamptonshire* (RCHM 1980), which summarises and updates the inventories, provides an unusually good opportunity to make comparisons between sites of different periods, or to study the geological and other factors which condition the discovery of sites.

The county has an area of $c.2370km^2$ (915 sq. miles), and a varied landscape formed by rivers and their many tributaries which have cut down through glacial deposits to expose the underlying rocks and to form alluvial terraces. The influence of these variations upon the discovery of sites has been noted above. The total of over 600 Roman sites has an average density of one in every $3.6km^2$ ($1\frac{1}{4}$ sq. miles), but in well-researched parts of the Nene Valley the density rises to one in $1.5km^2$ ($\frac{1}{2}$ sq. mile). The county contains three small walled towns (Norton, Towcester and Irchester; two more, Water Newton and Great Casterton, lie just beyond its north-eastern boundaries), and 15 large settlements of over 10ha (24¾ acres), some of which may be small towns or vici; four rural temple sites are also known. 59 villas and c.600 settlement sites are included in the Atlas, along with a further 60 ironworking and pottery-making sites. Many more potential settlements are indicated by surface scatters of Roman pottery. The total number of Roman sites or other findspots on the Atlas is around 900.

The density of villas is one per 40km² (15½ sq. miles), but their distribution in the county is particularly uneven; in the 10km² of the National Grid to the north-east of Irchester, there are ten. Many of the remainder are dotted along other parts of the Nene Valley. Not to be forgotten are pre-Roman sites, whose complexity has recently been underlined by Knight's detailed research (1984). 'In some places the density of Iron Age settlement approaches that of the Roman period and covers the same variety of limestone, sand, clay, and glacially derived soils. In these areas the heavy Roman occupation seems to be merely an intensification of an earlier and almost equally heavy Iron Age settlement' (Taylor 1975, 118).

Unfortunately, no analysis of the date-ranges of Northamptonshire's rural sites has been attempted, but there do not seem to be any marked periods of abandonment or decline: 'Settlements which seem to have been occupied during the greater part of the Roman period appear to be as common on the heavier soils as on the light ones. Likewise all soils have sites which have evidence suggesting they were mainly occupied in the later Roman period' (Taylor 1975, 117). Discovery of sites still continues – in a relatively unproductive season (1982), 21 hours of aerial survey revealed 146 sites; 53 were new, and further details were added to 16 of the 93 already known. The researchers commented that '. . . the season's work was valuable in continuing the process of gradual accretion of information, which in some areas is leading to the slow combination of settlement, religious, field system and related evidence to produce a more continuous picture of sections of earlier landscapes' (Brown 1983, 178–9).

As in other provinces of the Roman empire, the kind of fieldwork conducted in Northamptonshire, which is typical of much carried out in other parts of lowland England, raises serious questions about the Roman economy. How did such an intensely populated countryside relate to town life? How large were the agricultural surpluses? Who consumed them, and through what means of marketing and distribution? Perhaps the most profound question is that of the size of the population. At the 1801 census, 121,600 people lived in Northamptonshire. With over 600 known Roman sites in the county, it is obvious that this number could easily be accommodated at the rate of a few thousand in towns or vici, and the remainder as two or three family groups on each of the rural settlements. The fact that the known sites undoubtedly provide an underestimate of their original numbers may compensate for the probability that not all were simultaneously occupied. A population of between 100,000 and 150,000 for Roman Northamptonshire seems quite reasonable. To examine the form of agriculture practised in the area, aerial photographs of field systems, and many samples of plant and bone remains from sites are needed.

ROMAN SETTLEMENT IN THE MILITARY NORTH

Northern Britain was conquered much later than the south-east of England. A legionary fortress was established at York in the AD 70s, and campaigns conducted by Agricola took Roman troops as far north as Moray Firth in the early 80s. Although it seems likely that permanent occupation of the whole of Scotland except for the Highlands had been envisaged, troop withdrawals led to the progressive abandonment of territory south to the Tyne-Solway line by the end of the first century AD. This line remained as a frontier for most of the three remaining centuries of Roman rule; in the 120s AD, it was impressively fortified with a continuous stone wall by the emperor Hadrian. The Tyne-Solway region therefore possessed a thoroughly military character, with forts along the frontier, outposts to the north, and a comprehensive network of forts in the hinterland extending southwards into Yorkshire, Derbyshire and Lancashire. It is therefore of great interest to examine the effects of this intense military occupation upon the native population of the frontier lands, and to assess the extent of the development of characteristics of the civilian south such as towns, villas, etc.

The Solway Firth

We have already seen from examples in Italy and France how fieldwork can transform our know-

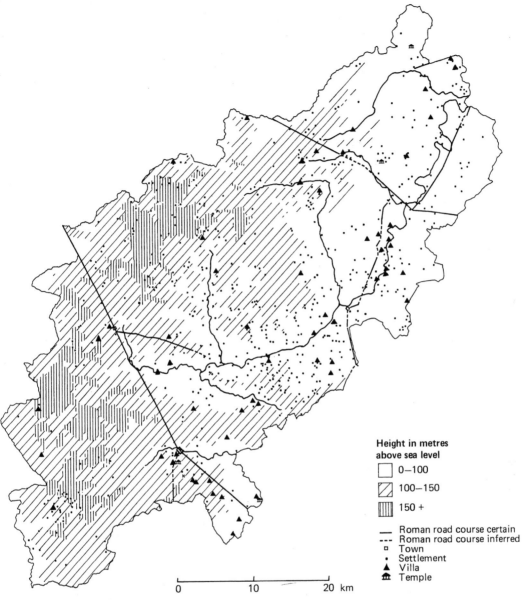

Height in metres
above sea level

☐ 0–100

▨ 100–150

▥ 150 +

——— Roman road course certain
- - - Roman road course inferred
▫ Town
· Settlement
▲ Villa
🏛 Temple

0   10   20 km

ledge of the pattern and intensity of rural settlement, particularly when aerial photography has been involved. This is very true of the lands either side of the Solway; the plain to the south of the western end of Hadrian's Wall was considered to be thinly occupied except for vici and native settlements in the vicinity of Roman forts and roads. In fact, this pattern was a clear case of sampling bias, for aerial photography had only taken place around known Roman military sites and along the roads which connected them. The drought conditions of 1975 and 1976 in particular

51. The Roman sites of the county of Northamptonshire have been published in comprehensive inventories by the Royal Commission on Historical Monuments. However, even in a well-researched area like this, many gaps and concentrations in the distribution of sites are demonstrably the result of biases in modern observation, rather than a true reflection of the original pattern. The dense settlement of the river valleys may have been equalled on higher ground, but modern conditions make the discovery of sites less likely there. (Audio-Visual Centre, University of Newcastle; based on RCHM 1980)

were exploited during a campaign of systematic overall aerial photography initiated by Jones and Higham in 1973, which had already begun to indicate the true numbers of sites (Higham and Jones 1975). 183 'site nuclei' had been recorded in an area of c.690km² (266 sq. miles) by 1982. Exploration was also conducted in Scotland on the northern side of the Solway, where 82 sites were located in an area of 800km² (309 sq. miles). The site densities are very different, 1 to 3.77km² (1½ sq. miles) south of the Roman frontier, 1 to 9.75km² (3¾ sq. miles) to the north, despite rather more favourable conditions for the detection of sites in the latter area.

The sites involved are circular or sometimes rectangular farmsteads, often with associated field systems; some sites are enclosed by several defensive ditches. Differences in shape have been observed which, like their density, demonstrate contrasts between the areas south and north of the Solway. To the north, none of the sites has directly associated fields, and fewer rectangular sites have been found; however, nearly 20 per cent have multiple defensive ditches, compared with less than 2 per cent to the south. The implication is obvious: the protection afforded by Hadrian's Wall provided better conditions for peaceful agricultural development within the frontier than beyond it. The farmsteads in both areas show every indication of having pre-Roman Iron Age predecessors, an observation paralleled by Taylor's fieldwork in Northamptonshire. The number of known settlements – again, it must be stressed, a minimum estimate of the original total – is roughly equivalent to the number of modern farms in the same area of Cumbria.

However, Jones and his co-workers take a very sanguine view of the Roman developments south of the Solway: 'So what we see here is not so much an outright success but rather a success in a limited sense; by that we mean that there is no hierarchic development of settlement, simply more of the same, more farms, and little progress towards full urban settlements' (Jones G. and Walker 1983, 191). This judgement is interesting in the light of Leday's discussion of how 'Romanisation' should be assessed (above p. 120); certainly, the Somme valley and Northamptonshire are not notable for large nucleated settlements, let alone towns. 'Within Roman Britain, a hierarchical settlement pattern stretching from coloniae, cantonal capitals, small towns, villages, villas, hamlet to farm, large and small, can be discerned. In much of the north, and more specifically in the north-west, however, the dominant pattern is more restricted namely, fort, vicus, farm' (ibid. 191). While it is obviously true that villas are notable by their absence in the area concerned, it does not seem fair to judge the extent of Romanisation, or its failure, in terms of the extent of urbanisation.

Natives north of Hadrian's Wall in Northumberland

Our knowledge of the Solway region in the Roman period relies mainly upon recent intensive aerial fieldwork. In contrast, the study of settlement in Northumberland has developed steadily over several decades, combining fieldwork, aerial photography and selective excavations, all aimed at elucidating the long-term pattern of occupation from prehistoric times. In the Roman period Northumberland was a frontier region, with Hadrian's Wall running through its southern edge, whilst the Cheviot hills formed a geographical dividing line which later became the Anglo-Scottish border. The whole county was only fully incorporated into the Roman empire for brief periods in the late first and mid-second centuries AD, when Roman occupation was extended into Scotland. However, the local tribe, the Votadini, is usually assumed to have been friendly (or at least not actively antagonistic), because its territory contained no permanent garrison forts until the later second century AD, when outposts were established on the main road north to Scotland in an area on the tribe's western borders.

The extensive upland areas of Northumberland have long been known to contain numerous and easily visible remains of settlements, comprising curvilinear walled enclosures with round huts on the fringes of the Cheviots, and rectangular enclosures further south (Hogg 1943, 144, fig. 4). The latter were interpreted by Hogg as the homes of settlers transplanted from the Danube region by the Romans in order to provide a pro-Roman population to farm the area; subsequent writers often assumed that their rectilinear form must reflect the influence of Roman buildings. However, excavation has shown that stone-built rectangular settlements often overlie timber sites of the same form, which stretch back into the pre-Roman Iron Age. Construction in stone does seem to be a phenomenon of Roman date, presumably because supplies of timber had become sufficiently scarce to make the investment of time and effort involved in their building worthwhile.

Aerial photography has confirmed that settlement was by no means an upland phenomenon in north-east England. Wherever conditions allow discovery, settlements have been recorded throughout the lower-lying land in the valleys and on the coastal plain, which was once assumed to have been covered by woodlands and difficult to cultivate because of heavier soils. This occupation evidently involved extensive agricultural exploitation, for the excavation of several military structures along Hadrian's Wall has revealed that the ground surfaces buried at the time of their construction in the 120s AD consisted of fields under cultivation (Smith 1978).

Many of the stone-built native settlements of the Cheviots can be examined without excavation, and study of their plans has enabled some interesting observations to be made about the impact of the Roman occupation. The most obvious contrast with the Iron Age is that the characteristic heavily defended hill-forts went out of use; in many cases, Roman huts and enclosures were actually built over their abandoned ramparts and ditches. Furthermore, many of the small settlements show signs of expansion, with additional huts and enclosures packed into or added onto their original plans. These have been examined in detail by George Jobey (1974), who has carried out most of the relevant fieldwork in Northumberland; he has recorded that up to 31 per cent of known sites show signs of expansion in this period. Many cases of expansion could have taken the form of building a new settlement at a different location, of course, which would not be detectable in the same way. Where it can be measured on individual sites, the extent of expansion can be as much as 37 per cent. Numerous assumptions underly this kind of quantification, but it probably under- rather than overestimates the apparent increase in the intensity of Roman settlement.

Such sites do require excavation if dating is to be provided, and few artefacts tend to be found. It may have been the case that expansion took place not primarily as a result of prosperity brought about by the opportunity to supply the Roman army's demand for agricultural produce, but simply because the Romans prevented the kind of local and tribal warfare against which hill-forts had formerly provided essential defence. The impact of Rome may therefore have been nega-

tive rather than positive; the landscape was already cleared and cultivated (fig. 52), and surpluses had been sufficient to support a hill-fort building aristocracy engaging in tribal warfare. The disappearance of the latter allowed some rural intensification rather than expansion, but little in the way of Roman trade goods reached the native settlements north of Hadrian's Wall, compared with those to the south, whether in Northumberland or in Cumbria (Greene 1978b; Jones G. 1978).

Conclusions

As we shall see, the picture which emerges from Northumberland and the Solway region is similar to the phenomenon of settlement in the Libyan pre-desert. The Roman period was not marked by drastic changes or colonisation by 'Romans' in either area, and there is no evidence that the intensification of existing native settlement and agriculture took place under the official direction of the Roman authorities. The principal causes probably included favourable climate, the relatively peaceful conditions provided by Roman conquest, good communications, an economy which involved cash payments and taxation, and the existence of military and civilian consumers requiring surplus products.

THE UNESCO LIBYAN VALLEYS SURVEY

This particularly interesting project began as a direct result of Colonel Gaddafi's own recognition of the remains of settlements and fields while he was still living as part of a nomadic group on the fringes of the Sahara desert. The question to which he wanted an answer was an entirely practical and modern one, namely whether settled agriculture could be re-established in the area; however, the results are also very informative about the Roman period. Several large areas extending from c. 100km (62 miles) to 300km (186 miles) inland have been examined, south of the coast on which lies the modern city of Tripoli, and the well-known Roman cities Sabratha and Lepcis Magna. Sufficient rain falls in the coastal region and in the northern parts of the survey area to permit settled mixed farming including intensive olive and wine production (Arthur 1982), but rainfall is scarcer and very sporadic further south. The pre-desert landscape consists of a plateau broken up by numerous dry valleys (wadis) which soon carry away water from the few heavy cloudbursts that occur; the pattern of rainfall as

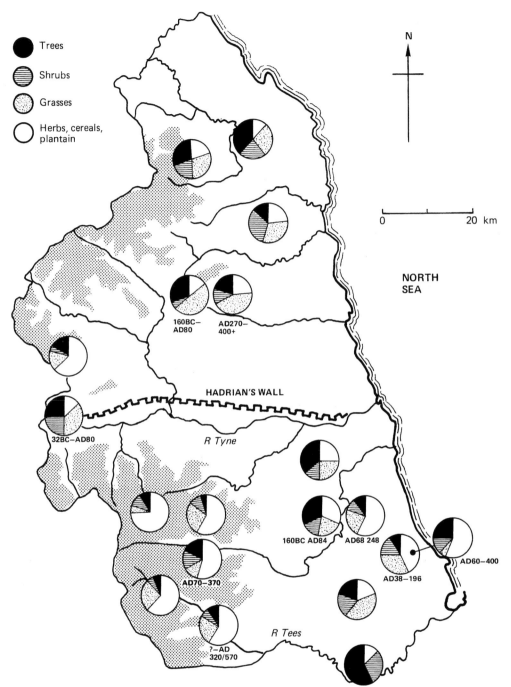

52. The vegetation of north-eastern England in the Roman period has been studied by the analysis of a large number of pollen samples. It is clear that the area was not heavily forested, for the amount of tree pollen is less than 25 per cent in most samples. North of Hadrian's Wall, grassland made up a higher proportion of open land than to the south; this may indicate that stock-raising was more important than arable farming beyond the frontier, while the forts of the Wall and settlements in its civilian hinterland provided markets for locally-grown cereals and other crops. (Audio-Visual Centre, University of Newcastle; based on Clack 1982, 389, fig. 5)

much as its scarcity is a governing factor for life in this area (Shaw 1984).

It had long been recognised that Roman farming took place in many north African areas which are now deserted; the distinctive remains of stone olive-oil processing 'factories' and the presses themselves have received considerable attention (e.g. Gsell 1901; Oates 1953; Barker G. and Jones G. 1980–1981, 32, fig. 10 is a typical olive farm in Libya). Because so much of this evidence lies beyond the present limits of settled agriculture, severe climatic change has often been invoked as the reason for their abandonment (Shaw 1981). For this reason, the survey project has involved environmental scientists as well as archaeologists. An assessment of the date, intensity and duration of various types of settlements was an obvious prerequisite of this research, and it was carried out by the normal archaeological methods of surface inspection, surveying, collection of artefacts, and selective excavation. These could be conducted much more easily in Libya than in Italy, as the area had not been overlain by later settlements or disturbed by modern mechanised farming methods. The results of the survey have been published in a series of papers in the periodical *Libyan Studies* since 1980, with additional articles on specific aspects of the survey.

The Romano-Libyan period was indeed an exception in the agricultural history of the Libyan pre-desert. Fieldwork demonstrated that the present form of semi-nomadic pastoralism with occasional cultivation of small patches of crops had been the normal system of the region in prehistoric times, which returned after the end of the Roman period. The physical remains which are associated with the Romano-Libyan occupation of the pre-desert comprise stone 'castles' known locally as *gsur*, courtyard farms, other houses and small farmsteads, and some hill-top villages (Barker G. and Jones G. 1982, 4). In addition, some burial sites are known with impressive stone memorials in a Roman architectural style, and, most important from the point of view of agriculture, extensive systems of walls on the wadi floors. According to pottery found on them, the date range of the sites extends from the first to the fifth century AD; the impressive *gsur* first appeared in the second century AD. The pottery includes Roman finewares such as terra sigillata and red slipped wares from Italy, Gaul and Tunisia which can be firmly dated in other areas where they are found. Most of the pottery recovered during the survey consisted of samples collected from the surfaces of unexcavated sites; fortunately, when farm LM4 was excavated, the much larger amount of pottery recovered confirmed that the surface scatter which had been collected previously provided an accurate guide to the history of the site (Dore in Barker G. and Jones G. 1984, 22–39).

Romano-Libyan agriculture

In the Roman period, concentrations of the structures outlined above are found in association with extensive systems of walls and water cisterns, particularly where several wadis with sloping rather than precipitous sides converge (fig. 53; Barker G. and Jones G. 1980–1981, 36, fig. 11); the wadi floor wall systems were able to control a large amount of water running both along and into the wadis. Evidence of a wide range of crops had already been deduced from carved reliefs on tombs in the area, but this has now been supplemented by studies of plant remains and animal bones. It is clear that sheep and goats were raised, and that fruits, figs, grapes and olives were grown in addition to cereals (fig. 25; Veen 1980–1981). These species require between eight and 40 times the amount of water provided by normal rainfall: since there is no evidence to suggest that wetter conditions prevailed in the early Roman period, their cultivation must reflect successful control of rainfall by the wadi wall systems. Instead of rushing away in 'flash-floods', rainwater was made to run slowly so that it would soak in and deposit its fertile sediments, whilst some of the excess was diverted into storage cisterns. Complex sluices, which once possessed platforms for the operation of control gates, were situated at the main entry points to wall systems (Barker G. and Jones G. 1984, 31–42).

A recent paper has investigated the wadi walls in detail, and has proposed three 'models' of ways in which they might have been used for cultivation (Gilbertson *et al.* 1984). All three involve a combination of olive trees, cereals and pasturage for animals, but are by no means standardised:

> In general the locational and geomorphic data suggest the region was characterised by a mixed farming economy: the details of the mix varying from place to place according to climate, environmental and no doubt also socio-economic opportunities and constraints. Preliminary studies of the faunal and botanical samples collected in the field programme support this conclusion (op. cit. 66)

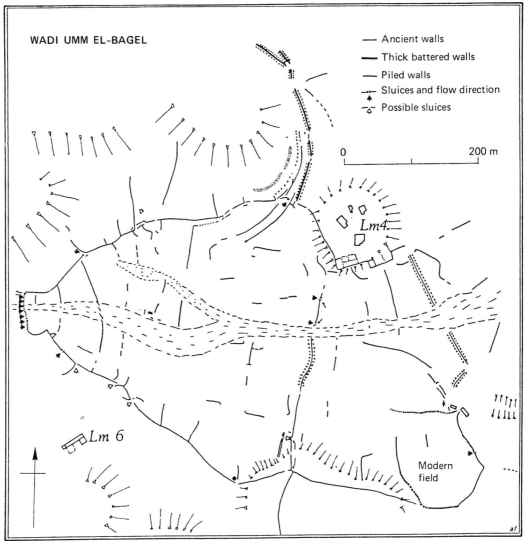

The great importance of botanical and zoological evidence, as well as surveys of sites, in determining the precise form of Romano-Libyan agriculture had already been emphasised (Barker G. and Jones G. 1982, 19):

A systematic programme of midden sampling is essential if we are to move beyond generalisations about ancient systems of cultivation and animal husbandry and tackle vital questions about the complexity of these systems: for example, were ratios of crops and animals uniform throughout the region and throughout the period, and were the production goals likewise uniform or variable? Were crops and animals exploited for subsistence or for producing a surplus for market? Were sheep kept for meat or wool? Were there different combinations of olives and cereals at different types of site, or in different

53. 'Lm4', a typical farming complex in the Libyan pre-desert, consists of a dwelling and subsidiary buildings, which included animal houses and an olive processing unit (see fig. 54). The site lies on a low hill overlooking a network of walls and sluices on the wadi floor. Any rainwater which flowed into the valley was captured and controlled, so that it soaked in and nourished the soil, rather than rushing through and causing erosion. (Audio-Visual Centre, University of Newcastle; based on Barker and Jones 1984, 33, fig. 17)

wadis, or in different periods? There is every reason to expect that we should be able to answer detailed questions like these if we can integrate our existing settlement and agricultural data with further data from carefully selected excavations'.

The excavation of a farm

The first of the selected excavations was published in 1984; the site, prosaically known by its survey identification code as 'LM4', consists of five stone buildings on the edge of a typical 'wadi-wall' irrigation complex (fig. 53; Barker G. and Jones G. 1984, 5, fig. 3). The buildings included a farmhouse with plaster floors and decorative columns on its facade, a possible animal house, and an olive-oil production unit with a full range of facilities for the pressing of the fruit, separation of different grades of oil, and storage in amphorae (fig. 54; 13–18). The capacities of the surviving vats and tanks show that it would have been quite possible to produce in excess of 2000 litres (440 gals) of oil in a season. The publication of the next part of the excavation report, which will include the study of the bones and environmental evidence, is eagerly awaited.

Interpretation

An interesting and important aspect of the interpretation of the results of the Libyan valleys survey is the question of the historical context of the observed pattern of settlement. In the 1950s and 1960s, the existence of orderly stone-built structures was assumed to indicate direct Roman intervention in the area, probably in the third century AD, when it was thought from a reading of historical sources that frontier troops were encouraged to engage in farming. The dating evidence for the structures has turned out to be up to two centuries earlier, however, and a different view has been taken by Barker and Jones, who suggest either a 'deliberate colonising strategy by the Romans, or a more complex process in which

54. An olive-processing building at farm Lm4 in Libya (see fig. 53). In room 1, a timber beam was fixed between the *arbores*, and pressed down onto olives with the help of the stone counter-weight in room 2. The oil ran into a tank, where water would be used to float it clear of sediment. Fine grades could be ladled off into the adjacent vats, whilst the bulk flowed through the spout into room 5, where it was loaded into amphorae whose bases had left impressions in the floor. (Audio-Visual Centre, University of Newcastle; based on Barker and Jones 1984, 14, fig. 9)

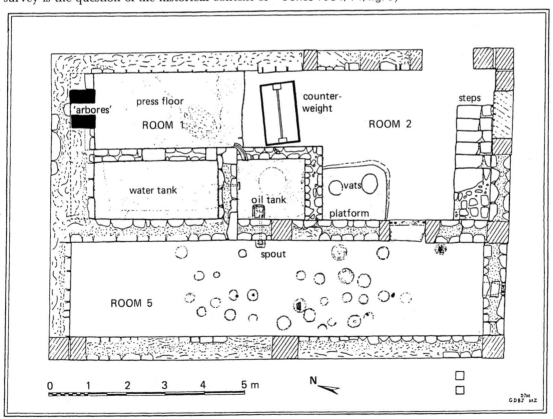

indigenous élites responded to the increasing market opportunities of the coastal zone, presumably supported by capital investments from outside' (Barker G. and Jones G. op. cit. 20). In the northern parts of the survey area, the settled pattern of agriculture survived beyond the Arab conquest of the seventh century AD, whilst in the south, disruption of markets through insecurity in the late Roman period and perhaps also over-exploitation of the environment through over-population brought the phenomenon to an end after two or three centuries.

It will be very interesting to see the results of a full analysis of the chronological development of the sites recorded by the UNESCO survey project. There are inherent difficulties, of course; sites are normally dated according to recognisable categories of imported pottery found on them. Does their absence mean that occupation of a site had ceased, or simply that it no longer had access to the network of Roman trade? Dendrochronological study and radiocarbon dating of wood or other organic materials should help to solve this problem (Greene 1983, 108–115). If the region is resettled, it will be very interesting to study the long-term effects of renewed agriculture; will the threats of erosion and salinity (Barker G. *et al.* 1983, 84) prove too difficult to overcome on a permanent basis? The replication of a Nabataean farm of the Roman-Byzantine period in the Negev desert has made it quite clear that present climatic conditions can allow very productive agriculture to be practised in conditions that demand even more elaborate water catchment and control systems than those of the Libyan pre-desert (figs. 27, 60; Evenari 1971). Archaeology would not be the only beneficiary if the economic priorities of Libya prove sufficiently flexible for experimental testing of models of Roman agriculture, such as those proposed by Gilbertson (1984); they do, after all, have implications for the whole 'famine-belt' of the Sahara.

COASTAL CITIES AND THE MILITARY HINTERLAND OF NORTH AFRICA

The UNESCO Libyan valleys survey is an excellent example of a fieldwork programme in which archaeology, the environment and the economy have been studied through an integrated approach. However, the pre-desert is only one of a number of different zones which underwent agricultural exploitation in the Roman period. From Libya west to the Atlantic coast of Morocco, a band of mountainous land separates the Sahara desert from the fertile Mediterranean coastal strip. The coastal zone is characterised by numerous cities which participated in the flourishing maritime activity of the time, whilst to the south a complex system of forts, roads and boundary ditches marked the edges of the empire, and watched over semi-nomadic peoples who entered and left the empire according to their seasonal needs for fields or grazing. The cities have been studied in detail because of modern French colonisation of the coastal strip, whilst the military works have attracted attention from students of Roman frontier policy. The economic development of the civilian and military zones has received much less attention, but survey work can once again provide the foundation for its interpretation.

Roman literary sources leave the reader in no doubt about the importance of North African agriculture, and the area was famous for the size of its estates, whether in private or imperial ownership. Numerous inscriptions survive to fill out details of estate management, tenancy agreements and methods of cultivation, and many African mosaics show elaborate scenes from rural life. In the last chapter, we have seen how a study based on an inscription, place-names and surface evidence in Tunisia (Peyras 1975) can allow a Roman estate to be studied with a greater degree of confidence than is imaginable in most provinces, where later occupation has destroyed all three categories of evidence to a much greater extent. North Africa is also important because its mixture of military and civilian territories resembles that of other frontier provinces such as Germany or Britain.

Caesarea and its rural hinterland

The city of Caesarea lies on the coast a little to the west of Algiers, and its hinterland has been studied in great detail by Leveau (1975; 1982; 1984). Two main classes of settlements existed – villas and villages (fig. 55). Although architecturally impressive, less than 20 per cent of the villas have traces of the provision of residential rooms for their landlords, implying that they only visited these establishments for short periods – perhaps during the critical stages of the harvest. The buildings are principally devoted to intensive oil and wine production. The peasant villages, a few of which were of quite large extent (up to 12 hectares), were either located away from the areas

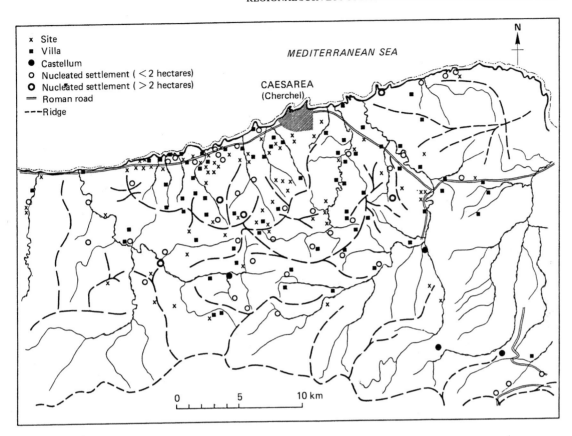

55. Rural settlement around Caesara (Cherchel), Algeria. In addition to the pattern of dispersed villas and settlements familiar from surveys on the north side of the Mediterranean, the hinterland of the city contains several large nucleated settlements. (Audio-Visual Centre, University of Newcastle; based on Leveau 1984, 482, fig. 249)

where villas existed, or, conversely, clustered around individual villas, on which they were obviously dependent (1975, 860). Thus, occupation of the land was continuous from the plains to the hills, but villas were only found near towns or along roads; a stark contrast between 'Roman' farming on the coastal plain and 'native' occupation of the mountains is, in Leveau's view, a modern notion derived from the experience of modern French settlers, whose exploitation of the land depended upon their need to use heavy ploughs on level ground (ibid. 869–870).

The prosperity of the region was greatest in the first two centuries AD, and declined from the third, although Leveau stresses that the life of the villages may well have continued, but with re-

duced commercial activity which allowed the purchase of datable types of pottery (ibid. 865). It will be interesting to compare the results of recent surveys around Carthage with those published by Leveau; Joseph Greene has indicated that there was a steady rise in the number and complexity of rural sites in the Punic, Roman and Byzantine periods, which finally ended after the Arab conquest in the seventh century AD (Keller and Rupp 1983, 198–199).

Army veterans in southern Numidia

Fentress has studied the impact of the Roman conquest upon the area of Algeria and Tunisia which made up the province of Numidia (1979). She has summarised the results of several surveys in the environs of Diana Veteranorum, a town over 100km south from the Mediterranean coast (op. cit. 210–214). Forty-four sites are recorded in this area of c.20 × 30km (12½ × 19 miles), most of which lay on the interface between pasture and arable land which had been subdivided by field boundaries (212, map 11); some large irregular sites away from the arable land may have specialised in stock-raising. Only one villa lay in this area, which otherwise contained farms and/or hamlets of a predominantly small size; the existence of more small sites is suspected, but new surveys are needed to check the whole area. Occupation certainly continued in the late empire, for several churches were built at that time.

Towns such as Diana Veteranorum, and other better known cities such as Timgad, provided a focus for the initiation of agricultural exploitation which would provide supplies for the army in this frontier region. Retired soldiers (the veterans of the town's title) were an obvious choice for '... the creation of a romanised class of peasants with, perhaps, a certain amount of capital to invest in the land' (op. cit. 125); other veterans were given leases of good-quality land on imperially-owned estates (135). In addition to foodstuffs which could be sold to the army, the area produced items which could be exported to more distant markets, notably olive oil and wool or woollen garments.

GREECE AND THE AEGEAN

Greece was absorbed into the Roman empire in 146 BC; the mainland and the islands had undergone a complicated social and economic evolution for several centuries prior to their conquest, and Greece had already exerted considerable influence over many aspects of Roman life. Greek colonies had been established as far west as Spain and southern Gaul since the seventh century BC, and long-distance trade had flourished. The maturity and sophistication of Greek civilisation was unlikely to experience fundamental change after the Roman conquest. Field surveys in Greece have in the past understandably concentrated on prehistoric and classical Greek periods, and have neglected their Roman and Byzantine aftermath. However, the newly developed interest in multiperiod examinations of the evolution of settlement has begun to rectify this situation; the 'model' survey of the island of Melos has already been held up as an example of the way in which such work can be used to maximum effect (above p. 101). On the mainland, relevant surveys are underway at a number of locations, but few have been published in any detail (Keller and Rupp 1983, 11, fig. 2).

Nichoria

In an area on the coast of south-western Greece, the pattern of settlement around Nichoria in the ancient state of Messenia has been investigated (Rapp and Aschenbrenner 1978). A marked shift in settlement occurred between the late Helladic (1100 BC) and Roman periods, by which time only 27 per cent of sites occupied in late Helladic times were still in existence; there was a continuous trend towards occupation of sites near the coast (96, figs. 7.12–7.13). In the pre-Roman period, the literary and archaeological evidence indicates the existence of scattered rural settlements, and small towns in which trade and crafts were centred. The Roman period saw an overall reduction of sites, but an increase in their density in the most fertile areas around the town of Korone; Rapp and Aschenbrenner suggest that Roman settlers or landlords were attracted to the area (op. cit. 97). Citing the authority of the Roman writers Cato and Varro, they envisage an integrated economic pattern of urban and rural markets, the latter being provided by the large estates.

The identification of sites as villas was made according to a list of four criteria, which are clearly stated and thus permit comparison with site classifications used by Dyson or Potter in Italy (Rapp and Aschenbrenner 1978, 99). The criteria were (1) the presence of baths; (2) the use of marble in construction or decoration; (3) size, in terms of the extent of surface remains; and (4) location in relation to land, water and communications. The villas fitted into a hierarchy of sites – large town, small town, villa and farm; this may be compared with the hierarchy proposed for the late Helladic period: capital city, provincial town, village, estate and farmstead. The similarity of complexity of these hierarchies is attributed to their economic systems, in which large centres provided major services, and lower level marketing took place on the smaller sites:

> These services probably included the collection and redistribution of goods, a marketplace, an administrative centre, defense, and so on. It should be noted that although Petalidhi and Nichoria may have functioned as major weekly marketplaces, daily markets were probably held in the smaller towns and villas throughout the area. This type of a mobile (periodic) market economy was quite common in antiquity and was probably in use during the late Helladic and Roman periods. (op. cit. 103)

The main difference between the Bronze Age and Roman periods was a greater emphasis upon coastal sites, reflecting the long-distance trade and improved security of the latter period. Developments within the Roman period are not discussed by Rapp and Aschenbrenner, but the sparse nature of Byzantine occupation indicates that a decline had indeed taken place.

The Nichoria survey could be criticised for forcing its data too rigidly into interpretations derived from historical sources, with obvious dangers of circular argument. The principal lesson for the Roman economy is that complex site hierarchies existed well before the Roman period; the opportunities provided by the 'world market' and coin-based economy of the Roman empire did not produce any spectacular advance upon the late Helladic situation of around 1200 BC. Archaeologists working in the north-western provinces of the empire would do well to note that Roman conquest was not the only route to economic complexity. In central Italy, the kind of settlement pattern which developed in late Helladic Greece is not encountered until the last few centuries BC, when it contrasts sharply with the continuity of settlement which had remained little changed since Neolithic agriculture was first introduced 4000 years earlier (Barker G. 1981, 219). However, any areas of Italy in which Greek colonies had been established may have a more complex history, as the long-term survey of the Metaponto region at the southern end of the Italian peninsula indicates (Keller and Rupp 1983, 191–2). There, the intensity of Roman settlement may be matched or even exceeded by sites of the fourth century BC associated with the Greek city founded around 650 BC.

Melos

The methodology of the Melos survey has been discussed in the introduction to this chapter. Unlike the Nichoria survey, all sites of all periods from the earliest to the modern have been assimilated into a study which aimed to reveal the shifting patterns of socio-political organisation, of which settlement patterns were assumed to be an accurate reflection. This long time-span, with its emphasis upon the informative value of comparisons, made probabilistic sampling essential if valid judgements were to be made. The starting point for the Melos survey was provided by excavations at Phylakopi, an important Bronze Age centre which was the first 'city' on the island, and which stood out from contemporary sites because of its size. The 6000-year perspective into which the island's Roman sites can be placed (fig.

56) is summarised on a single table (Renfrew and Wagstaff 1982, 252).

The Roman period (164 BC to c.AD 500) is characterised by highly dispersed and differentiated settlement: 'Primate settlement dominates densely packed rural landscape; some recognisable industrial/commercial sites' (fig. 57). The estimated total of sites on the whole island (projected from the numbers found in the sampled areas) was 150 – almost one per km^2; this was the only period between c.2000 BC and c.1900 AD when all three trends of population, site numbers and settlement density were upward. The estimated population rose from 2–3000 in the three centuries preceding Roman rule to c.5000; a decline to less than 2500 had taken place by the fifteenth century AD, and there has been a further reduction from a seventeenth-century peak of 5000 to 4500 in 1971 (fig. 56).

THE ISLAND OF CRETE

Crete has attracted considerable archaeological attention because of its Bronze Age Minoan civilisation with its remarkable palaces such as Knossos. Several archaeological surveys carried out on the island have been published, aimed at elucidating particular periods or areas. Two of these surveys illustrate the benefits of an intensive multi-period approach, while the third demonstrates the broader conclusions which can be derived from a regional examination of a single period.

The Ayiofarango valley

Blackman and Branigan have published an intensive survey of 6–7km (3¾–4¼ miles) of this small river valley which is located on the southern coast of Crete, south of the Roman city of Gortyn (1977). After a phase of occupation in the Bronze Age Minoan period, consisting of small settlements and farms which exploited the valley's patches of arable land (ibid. 66, fig. 34), it appears to have been deserted until the fourth century BC. Farms then reappeared in the same kind of locations as before, reaching a peak in the first century AD; the abandonment of a religious centre seems to have led to a decline, and settlement may have been attracted away from the valley towards the city of Gortyn.

Since only one site seemed large enough to be a village, the Roman settlement pattern apparently consisted of dispersed farms (op. cit. 76). The Roman sites dwindled to the point of extinction,

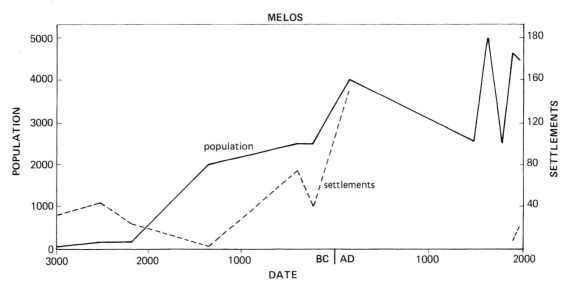

56. The meticulous survey of the island of Melos in the Aegean (see fig. 41) allowed trends in population and settlement density to be estimated. It can be seen that a population comparable with modern levels was achieved in the Roman period; however, Roman sites were very dispersed in contrast to those of recent periods, which had a small number of large nucleated centres. It should not be forgotten that these estimates are only as reliable as the data upon which they are based, and their validity is not equal in all of the periods studied. (Audio-Visual Centre, University of Newcastle; based on data from Renfrew and Wagstaff 1981, 252, table 19.1)

leading to another period of abandonment from the seventh to eleventh centuries AD. The number of sites known in the Bronze Age and Roman periods both totalled 11; as a comparison, only 18 farms and two villages of Byzantine, Turkish and modern date are known (77, fig. 36). Considering the greater likelihood of discovering modern sites, it would seem that approximately equal densities of occupation existed in the Minoan and Roman periods, which have never been matched since. Geomorphological evidence revealed by excavation suggests that the Roman exploitation of the valley for grazing may have caused serious erosion (fig. 32), leading to the deposition of a considerable quantity of soil from the first century AD on the site of an abandoned settlement (23).

The Lasithi plain

A rather larger area has been surveyed in the eastern part of Crete, where the Lasithi plain forms a high oval plateau 800m (2625 ft) above sea level, c.9 by 5km (5½ by 3 miles) in size and surrounded by mountains (Watrous 1982). In the Minoan period, the fringes of the plain were occupied by many sites (ibid. maps 5–9), but, like the Ayiofarango valley, it had become depopulated by the immediately pre-Roman period (maps 12–13). A contemporary writer, Theophrastus, blamed this upon a deterioration of the climate, but Watrous stresses the effects of interstate warfare between rival cities (23). After the Roman conquest in 69 BC, the island in general became repopulated, partly with the help of Roman settlers. Sites in the survey area became as numerous as at any time in the past, and extended onto the plain itself for the first time, perhaps assisted by drainage schemes. In the fourth century AD, there was a hierarchy of sites, ranging from a single dominant centre on one edge of the plain to a 'plethora of small sites, probably farmsteads'; four communities consisting of a few houses lay between these two extremes (24, and map 14).

There is a striking similarity between the pattern and intensity of Roman settlement in the Lasithi plain survey and the island of Melos. Watrous does not give any detail about the decline of Roman settlement, but only states that it was at its height in the fourth to seventh centuries AD. However, he provides an extremely

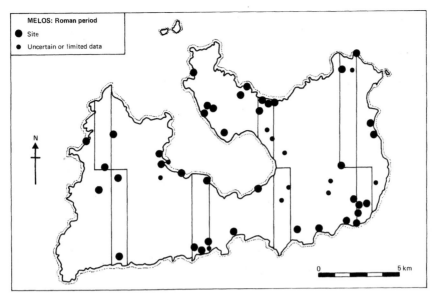

57. Roman settlement on Melos, showing the widely dispersed pattern; see also figs 41 and 56. (Audio-Visual Centre, University of Newcastle; based on Renfrew and Wagstaff 1981, 22, fig. 2.8)

informative account of the well-documented medieval Venetian occupation, which might hold interesting analogies for the effects of Roman occupation in many areas (25–29). The plain was cleared of its inhabitants because of local resistance to Venetian rule in the thirteenth century AD. Animal herding was banned, and the plain was dedicated to cereal production, although the necessary preparations took half a century to complete. Settlers were introduced, and the plain was subdivided into farmings plots by a grid of drainage ditches which resembles Roman centuriation (map 15).

The tenants were meant to live in hamlets around the plain and take a share of the crops, and were discouraged from building permanent houses lest this should lead to vine and fruit growing. In fact, the system was not observed, and unauthorised farming, subletting and tree-felling took place; by the end of the sixteenth century the plain was suffering from depopulation, disease and flooding, and the cereal crops were small and of inferior quality. One is forced to wonder how often this was also the result of the colonisation, centuriation, large estates and share-cropping tenancies of the Roman period. The complaints of tenants against the abuses of their overseers are recorded on north African inscriptions (Kehoe 1982); was the boot occasionally on the other foot?

The plain of Mesara

The conflict between small intensive fieldwork projects and larger regional surveys is emphasised by another Cretan study, of the Mesara plain on the southern side of the island (Sanders 1976). Sanders' map actually includes the Ayiofarango valley, but incorporates none of the small sites discovered by Blackman and Branigan (132); there is no discussion of the methods by which the 74 sites in the 36,000 hectare area were recorded. A shift in settlement is proposed from the Greek to Roman periods, as the new conditions of security led to the relocation of the former small independent cities on lower ground. Rural sites expanded in the 'early' Roman period (up to AD 400), and then declined, but continuing occupation and prosperity is indicated by the existence of many fifth-sixth-century churches (137). In the same period, the existence of some large villas may indicate a move away from towns by landowners, in the manner detected centuries earlier in northeastern Spain (above p. 114).

Sanders divided the plain of Mesara into three areas with rather different settlement patterns. One was characterised by small towns surrounded by villages, another around Gortyna was devoid of rural sites, and on the southern edge of the plain was a string of 'planned estates' (134–137). Given the remarkably small number of sites involved in the area in question, it would seem likely that a sampling strategy similar to that used on Melos, modified to investigate the full range of soils and terrains, would have provided a much firmer base for the interpretation of the plain. Also, the benefits of comparison with the Minoan, medieval and recent periods are lost by selecting only sites of Roman date. Despite these criticisms, it remains true that Sanders' general survey does provide a good starting point for further investigation of economic factors; for example, was the blank area around the city of Gortyna farmed by the town-dwellers? If so, what was different about the other towns which are surrounded by villages? Did the villas and their estates exploit any particular kinds of soils for intensive arable farming or stock-rearing?

SYRIA AND THE NEAR EAST

The eastern Mediterranean provinces of the Roman empire had already experienced a long background of civilisation before their conquest and absorption in the first century BC. Unfortunately, fieldwork projects which encompass the Roman period in a detailed manner are only just beginning to be carried out in Greece and the Near East, and so far their results are only available in summaries. In compensation, there is an excellent study of an area of Syria, and considerable literary evidence from Egypt; the latter allows vivid insights into the countryside, farming and village life. Egypt has further significance, because it was an important source of grain which was shipped in bulk to Rome. This was a case of intensification rather than innovation, for the great city of Alexandria had already relied on similar shipments from the Nile valley in pre-Roman times. For the purposes of this chapter, only the Syrian and other Levantine fieldwork will be discussed, for the Egyptian documents have recently been explored and published in a very readable form (Lewis 1983).

SETTLEMENT AND AGRICULTURE IN NORTHERN SYRIA

Georges Tchalenko's *Villages antiques de la Syrie du nord* (1953) is one of few fully-published regional surveys of rural settlement in the eastern provinces of the Roman empire. The region in question lies around 50km (31 miles) inland from the ancient city of Antioch, at the northern end of the east coast of the Mediterranean. It was heavily occupied in the Roman period (fig. 58),

but had been virtually deserted from medieval times until the present century. Because the survey area consisted of limestone uplands, where the soil cover was thin and stone plentiful, the remains of stone buildings were easily identifiable (fig. 59). After several centuries of rule by Hellenistic kings, Syria became a Roman province in 64 BC, although further areas were added to its eastern borders in succeeding centuries. It flourished until the seventh century AD, when a period of growing instability culminated in the Arab conquest.

Tchalenko outlined an elaborate hierarchy of Roman settlements, which he placed into a clear social, economic and historical context. The hierarchy ranges from poor villages of labourers and humble shepherds' buildings, through better-built peasant villages to substantial villas with courtyards and two-storey accommodation. There are two immediate contrasts with Italy, Gaul or Britain; the villas have local architectural antecedents, and are not especially 'Roman' in appearance, whilst the 'non-villa' buildings are always clustered into villages, rather than being evenly scattered over the countryside in small units. The villages are by no means uniform, however, and range from specialised olive-oil processing communities on high ground to commercial and industrial centres on lower ground adjacent to important roads. Two particularly large agglomerations of settlements, Brad and El Bara, emerged by the late Roman period; the latter extended over 40km² (15½ sq. miles), and was marked by easy access to roads, land for farming grain, vines and olives, and the presence of a good spring (op. cit. 387–390). Although such large centres included churches, oil production centres, markets, baths and other meeting places, they had no formal 'urban' layout, and their specialised buildings were not located centrally or marked by special architectural treatment (ibid. 399).

The impact of the Roman empire is most clearly marked by the appearance of villas in the settlement hierarchy. The Hellenistic pattern was one of peasant villages whose agriculture consisted of cereal farming on low-lying fertile ground; however, private estates characterised the Roman period, and coincided with the introduction of an intensive olive cultivation (Tchalenko 1953, 400). Evidence from inscriptions shows that the villa owners were not absentee landlords, but perhaps a mixture of army

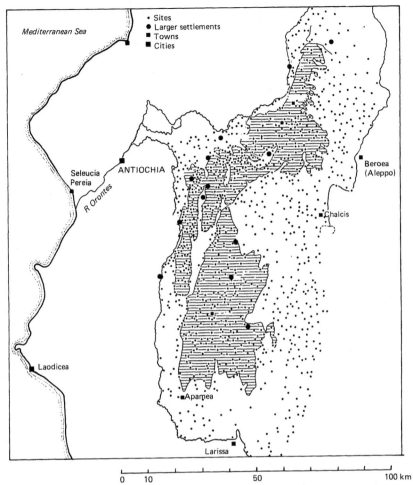

58. Tchalenko's survey of the plateau inland from Antioch in Syria recorded hundreds of well preserved stone-built sites lying on formerly fertile limestone from which most of the soil had been eroded. The success of settlements in the Roman period was probably a result of the economic circumstances of Roman control, which gave producers of olive oil access to a large overseas market. Settlement intensified in the late Roman period to an extent not paralleled in the western provinces of the empire. (Audio-Visual Centre, University of Newcastle; based on Tchalenko 1953, pl. 35)

veterans, officials and local native notables (ibid. 382, 404), and the number, size and distribution of villas argue against the dominance of very large estates (*latifundia*) in the region.

Tchalenko points out some significant implications of the introduction of olive cultivation. A considerable investment of time and effort is involved in the preparation of land and planting the trees, which will not produce fruit for ten to twelve years, although they demand skilled attention during that period. Such an investment implies estate owners with wealth, perhaps assisted by encouragements from the state, such as tax concessions of the kind which are documented in north Africa. Long-term skilled labour would also have been required, possibly under special forms of contract which eventually resulted in ownership of part of the land (op. cit. 413–415). The villa farmers required seasonal labourers to harvest and process the crop, using the communal presses of large villages to which villas were often attached. The oil would then be sold through the local markets and then transported to Antioch and other towns or rural areas where olives were not grown. The remaining surpluses would have been disposed of overseas via ports on the Medit-

59. A Roman burial monument near Barad in Syria, photographed by Gertrude Bell in 1905. The barren limestone landscape is clearly visible in the background, and its abandonment assisted the survival of the Roman remains which were studied by Georges Tchalenko in the 1930s. (Bell archive, University of Newcastle)

erranean coast. In fact, this specialised monoculture in the upland areas survived through many vicissitudes in the later Roman period, until shipping was finally disrupted in the seventh century AD.

The presence of churches and monasteries on many rural sites in northern Syria demonstrates their continued existence in the late Roman/early Byzantine period. Indeed, Tchalenko draws analogies between these institutions and their lands and dwellings and villa estates (op. cit. 396–398). By the time of the supremacy of these religious foundations, the earlier villa estates had diminished in significance through the subdivision of their lands, to be replaced by villages containing many individual buildings resembling small villas, each with an individual olive press (ibid. 408). The density of occupation intensified in this late period, perhaps because of the need to replace supplies of oil from Africa or Spain, which had been conquered by Germanic barbarians in the fifth century. Thus, another contrast with Italy is clear; population and settlement did not decline during the early Roman empire. A similarity with Italy, Gaul and Britain is the importance of non-urban settlements, whether farmsteads, hamlets or large villages.

Tchalenko also emphasises an aspect of rural life which can be supported by archaeology in the western provinces, but which runs counter to any idea of self-sufficiency on farms or agricultural estates in the countryside. There is no evidence in this area of Syria for the presence of crafts or industries located in the villas or upland villages; all essentials had to be brought in from outside, presumably from the towns by means of the same routes and roadside villages through which agricultural surpluses were exported (op. cit. 411). The extent to which imported pottery reached rural sites in Etruria or the Solway plain can also be explained by a similar system of widespread trade on a number of levels, from major centres down to small-scale local transactions. The extent of these networks, greatly facilitated by the use of a wide range of coin denominations, cannot be found again in Europe for 1000 years or more. The Roman empire provided a unique opportunity for rural development; in the case of northern Syria, 'its ... prosperity resulted from the Roman organisation of the Mediterranean world and the opportunities which depended upon it. As a fruit of the Roman conquest of Syria, it was unable to outlive it' (Tchalenko 1953, 438).

Abandonment and erosion

Other areas of the Near East show vivid evidence for abundant settlement in Roman and Byzantine times, which came to an end after the Moslem conquest of the region (Sperber 1977, 428–432; Guy 1954, 78–79). On the Golan heights between Israel and Syria, Dauphin claims to have found a situation in which isolated villas of the Roman period evolved into small Byzantine towns in a very similar way to those recorded by Tchalenko (Dauphin and Schonfield 1983, 196). In the rocky Negev desert, Nabataeans occupied farmsteads beside wadis which employed walls and terraces to trap water (fig. 60) in the same manner as in the Libyan pre-desert; settlement grew and peaked from 300 BC to AD 700 (Evenari 1971, 18). In a review of discussions of the reason for the subsequent decline, Ashtor has pointed out that: 'It would however be erroneous to believe that after the Moslem conquests there was a real cataclysm in the agricultural history of this region. In fact there was rather a progressive decline' (1976, 55). Evidence from various parts of the region suggests that depopulation and the different objectives and nature of Bedouin agriculture caused decay of irrigation systems and massive erosion of soils – whether exacerbated by climatic change or not (ibid. 45–55). The effects were not restricted to the former Roman areas, but occurred through much of Mesopotamia (ibid. map pp. 56–57).

TOWNS AND AGRICULTURE

An important observation which has emerged from fieldwork studies of the Roman countryside in Spain, Gaul, Britain and Syria is the peripheral nature of towns, which indicates that a wide range of trading transactions must have been conducted in rural markets. Of course, ancient historians have stressed for some time that no sharp division really existed between urban and rural life, and that their separation is an intrusive concept from the medieval period or the modern industrialised world. In the Mediterranean area, substantial sections of the populations of many towns have farmed the surrounding areas from their urban base right up to the present day. Literary sources make it clear that wealthy Romans owned large town houses and also country estates; in the provinces, some administrative capitals may have held that rôle not because of any intrinsic importance, but simply because they were located at a convenient meeting-place for the wealthy members of the town council, the curia (Salway 1981, 592). Recent archaeological research in the gardens of Pompeii (fig. 38) and the 'black earth' of London (fig. 29) has demonstrated that the division between town and country should be blurred even further, both in early Roman Italy and late Roman Britain (above pp. 80, 94).

Detailed historical and archaeological studies of individual towns are common; analyses which also consider their regional hinterland are rarer, but Wightman's book on Trier and the Treveri (1969), and Liebeschutz's on late Roman Antioch (1972) are good examples. Wilson's account of the decline and subsequent reappearance of defended urban centres on Sicily (1985) has been cited above, and is of particular interest because it remarks upon the generation of minor centres in the countryside to serve a dispersed rural population. Centres of this kind are also noted in Gaul and Syria by Leday and Tchalenko (above), and their British counterparts were the theme of a conference published in 1975 by Rodwell and Rowley.

FURTHER READING

Most of the crucial historical texts and inscriptions which contribute to the understanding of the economies of regions and provinces of the Roman empire are discussed, and often quoted at length, in the five volumes of Frank's *An economic survey of ancient Rome* (1933–1940); the source-books cited

60. The experimental farm at Avdat in the Negev desert, Israel. The sinuous walls in the centre of the photograph channel rainfall from the valley sides to the fields and orchards visible on the valley floor (see fig. 27). Water conservation schemes such as this, and similar systems discovered in Libya (fig. 53), not only make use of the small amount of rain which does fall in arid areas, but also help to prevent soil erosion by uncontrolled floods. (Photograph by courtesy of R. Burns)

at the end of chapter 1 should also be consulted. The growing contribution of archaeology to this aspect of the Roman period has been discussed in general articles by Snodgrass (in the French periodical *Annales*, 1982), and by Dyson in *American antiquity* (1982). Barker has published a new review of Italian work, 'Landscape archaeology in Italy' (Malone and Stoddart 1985 (1) 1–19). Specific field-survey projects – many including the Roman period – have been reported in Keller and Rupp's *Archaeological survey in the Mediterranean area* (1983) and Macready and Thompson's *Archaeological field-survey in Britain and abroad* (1985). The best published example of a multiperiod, multidisciplinary survey project is probably Renfrew and Wagstaff's *An island polity: the archaeology of exploitation on Melos* (1982). Edith Wightman's magisterial historical, political and economic survey of *Gallia Belgica* (1985) is an excellent synthesis of a single region in a shorter period. It explores the pre-Roman background of the Roman province; for Britain, Fowler's *The farming of prehistoric Britain* (1983) is helpful. Many of the techniques involved in field-survey are outlined in my recent book *Archaeology: an introduction* (1983). The rôle of aerial photography in the study of the historical geography of a specific region is examined in great detail in Agache's *Détection aérienne de vestiges protohistoriques, gallo-romains et médiévaux* (1970); Bradford's pioneering *Ancient landscapes* (1957) is still useful. Wilson's *Air photo interpretation for archaeologists* (1983) is also recommended.

SIX

Metal, stone and pottery in the Roman empire

INTRODUCTION

The chapter on agriculture began with a quotation stating that almost all of the Roman population was involved in low-level agriculture '. . . while industry depended on a backward technology and was rarely organised in large units' (Duncan-Jones 1974, 1). 'Low-level' and 'backward' are terms loaded with subjective judgements. Even in the 1970s the issue of the introduction of appropriate rather than advanced technology into the economies of 'developing' countries was already under discussion (Dunn 1978). The benefits of size have also been debated in industry; the phrase 'small is beautiful' has passed into common English usage as a result of reactions against large conglomerates and multinational corporations (Schumacher 1973).

The crisis in international banking which has followed the vast loans of the 1970s gives a rather different aspect to Duncan-Jones' assertion that the Roman economy 'remained a primitive system which would today qualify the Roman empire for recognition as a "developing" country' (op. cit. 1); nor is Duncan-Jones alone in his preoccupation with development (Deman 1975). Many Third World nations would gladly abandon high-technology low-labour industrial developments in favour of low-level agriculture and the production of simpler goods which could employ more people and enter the markets of the 'developed' world. In a paper published in 1965, Finley concluded that technical innovation was conspicuous by its absence in the ancient world; but in 1952, Thompson had already drawn attention to the innovative concepts included in an anonymous late Roman manuscript, *De rebus bellicis*.

Before we may make any judgements about the quality of Roman technology and industry, we must first suspend any modern notions about the importance of progress and productivity. The principal question should be, did Roman technology allow the Romans to exploit the resources they needed? If it is found that the answer is positive, and that labour and resources were quite adequate without any elaborate technical developments, we can hardly judge the Roman empire harshly for not making them. This chapter will attempt to present the evidence which archaeology has provided for the exploitation and/or manufacture of three important materials – metal, stone and pottery.

Sources of evidence

There is abundant evidence for the exploitation of the resources of the Roman empire; much of it is contained in legal texts, reference works such as Pliny's *Natural History*, or technical treatises such as Vitruvius' *De Architectura*. Pliny is a particularly valuable authority on mining in Spain, for he actually saw it in action in AD 72–74 while he held an official post (Bird 1984). However, Ramin has pointed out the inadequacy of the picture of Roman mines in Gaul which could be obtained from written sources (1974, 437). Many crafts and industries are also named and sometimes illustrated on grave memorials or other carvings (Loane 1938; Zimmer 1983; Squarciapino n.d.). Historians of technology have used these sources of evidence for their own purposes (Landels 1978), whilst archaeologists have taken serious account of the technical factors involved in the production of classical architecture and the manufacture of works of art or utilitarian objects in stone, metal or clay (Strong and Brown 1976); the combined skills of historians, archaeologists and scientists have made considerable progress in clarifying this aspect of Roman economic life.

THE EXPLOITATION OF METAL RESOURCES IN THE ROMAN EMPIRE

The first use of metals occurred in the late Stone Age, when gold and copper were fashioned into ornaments or versions of contemporary stone tools and weapons. In the Near East, such uses began around 8000 BC, and in Europe, soon after 6000 BC. The reason for the initial choice of these two metals is that both can occur naturally in their pure form, and may be worked directly without smelting or casting; their technology would not have seemed greatly different from stone working. However, the use of heat expanded the ways in which they could be fashioned; in fact, it is impossible to work copper successfully without regular heating (annealing) to prevent brittleness and cracking. Melting the metal is a different matter, however, for pure copper demands a forced draught to reach the required temperature of 1084°C (Tylecote 1976, 2).

The earliest appearance of smelting rather than the use of native copper is now seen as the mark of the beginning of the 'Bronze' Age; the extraction of metal from ores coincided with the appearance of pottery kilns, which also demonstrate the ability to control fire for intense heating (Tylecote 1976, 5). Bronze first appeared in the Near Eastern civilisations between 3000 and 2500 BC, and copper was replaced by bronze in Italy by 1800 BC. Molten copper or bronze can be cast into shapes which require little finishing, and the adoption of casting rather than cold-working and annealing optimised the use of metal's advantages over stone. Other metals which can be extracted and utilised through smelting of ores and casting include silver, lead and tin; alloys can also be made, of which the commonest in prehistoric times was bronze, consisting mainly of copper and tin, to which small quantities of lead or other metals might be added to obtain special properties. Most non-ferrous ores are found in volcanic rocks in highland areas, either in their original position or redeposited in river beds through erosion.

The metallurgy of iron is rather different from that of the metals mentioned so far, for its ore is found over very wide areas (Cleere and Crossley 1986). Furthermore, with the exception of China, smithying was the only means of working it in the ancient world (Cleere 1976); the casting of iron, first developed in England in the eighteenth century, was one of the most significant advances of the Industrial Revolution. The use of iron smelted from ore developed in Asia Minor around 2000 BC, although some instances of the use of iron derived from meteorites have been noted at earlier dates (Tylecote 1976, 40). Iron technology was well established in Britain and Europe by 500 BC, but bronze naturally continued in use for many purposes which did not demand the tough resilience of iron.

Metals were put to a wide variety of uses in the Roman empire. Gold and silver were used in making coins, jewellery and ornaments, and high-class tableware (Painter 1977). Bronze was far commoner, and provided the bulk of the coinage, cheaper jewellery and all manner of fittings for vehicles, military armour, furniture, etc.; it was also the principal metal used in casting statues and making a range of cast and sheet metal vessels and containers from cauldrons to jugs. Lead and tin provided metal for alloying with copper to make bronze, or with each other for pewter or solder (Hughes 1977; Blagg and Read 1977). Lead on its own was invaluable for sealing roofs or water tanks, and for making the pipes which were important in the construction of water-supply systems and baths (Boulakia 1972). Iron had universal use for the production of strong, sharp and durable tools for agriculture and crafts, many of which are remarkably similar to their modern counterparts (Glodariu 1977, Taf 1–3; Manning 1976); their range and specialisation was noticeably greater than in the pre-Roman Iron Age (Gaitzsch 1980, 259–261). The Roman period did not coincide with any great developments in metal technology, but Roman occupation brought a greater intensity of exploitation and production than had ever been seen before.

One simple example demonstrates the order of magnitude involved. An aristocratic Celtic warrior in Britain on the eve of the Roman conquest might have possessed a chariot with some iron and bronze fittings, an iron sword, and in a few cases a decorated bronze helmet or shield (Fox 1958). His poorer followers probably carried simple iron spears, and their settlement would most likely boast only a few metal cauldrons or other vessels. A Roman legion would have contained 5000–6000 men equipped with chain-mail or other body-armour, helmets, swords, daggers and long spears all made from iron; their belts and kilts bore numerous intricate cast bronze fittings (Robinson 1975). Campaign equipment included several bronze and iron cooking vessels. After its conquest, Britain was garrisoned by four legions and an even greater number of units of well-equipped auxiliary soldiers: the demand for metal for repairs and replacements would have been far greater than that needed by a small number of pre-Roman warriors. When the thousands of iron nails used in timber forts, the tons of lead required for stone forts, villas and town buildings, and the gold, silver and bronze included in coins, are added to the list of military requirements, the dramatic impact of this aspect of 'Romanisation' may be appreciated.

MINING

The guiding principle in the collection of ores for smelting is, naturally, the expenditure of the minimum effort. Underground mining in the Roman period was, therefore, a last resort, reserved for precious metals. Despite several thousand years of metal use, many sources of ores were probably still exploited by means of opencast workings on surface outcrops of rocks containing ores. Evidence for these is difficult to find, for such outcrops will almost certainly have been removed by subsequent activity, particularly in recent centuries (fig. 61; Jones G. 1980). More elaborate techniques depend on the geological nature of ore-bearing deposits, and whether the ore is in its primary position or has been redeposited by

erosion. Patches or veins of ore lying near the surface can be reached by digging simple pits or trenches until they become too deep, at which point some form of shafts or tunnels may be necessary. Tunnels will involve the investment of more labour, particularly if systems of ventilation and drainage are required. As we shall see, some sites of Roman gold mines in Wales and Spain show a progression from simple to complex methods as the easier deposits became exhausted.

In the case of ores which have been eroded and redeposited in river gravels, rather different techniques may be found, exploiting the nearby availability of water to wash away large areas of sediment to leave the heavier metal ores behind (fig. 63). The principle is the same as in the method of panning for gold familiar in 'Western'

61. Ancient and modern mining at Rio Tinto, Huelva, Spain. An extensive dark area of copper ore is being totally removed by blasting; the exposed workface is over 100m high, and several Roman mine shafts have been cut through in the process. Although mining had occurred on the site in earlier times, the exploitation in the Roman period was unrivalled in its intensity until modern times. (Photograph by courtesy of Prof. G. D. B. Jones)

films of the Klondike gold-rush period; some sand and water are scooped up in a flat pan, and the water spills out carrying away lighter material until – it is hoped – heavy grains of pure gold remain in the bottom of the pan. The use of water power is not restricted to riverside sites, however, for water released from carefully located dams could be used effectively in opencast mines to clear away surface soil and loose rock, whilst continuous flows of water could be utilised for washing and sorting crushed ores after mining. From the prehistoric period until the advent of drills and explosives, fire-setting was one of the most effective methods of breaking up solid rock, both in opencast mines and tunnels. Large bonfires would first be lit to heat up the area of stone under attack, which would then suddenly be flooded with cold water so that the thermal shock would shatter and crack it, making the ore easier to remove.

The Dolaucothi gold mines

Detailed inspection of the remains of gold workings at Dolaucothi, near the village of Pumsaint, in Dyfed, south-west Wales, has revealed evidence of all the important stages in the mining of gold ore, and has demonstrated the importance of water as a powerful ally of the miners (Lewis and Jones 1969). The site has been considerably disturbed by renewed mining at various times since the Roman period, particularly in the nineteenth and twentieth centuries; much Roman evidence must have been removed by the large opencast mine which is conspicuous today. The gold deposits and the mines lie at the end of a steep-sided narrow ridge flanked by small rivers, the Cothi and the Annell. The opencast areas are complex, and contain a number of tunnels, whilst fieldwork has revealed water channels and reservoirs on the hillsides above them. Using ancient descriptions of mining, largely provided by Pliny the Elder, it is possible to reconstruct the sequence in which the various available mining techniques were applied at Dolaucothi.

The gold-bearing veins of rock rise to the surface at an angle of around 35 degrees. It is likely that their exposed outcrops had already been explored by prehistoric workings, but efficient exposure was achieved in the Roman period by bringing aqueduct channels for nearly 10km (6¼ miles) along the ridge from a suitable point further up the river Cothi. Tanks were constructed directly above the slopes where buried ores were known or suspected, and then intentionally breached to allow a large volume of water to rush down, removing the overlying soil and loose rock. This technique is known today as hushing, probably because of the noise made by the water. The exposed outcrops of ore could now be quarried by firesetting or undermining, and the aqueduct used to provide a continuous source of water for washing the crushed ore to separate out the parts containing gold which were to be smelted.

Only when opencast mining became impractical did any tunnelling take place; at Dolaucothi, it was necessary because of the way in which the ore-bearing veins dipped. A deep vertical shaft was dug, and horizontal galleries (stopes) were opened out on three levels. The shaft and other tunnels connecting the galleries had to be sufficiently large to allow ore to be removed, and for adequate ventilation and drainage. Fragments of a large wooden water-wheel have been recovered which demonstrate that a mechanical system existed for draining the deep workings (Boon and Williams 1966). Such wheels lifted water by acting in the opposite way to mill wheels; much labour would have been required to turn them, as a series of wheels probably lifted water in stages to the surface (fig. 62; Luzon 1968; Palmer 1926–1927, pl. 16). Thus, Dolaucothi illustrates all of the stages of ore extraction from simple surface working to deep mining. Surface observations suggest evidence for additional uses of water, as a series of sieves and tables for ore washing may have been situated on steps down a hillside (Lewis and Jones 1969, pl. 50a–b).

Mines in Spain

Fieldwork in Spain has produced parallel evidence for similar techniques employed in the search for precious metals (Lewis and Jones 1970; Bird 1972; Rothenberg and Blanco-Freijero 1981; Domergue and Herail 1978). The scale of mining can be gauged from Bird's gazetteer of 231 sites in the north-west of Spain alone (1984, 364, 355–316 and fig. 12.1). It must be stressed that indications of surface traces of mining are not always easy to interpret; the nature of one of the Dolaucothi aqueducts and a supposed reservoir has been disputed (Boon and Williams 1966, 122, note 6), on the grounds that hushing would have been inappropriate for the geology of the site anyway. On the other hand, Domergue considers that the rôle of hushing has been underestimated by Lewis and Jones, and that it would be used extensively in the removal of ore, not simply the overlying debris (1974, 513). In his detailed commentary on Pliny's account of mining, Domergue also emphasises the importance of a further technique, *ruina montium* (fig. 63), by which water was led through vertical and horizontal tunnels in the working face of an opencast mine, until erosion caused the face to collapse in the manner achieved by explosives in recent times (Domergue and Hérail 1978, fig. 35c–d).

The most spectacular scale of mining was undoubtedly found in the Huelva district of southern Spain, notably at the Rio Tinto mines, where modern exploitation has uncovered many traces of earlier activity. Analysis of waste and slag from a deep stratified deposit has shown development of the pattern of working from prehistoric to Carthaginian and Roman times (Rothenberg and Blanco-Freijero 1981, 163–182); in these historical times, silver was the principal attraction, but copper continued to be extracted as well. The Roman period brought intensification rather than innovation in methods

62. Remains of a pair of Roman water wheels discovered in the course of mining operations at Rio Tinto in the nineteenth century. A series of similar wooden wheels, operated by human labour, would have lifted water in stages from the mines. (Palmer 1926–1927, pl. 16)

of exploitation; under Augustus, existing mines expanded and new mines were dug, using extensive shafts and underground galleries:

> Huelva was the most important metal producing area in the Roman Empire and one of the most important metallurgical regions in the ancient world . . . almost all of the presently operating and most of the old abandoned copper mines of Huelva had previously been operated in Imperial Roman times and had produced silver as well as copper. (Rothenberg and Blanco-Freijero 1981, 173)

Southern Spain and Portugal have provided examples of actual tools and other artefacts used in mines (Healy 1978, pls. 21–37), and technical equipment used in drainage, including substantial remains of water-wheels of the kind known from Dolaucothi (Luzon 1968, 106–7, figs. 4–6). Mechanical bucket-chains, Archimedean screw-pumps and even double-acting pumps with non-return valves were in use (ibid. 111–120); the labour which drove them was human, of course. The organisation of the mines and their labour is an interesting question, and the synthesis of information which can be made from references to Spain in the works of Roman writers has been extended by the discovery of the remarkable inscribed bronze tablets from Vipasca, in the modern district of Aljustrel, Portugal, which give many details of mining practices in the course of the regulations which they record (Domergue 1983).

The organisation of mining

In general, metal resources seem to have been under state control in the Roman empire, following the precedent of many earlier states and kingdoms (Finley 1970). In many cases, mines were not worked directly by the state, although the army may have been involved in the initial exploitation of newly conquered provinces (Noeske 1977). Richardson has discussed the 'gold-rush' of Italians to Spain in the republican period, and has stressed the importance of exploitation by comparatively small-scale lease-holders rather than the huge companies who 'farmed' taxes (1976, 151–2). The names of individuals and companies (*societates*) have been found cast or stamped on unused ingots of metal (Colls *et al.* 1975). In a study of stamps on lead ingots recovered from the sea near the port of Cartagena ('New Carthage') in south-eastern Spain, Domergue has observed the change from

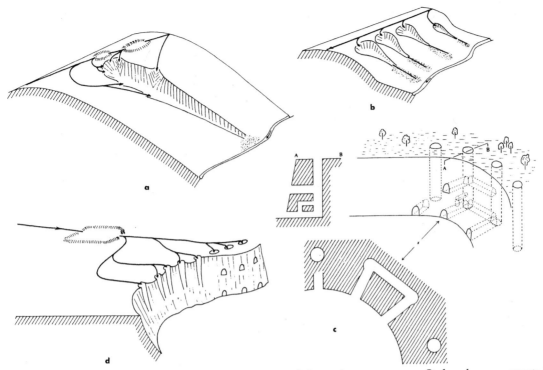

63. Methods of removing gold-bearing ore from sedimentary deposits in northern Spain, where various forms of artificial erosion by water were utilised in order to flush away unwanted material. In a and b, aqueducts lead to simple opencast workings; in c and d, deeper opencast workings are created with the assistance of *ruina montium,* which fed water into tunnels to cause the collapse of a workface. (Domergue and Hérail 1978, fig. 35)

large companies to individuals by the time of Augustus (1966, 65–66). During the empire, state control increased, and new areas of mines were exploited directly (ibid. 67–68). New conquests evidently affected the output of different mining areas, for ingots in south-western Gaul imply that the port of Narbonne changed from acting as a transit point for Spanish metal on its way north, to being an intermediary for supplies from Britain on their way to Italy and the Mediterranean (Laubenheimer-Leenhardt 1973, 199, 201).

Ideally, the Roman authorities should have been able to meet their requirements of metals of all kinds without having to undertake any direct mining at all, by balancing the demands made upon lease-holders against the need to encourage

mining when necessary. It has been suggested that the massive scale of exploitation undertaken at Rio Tinto was too great for the operation of companies with leases, rather than by the state (Rothenberg and Blanco-Freijero 1981, 173); the scale of some of the north-west Spanish workings has led to the same conclusion (Tranoy 1981, 233). However, it must be remembered that the Roman government felt able to run the vital supply of grain to the capital on a very large scale on a contract basis, as well as the distribution of stone (Rickman 1980; Ward Perkins 1980, 334). Some areas were placed under the control of an official, entitled *procurator metallorum,* who regulated mining activities and supervised the leasing of workings to individuals and companies (Dušanić 1977, 79–85). Many of the leases were operated on a system similar to agricultural tenancies, based on the sharing of the products with the state. In the provinces along the river Danube, it has been suggested that the state organisation of mining inhibited 'normal' progress towards town-centred Romanisation (Dušanić 1977, 93).

Labour in mines must always have been dangerous and unpleasant, and the ancient writers give frequent instances of the use of slaves, criminals and forced labour (Healy 1978,

147

135–137). The use of free contracted labour may well have been underplayed for dramatic effect, however, and holders of leases in mining areas would have needed to secure skilled and experienced labour (Mrozek 1977, 102–109); an analysis of inscriptions from Galicia in north-west Spain shows that workers were attracted from other parts of the Peninsula (Tranoy 1981, 233). The Vipasca tablets give details of leasing arrangements (Healy 1978, 130, 138; extracts translated in Lewis and Reinhold 1966, 188–194). There are mining regulations relating to safety, measures aimed at reducing fraud by mineowners, and even details about other occupations in the area such as the operation of baths, shoemakers, and tax concessions for teachers. They give the impression of a community with essential facilities to attract leaseholders and labourers to a remote district; however, Rothenberg and Blanco-Freijero argue that the documents only apply to a small community, and need not be representative of what happened at larger centres of exploitation (1981, 173).

Metallurgy

A clear consciousness of metallurgy is evident in Roman metalworking, particularly in the case of alloys of copper, notably bronze and brass. Coins demonstrate the consistency with which either pure metal or alloys could be produced, albeit by rule-of-thumb rather than scientific control. Early silver denarii were virtually pure, but declined with the progressive addition of bronze until only 2–3 per cent of silver remained (fig. 21). An appearance of higher silver content was sometimes attempted on large bronze coins of the fourth century, which contained less than 2 per cent, by chemically enriching the silver content of the surface layer, dipping in molten silver, or even encasing a coin in thin sheet silver (Tylecote 1976, 59). The 'bronze' coins of the early empire in fact consisted of brass or impure copper, whose colours gave added visual distinctions to the different denominations (fig. 16). The very gradual changes in the constituents of Roman coins bear witness to the degree of control which existed.

Different alloys have different properties, both in manufacture and use, and once again metallurgical analysis has demonstrated a sound knowledge present amongst Roman metalworkers, although it should be stressed that comparable knowledge had been acquired much earlier in simpler prehistoric societies. In the case of bronze, it is possible to compare actual Roman 'recipes' for alloys with the results of modern scientific analyses of actual objects (Brown 1976, 39–41). The analyses show that levels of tin and lead contained in cast objects, and both cast and sheet-metal vessels, were carefully controlled so that the finished products were not adversely affected by potentially negative properties. Thus, for thin metal vessels lead was kept down to around 1 per cent, lest it softened the alloy, whilst it ranged up to 35 per cent in cast objects and statues. Tin is found in both categories, but never over 14 per cent, at which point it leads to brittleness. Despite problems in translating terms which it is possible that Pliny the Elder may not himself have fully understood, the same distinction between thin vessels and castings is apparent in his lists of ingredients (ibid. 39). His comments on soldering silverware have been discussed in a recent publication of a programme of scientific analysis and microscopic examination of the techniques involved (Lang and Hughes 1984).

A wide range of casting methods was employed in the Roman period, using a variety of different forms of moulds, but it must be remembered that most of these methods had already been in use for several thousand years. In the early Bronze Age, simple depressions in stones had been used to shape molten metal into ingots or artefacts which would be finished off by hand. The use of two-part moulds allowed objects to be shaped on both sides, whilst the insertion of a separate clay core permitted cavities (such as sockets) to be made. Most early moulds were made from carved stone, but further development using clay allowed greater sophistication. For instance, two-part moulds could be made by enclosing a suitable existing object in fine clay, cutting it open, removing and firing the clay, and then using it to make replicas of the object. Multiple moulds could thus be made quickly from expendable material rather than carefully carved fine stone.

Another development was the 'lost wax' process, which enabled metalworkers to use beeswax to fashion elaborately decorated objects such as ornaments, which would then be coated in clay and fired. The wax would of course be 'lost' as it melted and escaped through a hole, into which metal could subsequently be poured to fill the void and produce an equally elaborate object. The mould would have to be destroyed in order to extract the object, but the price commanded by elaborate artefacts must have justified the fact

64. Life-size bronze head from a statue of Hadrian, found in the Thames at London. Hollow castings on this scale were a major technical achievement, involving the production of complex moulds and cores. Corrosion has revealed a hole in the neck, which was the result of a flaw in the original casting. It can be seen that a shallow rectangular area was cut out around the hole, so that fresh metal could be cast on and filed down flush with the surrounding surface. (Photograph by Audio-Visual Centre, University of Newcastle)

the latter through a suitable opening such as the statue base; the fixing pins were filed down flush with the surface. A very large hollow object requiring the minimum essential amount of metal could be made in this way. If the outer layer of the clay mould was carefully cut into sections before firing, it could even be reassembled and used more than once, perhaps to produce many copies of portrait-busts of reigning emperors for distribution to official buildings and army camps throughout the Roman empire.

The use of a wide variety of metals in Roman metalwork demonstrates a clear control over technology, and it is, of course, implicit that similar competence existed in the whole chain of processes from the mining through the preparation and smelting of the ores. For example, Cope found that Roman copper smelting for coinage reached a level of purity comparable to the very best modern practices (1971). Improvements in technique are apparent, but no revolutionary innovations; it is the scale of extraction and use which distinguishes the exploitation of metals in the Roman period from that of earlier times, or indeed pre-industrial Europe. For example, although the mining of iron and its subsequent processing into steel made the province of Noricum famous in Roman times (Alföldy 1974, 113–114), the technique of producing *cast* iron was not perfected until the late eighteenth century, when it allowed significant advances in the manufacture of tramway rails and building elements of great strength (fig. 65).

THE USE OF STONE IN THE ROMAN EMPIRE

The significance of stone as a resource in the Roman empire is well attested by the substantial and impressive remains of surviving Roman buildings; in many parts of north-west Europe, the Roman period was the first in which stone was used extensively for construction. The techniques of building could at times demand considerable sophistication of design and execution, and the study of Roman architecture is a discipline in its own right (Adam 1984; Boëthius and Ward-Perkins 1970). As well as the actual building processes, the skills of prospecting, quarrying, transportation and stone preparation were all involved. The related use of painted wall plaster, mosaic floors, and the making of concrete and mortar all emphasise the complexity of the Roman building trade.

A distinction must be made at the outset

that only one could be produced from each mould.

The lost wax process was also suitable for making very large objects such as bronze statues (fig. 64). A clay core would be made first, and coated with a layer of wax on which any fine detail could be modelled. Bronze pins were inserted through the core and wax into the layer of clay which covered the finished wax surface, so that the core remained in place when the wax was removed. After casting, not only the outer clay mould but also the inner clay core were removed,

149

changed by Roman rule. Mud-brick was preeminent in much of the east, whilst forms of stone architecture also existed wherever suitable sources of local stone had been exploited since pre-Roman times. Italy itself had been subject to influences from Greece for several centuries before Roman power extended over the whole peninsular, and therefore much in the way of style and technology was inherited from the Greek cities of the south or the Etruscan area of central Italy.

65. Although many of the forms of Roman iron tools were already known in pre-Roman times, they were certainly far more plentiful and specialised in the Roman period. This photograph includes a range of tools associated with stone working, from a wedge and hammer suitable for quarrying, to smaller hammers and chisels used in trimming blocks of stone, as well as dividers and a pointing trowel. (Photograph by courtesy of Rheinisches Landesmuseum, Bonn)

66. The substructures of the Palatine hill beside the Roman forum are an excellent example of Roman engineering, being simple in form but immensely strong. They are made of concrete and tiles, which may have been fired in kilns belonging to one of the many aristocratic families who owned profitable clay deposits around Rome. Very few Roman buildings were constructed entirely in stone, unless they were built in areas with particularly good supplies; fine stones were used sparingly to create an impressive façade backed by poorer stone, or brick and concrete. (Photograph: author)

between the use of stone for prestigious official projects and for ordinary buildings (fig. 66). Whereas the former might exploit the possibilities of interprovincial supplies of fine stones such as marble, backed up by the wealth and organisational power of the emperor, less impressive buildings were strongly influenced by local geology in their choice of materials. Nor must the importance of timber, brick and tile as alternatives to stone construction be underestimated; all four in combination could find a place in a single building (Adam 1984, 133, fig. 282). Bricks were frequently stamped with details of their makers, which have been analysed in great detail around Rome (Helen 1975; Setälä 1977); even in a small area of south-western England, a bewildering range of methods of organising brick supplies has been deduced from their stamps (Darvill and McWhirr 1984), and geological analysis can add further refinement (Peacock 1977).

In many parts of the Roman empire, long traditions of building existed which were little

Stone had many uses beyond building, and these must not be forgotten in an overall view of the exploitation of stone resources in the Roman empire. Marble and other fine stones were employed in the decoration of buildings as well as in their construction, in the form of panelling, mosaics and furniture inlays. Precious and semi-precious stones were used extensively in jewellery (Higgins 1961); jet and shale provided raw material for carved beads, larger ornaments, and even trays and table-legs (Lawson 1975). Coarse sandstones and lava were quarried to make querns and millstones (Peacock 1980; Röder 1958). Stone was perhaps the heaviest item that regularly required transport in the Roman empire, and its sources and places of use were, if possible, directly related to the availability of water transport. Competent barges existed once water had been reached; the larger river boats found at Zwammerdam in the Netherlands may have been used to bring stone for building work in the adjacent Roman fort (above p. 31). Only exceptional stones like Egyptian porphyry (a hard mottled red or green granite) justified the extensive use of overland transport; 200-ton columns were taken 160km (99 miles) overland from these quarries to the Nile (Ward-Perkins 1971, 142).

As we have seen above, a plentiful variety of competent iron tools was available in the Roman period. Those used in quarrying and stone working can be studied from actual finds (fig. 65), from carved representations of masons at work, or by deduction from the traces they left on unfinished and completed architectural or sculptural elements (Asgari 1973, pl. 139, fig. 10; Blagg 1976). A comprehensive range from axes and adzes to fine chisels and files allowed stone to be finished to the precise degree of sophistication that was required for any particular purpose (Adam 1984, 34, fig. 45; Blagg 1976, 158, fig. 1; Varène 1974).

Quarries

Quarrying remained static from early times up to the nineteenth century, with a laborious technology which improved only slightly with the appearance of metal tools. No major changes took place before the advent of drills, explosives or large mechanical cutting wires and saws (Ward-Perkins 1971, pls. 8, 15b). Many quarries have been examined archaeologically, and have demonstrated the consistent use of a limited range of methods of extraction. The principal objective was to remove blocks of stone piecemeal, either by digging narrow separation trenches around each one (fig. 67), or, if possible, by driving in wedges to encourage splitting (Adam 1984, 29, fig. 30). Both techniques leave clear indications in quarries, either in the form of traces of trenches or wedge holes (ibid. 33, fig. 41). Iron wedges could be hammered directly into carefully cut tapering holes, or dry wooden wedges could be inserted and then soaked with water to split the rock as they expanded (Asgari 1973, pl. 138). Large single-piece building elements, such as columns, had to be shaped and removed individually by a modified form of the trenching technique (Adam 1984, 27, figs. 25–26); some examples survive in quarries, where they were abandoned after errors or the discovery of cracks or flaws in the parent rock (Ward-Perkins 1971, pl. 6).

67. Distinctive traces of Roman block extraction at the marble quarries on the Turkish island of Proconnesos, in the Sea of Marmara; the smooth vertical surfaces are the sides of separation trenches cut around large blocks. This island was an important source of an attractive, veined, grey-white marble used for statues, sarcophagi and architectural elements. It became particularly important in the late Roman and Byzantine periods because of its proximity to the new capital city of Constantinople, and its island situation made transport easy. (Photograph by courtesy of Prof. R. M. Harrison)

Blocks of stone of specific sizes must normally have been extracted with a particular use in mind to avoid wastage, especially in the case of architectural items such as columns and their capitals, or the sarcophagi (stone coffins) used for the burial of the rich in some provinces. Study of unfinished items shows that a considerable amount of detailed preparation was carried out at the quarry rather than at the building site, presumably in order to reduce the weight for transport (Ward-Perkins 1971, pl. 3a; Asgari 1973, pl. 142). Only the final stages of trimming building blocks or carving details remained to be conducted on site, demonstrating the close links between the stages of extraction and use of stone (Adam 1984, 39, figs. 63–67). These observations have allowed a number of deductions to be made about the organisation of stone supplies, at least where major building projects are concerned.

The organisation of stone supply

Much of the analysis of marble supply in the Roman empire was carried out by J. B. Ward-Perkins (1971; 1980), who was both an archaeologist and an authority on Roman architecture. He stressed that the massive building programmes of the early empire led to such a high demand that state ownership of quarries was introduced, stockpiles were created, and a certain amount of standardisation took place in the sizes of common items such as columns. Blocks of stone were frequently inscribed with dates of extraction, the name of the supervisor, and other details such as serial numbers. Masons worked at the quarry in roughing out architectural items, and travelled with the stone to finish it on the building site. The state system broke down in the third century, when political and military disruption reduced the amount of public and imperial building, but revived to a certain extent in the Byzantine period, particularly during the sixth century AD. Ward-Perkins envisaged a situation in which stone produced in surplus of state requirements was freely available to individuals or city administrations embarking upon building schemes, and that the actual transport and distribution was left in the hands of private commerce (1980, 37–38).

ARCHAEOLOGICAL STUDIES OF STONE USE

An instructive perspective upon the use of stone in Italy was provided in part of the south Etruria survey; Jones mapped the occurrences of specific building materials found on Roman sites in the *ager capenas*, and compared them to the surface geology (fig. 68). Approximately half of the area has tufa, a volcanic rock unsuitable for large-scale building on its own; *c*.5km ($3\frac{1}{8}$ miles) north lies a ridge of limestone, and in one place a small area of travertine, a veined grey-white stone suitable and popular for building both in the Roman period and today. The study of building material shows quite decisively how important local stone can be, for the use of limestone and travertine in the *ager capenas* was entirely restricted to sites on or immediately adjacent to their sources. Elsewhere, a different building technique was employed, in which small pieces of tufa were embodied in concrete in a regular diagonal pattern (*opus reticulatum*; Adam 1984, 142–144).

In northern Europe, Amand has examined the uses and distribution of building stone from quarries near Tournai in Belgium. His map shows the importance of rivers in the essentially local distribution of the stone, but some did reach the Dutch coast by river and road; he suggests that a return cargo of salt and shellfish explains this longer-distance trade. These observations from Italy and Belgium underline the fact that the transport of large quantities of building stone in the Roman empire was exceptional, and mainly restricted to large imperial and public buildings.

Stylistic comparisons of carving and identifications of types of stone of the kind used by Ward-Perkins have been explored to study architectural patronage in Britain (Blagg 1980). These seem to show that the construction of civic buildings in the south of the province from the late first century AD did not involve military architects and stone-masons, contrary to a long-held opinion derived from the historian Tacitus, who stated that official encouragement was given in the building of forums, temples and houses (*Agricola* 21). The stylistic links are with Gaul, rather than the buildings found on military sites in the north and west of Britain. Stylistic comparisons also allow the identification of local or regional workshops, which can reveal interesting economic patterns at a much lower social level than that of the patrons of public buildings or lavish villas; for example, Kewley has plotted the distribution of decorated stone altars from a centre in Co. Durham to military and civilian sites over a wide area of northern England (1974, 54, fig. 1).

Subjective comparisons of style are not always reliable, and are of little help in the study of utilitarian items such as millstones. Help can be

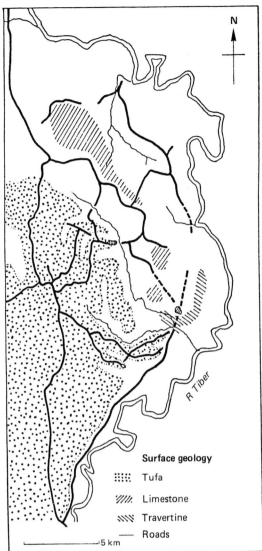

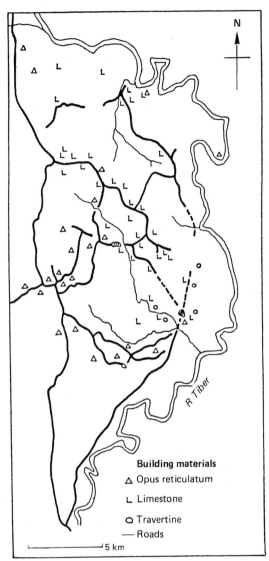

obtained from techniques of petrological analysis, which have been familiar to prehistorians for decades. At a fairly simple level, trade in such items can be studied by taking samples from the stones themselves and identifying the parent outcrops from which they were quarried (Peacock 1980, 51, fig. 1); the methods are similar to those used in the study of prehistoric stone artefacts (Greene 1983, 128–131). More sophisticated analysis of proportions of individual elements and their isotopes, which has been enormously successful in tracing the exploitation of sources of obsidian used for prehistoric stone tools (ibid. 130), has now been applied to the identification of marble. Such techniques are particularly useful in

68. The close relationship between surface geology and building materials is demonstrated by this map of their distribution in the *ager capenas*, a part of the south Etrurian survey area shown on fig. 43. Tufa was too light and breakable to be suitable for normal walling, but it was used in small square blocks inserted into thick mortar to produce a patterned surface known as *opus reticulatum*. Building stone travelled over long distances for special reasons only, such as its rarity or particular suitability for specific architectural functions. (Audio-Visual Centre, University of Newcastle; based on Jones 1963, 137, fig. 13)

153

the case of white varieties, which are difficult to distinguish by eye (Herz and Wenner 1981; Walker 1984; Walda and Walker 1984).

Archaeology has also revealed interesting information about stone resources used in rather different ways, such as lime and coal. Roman stone buildings normally involved the use of large quantities of mortar, which was made by burning limestone in large kilns. An example excavated in Northamptonshire was reckoned to have been capable of producing sufficient lime in one firing to make enough mortar for the construction of a stone building like the modest villas which appear in the area in the second century AD (Jackson *et al.* 1973). In Germany, a battery of six kilns in a walled compound was operated by the Roman army in a limestone area between Köln and Trier (Sölter 1979); the scale of their activity is an indication of the constant building, rebuilding and repair involved in maintaining forts on a garrisoned frontier. Coal, too, was exploited where available (Webster 1955); although most of the British finds concentrate around coalfields, an appreciable quantity found in the East Midlands may have arrived as return cargoes in boats which had carried grain to the eastern end of Hadrian's Wall (ibid. 201, fig. 1).

CASE-STUDY: THE FISHBOURNE PALACE

The most detailed and comprehensive analysis yet published of the sources of stone used in the structure and embellishment of a Roman building must be that included in the report on the excavation of the Fishbourne palace in Sussex (Cunliffe 1971, vol. 2, 1–42). The exact purpose of this building remains somewhat enigmatic, but it is usually associated with the family of the local tribal king Cogidubnus, whose co-operation during the conquest in the 40s AD may have been rewarded with a longer-term official function for which the 'palace' formed an appropriate setting. The site had a sequence of structures, progressing from an army supply depot built at the time of the Roman conquest (AD 43) to an elegant timber house lasting no longer than a decade, for which a replacement in stone was constructed in the 50s/60s AD. This 'proto-palace' was subsequently incorporated into the magnificent building begun around AD 75 (Cunliffe 1971, vol. 1, xxv).

The palace proper consisted of four ranges of rooms and internal courtyards around a rectangular garden nearly 100m (328 ft) long. Further gardens and perhaps more buildings

extended to a small navigable creek leading to the sea (ibid. 81, fig. 21). A grand portico and entrance hall faced Chichester to the east, and led across the garden to a large room which may have served for receiving visitors on official business. These features, combined with the presence of a large columned hall in another part of the building, underline the possibility of partly official functions. The structure was unique:

> Such elaboration in architecture and design was largely unknown in Britain at the time. It must have been the creation of large numbers of craftsmen imported from the Mediterranean world specifically for the job, and employed by a Romanophile possessing great wealth. (Cunliffe op. cit. xxv)

Exotic stone was even found in association with the timber buildings which preceded the 'proto-palace', used for kerbs and dry footings on which timber could stand. Although it consisted mainly of sandstones from Sussex, it also included Mediterranean limestones and volcanic rocks from Cornwall and the Channel Islands which probably reached the site as ships' ballast. The structure of the 'proto-palace' contained a variety of stone, including similar local and exotic types in the footings, whilst the walls were faced with blocks of Sussex stone. However, evidence for columns with carved Corinthian capitals was also found, made up from cylindrical blocks of sandstone from the Sussex coast with capitals of Mediterranean limestone.

The masons' yard

Fortunately for us, an idea of the internal fittings of the 'proto-palace' can be gained from remains found in a masons' yard associated with the building. Two areas covered by a layer of sand and stone fragments proved to have been the sites of the preparation of stone for its decoration (Cunliffe 1971, vol. 1, 58–61). Many fragments of Purbeck marble, a very fine limestone from Dorset, were found in one area, as well as red siltstone, possibly of Mediterranean origin, and a brown breccia from the Côte d'Or, France. The last of these was fashioned into thin polished slabs, and many flakes from the initial trimming of the other two were also found. The second floor seems to have been the principal working area, where many different fine stones were sawn up and smoothed. The excavation of the site recovered red, grey, blue, black, multi-coloured and white stones from numerous British and Continental sources, including the white marble of Carrara in Italy; many of them show clear signs of the processes of preparation. The original blocks were cut into thin sheets by multiple-bladed saws, smoothed to a fine finish, and then marked out for further cutting into geometric shapes suitable for decorated floors or wall surfaces.

Thinner fragments of more complex shape were probably intended for furniture inlays, and must have been cut up with some kind of hacksaws. All of the cutting would have been assisted by the abrasive properties of water and sand, which accounts for the quantities of sand remaining on the preparation areas; an account of stone sawing is contained in the *Natural History* of Pliny the Elder (36, 51). Quite near the fine stone working areas, further signs of stone masonry were found, indicating the trimming and shaping of the greensand blocks which were used for building the main structure of the 'proto-palace'. Thus, archaeological excavation has recovered detailed indications of the materials and methods used in the construction of a building which lasted only a few years before being adapted and incorporated into the main Fishbourne palace.

The main palace

Around AD 75, construction of the large palace began at Fishbourne (fig. 69a). Because its remains were more extensive and better preserved than those of the 'proto-palace', our knowledge of the construction materials is derived from the actual structure rather than preparation areas (Cunliffe 1971, vol. 1, 80–83). In the construction of the west wing, the foundations consisted of mortar containing flint pebbles, and the main superstructure was built of blocks of limestone from the coast of Sussex only 11km (6¾ miles) from the site. Quarrying had been minimised by collecting slabs which had already been eroded by the sea and simply required squaring-off; behind these facing stones the walls had a mortar and flint core. The other wings were faced with greensand blocks, probably from Pulborough, over 20km (12½ miles) north-east of Fishbourne; the walls may have included bonding courses of tiles as well. The garden was surrounded by elegant colonnaded terraces, with large stone gutters in front of them. The columns were made of single pieces of sandstone, some from south-western England, others from Caen in Normandy, France, and a few from an unknown French or Mediterranean source. They stood upon large blocks which all came from sandstone quarries on the eastern end of the Isle of Wight, while many of the gutter blocks came either from the Isle of Wight, or from near Pulborough in north-east Sussex.

Apart from painted wall plaster and stucco, the interior decoration of the palace incorporated a wide range of decorative stonework (fig. 69b), much of it drawn from different sources to those exploited for the 'proto-palace' (Cunliffe 1971, vol. 1, 140–145). White and pink-and-purple marbles came from Turkey, green and brown marbles from Gaul; from Italy came mottled violet and veined grey-and-white marbles; from southern France came brown-and-white and green-and-white marbles. In addition, white Purbeck marble from Dorset was extensively used as a substitute for true marble. The marbles were used in the making of mouldings, panels, veneers and inlays, and small pieces were sometimes incorporated into mosaics.

Implications

The Fishbourne palace, and its predecessor, the 'proto-palace', have several clear implications for Roman stone exploitation. First, it is evident that within 20 years of the conquest, the geology of southern Britain was sufficiently well known for several different types of limestones and sandstones to be selected for specific parts of the palace. Their strength and suitability for making architectural items varying in size and function, such as gutter blocks, facing stones or columns, was clearly understood. Secondly, skilled craftsmanship and the essential materials were available for the internal decoration of the building with paintings, plaster and mosaics, to the highest contemporary standard and fashion. It is inconceivable that the relatively small quantities of marble would have been individually ordered and transported from each of their many sources. The kind of stockpile envisaged by Ward-Perkins, perhaps in Italy or France, would obviously be the most convenient source, and experienced masons would also be drawn from similar areas. For general building stone, water transport was evidently preferred, but not exclusively, as stone from Pulborough or south-western England demonstrates.

Finally, Fishbourne demonstrates the importance of careful stratigraphic excavation, the precise recording of all finds, and post-excavation processing by specialists such as geologists to

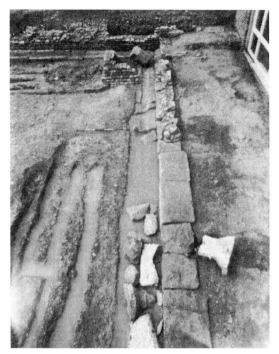 

maximise the potential information to be drawn from a site. Equally important, this specialist information is integrated into the conclusions of the excavation report.

POTTERY IN THE ROMAN EMPIRE

Roman pottery gives a unique opportunity to apply archaeology to the economy of the Roman empire. Pottery is the commonest class of artefact found on excavations, but precisely because it was so common, it received no significant comments from Roman writers; virtually everything known about it is therefore derived from archaeological research. Because it is made from fired clay, pottery has a very high survival rate, even in severe soil conditions which can badly corrode metal artefacts. Unfortunately, this advantage has a negative side: the very abundance of pottery from most Roman excavations makes it extraordinarily difficult to study and publish adequately, although scientific techniques and computers are beginning to be of great assistance (Peacock 1977; Greene 1984). There are also great variations in the degree of attention that Roman pottery has received from archaeologists. In Britain and Germany, detailed research has been devoted to the whole range of wares, from luxury table vessels to humble cooking pots (Dore and Greene 1977; Anderson and Anderson 1981).

69a and b. The Roman palace at Fishbourne in Sussex was a magnificent building constructed in the late first century AD around a square garden. Fig. 69a shows the north-west corner of the gardens, including trenches for ornamental hedges and flower beds. The large blocks of stone supported a colonnaded terrace; fragments of column shafts and capitals lie where they were missed or abandoned by medieval stone-robbers. At the top of the photograph, large gutter-blocks are well preserved in front of a wall faced with neat ashlar on a core of layers of rubble and mortar. Each of these architectural elements was composed of different limestones or sandstones selected from a variety of sources in southern England. The floors and walls in the interior of the palace were embellished with paintings, mosaics, or geometrical panels of exotic stones, many of them imported in blocks and cut up on the site (fig. 69b). (Photographs by courtesy of Sussex Archaeological Society)

On sites around parts of the Mediterranean, many excavators have only recently begun to keep potsherds, let alone study or publish them; the balance is now being redressed, fortunately (Riley 1981; Fulford and Peacock 1984).

Approaches to the study of Roman ceramics have widely differing objectives; some archaeologists may have a primarily art-historical interest in its form and decoration (Charleston 1955; Brown 1968); others may wish to use pottery as dating evidence for historical phases of excavated sites (Gillam 1957). The approach adopted influences the way in which the pottery will have been studied and published, and it may be very difficult to draw comparisons between work carried out with different objectives in mind. Precise details of individual wares and the quantities in which they occur on sites are essential if pottery is to be used as a sensitive indicator of trade routes, or in the examination of other economic questions (fig. 4; Young 1980). Technical problems of this kind must constantly be borne in mind, if valid conclusions are to be drawn from ceramic evidence and used in the study of the economy of the Roman empire (Peacock 1983, 160–172).

Roman pottery provided a comprehensive range of vessels for table and kitchen functions, and for use in storage and transportation. The range overlaps with items made from raw materials other than clay, of course. Much kitchenware was made from metal, and many table vessels were made of metal or glass, particularly in richer households (Strong 1966; Goethert-Polaschek 1977). Wooden barrels or even animal skins were used for transporting liquids, as well as clay amphorae. At the top of the quality scale were the fine wares, including terra sigillata, the universal glossy red tableware made in Italy and later in the provinces. Other fine wares had special finishes created by the use of coloured slips or glazes, and decoration which might be painted, moulded or formed by hand from wet clay. However, the bulk of Roman pottery consisted of less elaborate unglazed earthenware vessels (fig. 70), varying in colour from white through orange to grey or black according to the source of their clay and the method of their firing. Most vessels were made on a potter's wheel, and fired in carefully constructed kilns, although some widely distributed kitchen wares were hand-made and fired in simple bonfires (Swan 1984). Distribution patterns of individual wares varied enormously, from forms of terra sigillata which could be found throughout the empire, to local kitchenwares produced for a single locality. Some industries made wide ranges of forms, others concentrated on particular categories.

Roman pottery is particularly interesting because of the tremendous variety of wares, forms and modes of production and distribution in-

70. Pottery in the Roman empire ranged from coarse hand-made wares to fine table vessels. Utilitarian pottery for kitchen use (such as the two vessels on the left) was fairly plain, but could still be traded over considerable areas within provinces. More specialised forms such as *mortaria* (centre and back right) travelled much further, even between different provinces. The same is true of fine wares such as the colour-coated jug; drinking and serving vessels with decorative slips or glazes formed a regular adjunct to the principal tableware, terra sigillata (fig. 71). (Photograph of pottery from Ospringe, Kent, by courtesy of English Heritage)

volved. Furthermore, it survives in large quantities throughout the Roman empire. Whether the lack of relevant ancient writings about pottery is seen as a hindrance or not, it should be agreed that some of the studies of pottery which have been completed have significant implications for our understanding of the Roman economy. It may be best to begin by examining the largest of the categories of Roman pottery, terra sigillata, which in various guises provided the essential tableware requirements for millions of inhabitants of the Roman empire for many centuries (Oswald and Price 1920; Johns 1971).

TERRA SIGILLATA

British archaeologists describe the glossy red-surfaced tableware made in Italy as arretine ware, after the production centre at Arezzo, and that made in the provinces as samian ware, a term used by Pliny. Most European and American archaeologists call it terra sigillata; strictly, this

Latin term should only apply to decorated vessels, but it is used to describe the whole range of forms, the majority of which were, in fact, plain. To add to the confusion, technically and aesthetically comparable terra sigillata made in north Africa or late Roman Britain is known respectively as red-slipped and colour-coated ware rather than samian or terra sigillata. These differences in terminology cloud the importance of the essential unity of all of these wares; they were made for table use in a range of standardised forms, and were generally red in colour with a fine clay coating known variously as a glaze, gloss or slip. Red tablewares in the terra sigillata tradition were made and used in the Mediterranean region continuously from the first century BC to the Byzantine period (Hayes 1972).

Terra sigillata derives from a much older tradition of Greek pottery which includes a similar mixture of plain and decorated forms, whose principle difference was that their surface coating was black instead of red. The technical change from these Hellenistic 'black-glazed' or Campanian wares (some of which were made in Italy) to red terra sigillata occurred in the first century BC (Morel 1965; 1981). The pots were fired in an oxygen-rich as opposed to oxygen-starved kiln atmosphere; the reason for producing a red rather than black end-product was presumably determined by taste rather than technology. Differences in terminology should not be allowed to obscure the fact that for much of the Roman period, households in north Africa or southern Britain shared a common taste for red tablewares, despite the fact that their forms, styles of decoration and production centres differed.

The terra sigillata made in Italy, Gaul and Germany comprised both decorated and plain wares (fig. 71). The range of forms included large bowls embellished with moulded decoration, and plain bowls, cups, dishes and plates; in other words, a comprehensive service of serving, eating and drinking vessels (Hartley 1969). The forms were both standardised and continuously changing, so that, for example, similar plates would be made at the same date in several different manufacturing centres, which would then change in parallel ways over time. In the early empire, the terra sigillata made in Italy and Gaul is very precisely dated, thanks to detailed archaeological studies made of finds from forts situated on the frontiers of Germany and Britain, which can themselves be dated by sources such as the historical writings of Tacitus. Thus, the pottery and other finds found on military sites discovered east of the Rhine can be associated with the brief period between the campaigns conducted during the reign of Augustus after 16 BC, and the permanent abandonment of garrisons east of the

71. Mass-produced terra sigillata or related red-coated pottery provided the standard table-ware of most of the Roman world, and is even found on relatively humble rural sites. It comprised a comprehensive range of drinking, eating and serving vessels, including bowls with elaborate relief-moulded decoration. The vessels illustrated were manufactured in Italy and southern Gaul in the first century AD. (Photograph by courtesy of Rheinisches Landesmuseum Bonn)

lower Rhine after the disastrous defeat of his armies in AD 9 (Schnurbein 1982; Gechter 1979, 3–38).

We therefore have a considerable body of well-published evidence which allows a detailed knowledge of Augustan terra sigillata to be gained; this knowledge can then be applied to undated sites including the production centres of the wares involved. The Antonine Wall in Scotland provides a similar dated range of pottery belonging to the mid-second century AD, which can be compared with finds made on Hadrian's Wall, which was occupied both before and after the Scottish frontier (Hartley 1972). Some caution is essential, however, for circular arguments can easily build up in the course of this kind of cross-dating (Greene 1983, 101–102). Few finds of terra sigillata are as well dated as the group of bowls found at Pompeii in a burnt packing-case, which had presumably been delivered from southern Gaul shortly before AD 79 (Atkinson 1914).

The manufacture of terra sigillata

The technical stages in the manufacture of terra sigillata are of considerable interest because they not only reveal the technology involved, but also have implications for the organisation of the work. In common with other forms of pottery, the clay for terra sigillata had to be dug from selected deposits, and weathered to break down lumps and to allow organic matter to decompose. Some form of refining would have been necessary to remove stones or other impurities which might affect its working or firing qualities. The prepared clay would need to be brought to an optimum consistency for the particular manufacturing process to which it was to be subjected; this might involve wheel-throwing, forming or moulding, depending on which type of vessel was being made (Brown 1976).

A few terra sigillata vessels had closed shapes for which wheel-throwing was the only possible production method, but the majority of plain wares were mass-produced using shaping equipment. To form the interior of open vessels such as bowls or plates, clay was placed over a blank, probably lathe-turned from wood and mounted on a rotating wheel. The profile of the exterior could then be trimmed by a template, and the footring raised by hand. Decorated vessels were made in clay moulds, which had been wheel-thrown from very fine clay, and carefully shaped and smoothed inside to produce the desired shape of the kind of vessel to be mass-produced. Before it dried, this interior surface was impressed with small hand-held dies bearing individual animals, figures, leaves or other motifs, to make up the overall ornamental arrangement which was to appear on the finished bowls. The mould was then fired, and was ready for production. After it had been centred on a rotating wheel, clay was pressed to an even thickness inside it, and drawn up to create a hand-thrown rim projecting above the mould. The clay filled the impressed decoration in the mould, and therefore had to be allowed to dry long enough to shrink clear before being lifted out. When sufficiently hard, the moulded vessel was inverted on a wheel, and a footring was added by hand.

Both decorated and plain terra sigillata vessels required a coating of slip to produce their glossy surface when fired. The slip consisted of a very fine film of the same kind of clay as that used in the manufacture, probably suspended in water so that larger particles sank to the bottom. When dipped into the slip mixture, the dry unfired pots would have absorbed this water rapidly, causing a fine film of particles to be deposited on the surface. The finished vessels would then be thoroughly dried before firing in an oxygen-rich atmosphere, which caused the iron oxides in the clay to become red. The kilns were very large, and partly built from prefabricated elements such as clay pipes, by means of which the heat of the fire was channelled through the firing chamber without any risk of smoke spoiling the even red finish that was desired (Brown 1976, 85, fig. 146).

The terra sigillata potters

The complexity of the manufacturing process of terra sigillata from raw clay to fired vessel, combined with the vast quantities of the ware which were made by the workshops of Italy, Gaul and Germany, suggests that there may have been considerable division of labour. Parts of the process involved very specialised skills, such as mould making or kiln construction and firing, which could conceivably have given scope for specialists used by a number of workshops. We are able to avoid pure speculation thanks to the fact that the majority of terra sigillata vessels bear name-stamps which, together with longer inscriptions found scratched onto pots at some kiln sites, help to elucidate the organisation of production.

Some of the stamps found at Arezzo in Italy

bear two names, one featuring the *tria nomina* of a Roman citizen, and another (commonly Greek) which was probably that of a skilled slave. The possible size of the establishments involved is indicated by the number of slave names associated with a single owner's name; the average is between 10 and 20, but up to 60 are known. One notable owner, Cnaius Ateius, is known to have owned workshops in both Italy and Gaul in the Augustan period. The Gaulish workshops of the first century AD seem to have been smaller and very numerous, for stamps on plain vessels frequently take the form OFF.IUSTI or ALBVCI.OFI, incorporating the word *officina*, meaning workshop. Workers are indicated by stamps taking a different form, such as LABIO FECIT or PONTI.MAN, the former meaning 'Labio made this', the latter 'made by the hand of Pontus'. The qualifications are frequently abbreviated to a single O, F or M, and many names occur without any supplementary information.

Other forms of signatures exist, and it is possible to find more than one kind on a single pot. For example, many moulds for decorated bowls incorporated large 'advertisement' stamps into the design, carrying the name of the owner rather than the mould- or bowl-maker. Mould makers often wrote their names freehand in the damp clay of the mould in a position where it was normally obscured by the addition of the footring to a moulded vessel; some remain visible, however, and have to be read backwards. The interior or the hand-made rim of a moulded bowl were also stamped occasionally, showing yet another individual at work. Thus, a single bowl might preserve the mould-maker's name (freehand and backwards), a workshop name (amongst the decoration) and a bowl-finisher's name (on the rim or inside). Much confusion has been caused in the identification of distinctive products of particular workshops by the failure to distinguish between different forms of stamps (Johns 1963). At the simplest level of interpretation it is clear that the terra sigillata industry was subdivided into large numbers of small units employing a number of workers, whose numbers seem to have been smaller in Gaul than in Italy, and whose status in Gaul may have been free rather than servile.

It is highly likely that some activities may have been conducted by craft specialists on behalf of many workshops, or at least that large workshops might have allowed lesser ones the use of their facilities, no doubt for a suitable fee. The best evidence for such activities relates to the most vital stage of manufacture – kiln firing. A series of remarkable inscriptions written on flat terra sigillata plates has been found on several production sites, especially in southern Gaul. Each inscription seems to consist of lists of pots arranged by size, form and number, set opposite personal names, many of which belong to potters who are well known from name-stamps found on other vessels (Peacock 1983, 125, pl. 30).

The numbers of pots included in these lists add up to tens of thousands, reflecting the responsibility resting upon the kiln operator; they presumably acted as receipts for the unfired pots. Such firings of the products of several independent workshops make additional sense of the universal practice of stamping individual pots with their owner's or maker's name; this would assist the accurate allocation of the vessels after firing, and avoid disputes over ownership. The stamps would also have had a value in workshop organisation, if any kind of 'piece-work' payment by results operated. Another operation which suggests specialised workshops is the making and decoration of moulds; it is again conceivable that larger workshops might make moulds not only for their own use but for sale to smaller enterprises.

The diffusion of the terra sigillata industry

A particularly interesting aspect of terra sigillata production is its gradual dispersal from Italy to the provinces, and the progressive decline in the quality and distribution of the products of successive centres. It has already been noted that the workshops in Italy had 'branches' in Gaul, notably at Lyon. Indeed, an even clearer example of this phenomenon is presented by Aco, a manufacturer of a more specialised form of fine ware drinking vessels, who operated contemporary centres of production in both north Italy and Lyon. The distribution of two quite distinct groups of slaves' names associated with his own name on pots indicates that the two centres served separate geographical areas, north and south of the Alps (Vegas 1969–1970). In a study of Roman pottery lamp production, Harris has pointed out the existence of a mechanism available in Roman law by which managers could be placed in charge of branch workshops (1980, 140).

The production of 'arretine' terra sigillata in Italy and Gaul ceased in the early decades of the first century AD, and although the manufacture of terra sigillata continued in Italy, its export distribution was restricted to the Alpine region and the west Mediterranean coasts (Pucci 1981, 116–119, tav. xx–xxi). Even these areas were soon taken over by terra sigillata from centres in southern Gaul, notably La Graufesenque near the modern town of Millau (Aveyron). These centres flourished until the end of the first century, but by AD 100, new terra sigillata production sites in central Gaul had come into prominence. The Mediterranean was increasingly supplied with African red slip ware from Tunisia, which copied south Gaulish forms for a few decades before diverging along a different path of development (Hayes 1972).

Whereas arretine ware had reached as far as India and pre-Roman sites in Britain in the early first century AD, as well as supplying most sites in the north-west provinces and around the Mediterranean (Pucci 1981, 104–105, tav. xvii), south Gaulish ware was restricted to the western provinces. After its decline, several centres expanded in central Gaul and Germany, with still smaller distribution areas. Central Gaulish ware came largely from Lezoux near Clermont Ferrand, and was important only in Gaul and Britain, until imports ceased around AD 200; east Gaulish ware was made in several different places from Trier on the Mosel to Rheinzabern on the middle Rhine, and even in minor centres along the upper Danube (fig. 14; Peacock 1983, 117, fig. 60). East Gaulish ware was largely directed at local consumers, with limited exports to Britain from the major sites, and it continued well into the third century AD (King 1981, 64, fig. 6.4). Whilst African red slip ware and its east Mediterranean equivalents flourished throughout the late Roman period, terra sigillata production in the north-western provinces had devolved into purely local industries by the fourth century. Some late terra sigillata is almost indistinguishable from the output of producers whose products are normally described merely as colour-coated ware. A typical case was the industry based in the Oxford area of Britain in the late third and fourth centuries AD, which made red-coated table vessels with crude stamped or painted rather than moulded decoration (Young 1977).

The diffusion of terra sigillata production reflects two historical themes. First, historians have long emphasised the decline of the economic pre-eminence of Italy in agriculture, as Rome's

provinces developed in the early centuries AD; secondly, there was no control over the spread of technology through patents. Given the essential simplicity of the stages of terra sigillata manufacture, which involved processes already familiar in pre-Roman times, it was evidently possible for anyone with access to suitable clay deposits to set up a workshop, whether by buying experienced slaves or employing free craftsmen. In fact, prosperous workshop owners could themselves migrate, taking their equipment with them. As the forts, towns and countryside of the provinces generated a growing demand for 'Roman' artefacts to accompany a Romanised way of life, local centres could easily be created whose lower transport costs counteracted their diminished economies of scale, allowing them to make inferior products which could sell at much lower prices than those from major centres. Many insights into the diffusion of terra sigillata production can be obtained from the study of name-stamps on the vessels, which can reveal the careers and movements of individual potters (Hartley 1977).

The changes observed in the production and distribution of terra sigillata over several centuries have been deduced entirely from study of the ware itself and the sites on which it occurs. Close dating allows further observations, which show that the quality of the wares from each production area was by no means uniform, and that great changes could take place in individual centres in the course of a few decades. For instance, the superb Augustan art found upon arretine moulded vessels lasted less than forty years; later first-century Italian wares ranged from robust plain wares to thick coarse moulded wares made in shadowy imitation of south Gaulish ware. The erosion of Italian terra sigillata by provincial products is underlined by the crate of south Gaulish bowls which must have reached Pompeii before AD 79.

Early south Gaulish ware made at La Graufesenque in the 20s AD was fine and well made; it became very glossy but less elaborate by the 60s, and declined rapidly after the 70s. It reached a state in the late first century when moulds were hurriedly decorated with large, crude designs, and the bowls made in them were pulled out too soon, with the result that the decoration was scraped off or blurred during removal. It seems likely that these signs of haste reflect difficulties in the industry, such as lower prices, which demanded faster production. The best east Gaulish ware matched the average from central Gaul, but the general standard was far removed from the Augustan arretine terra sigillata, whose fineness, forms and decoration could stand comparison with those found on silver, bronze or glass table vessels of the same period. Provincial prosperity or consumer tastes may have converted a former luxury to an everyday item; the transition from fine and luxurious Wedgwood jasper ware of the eighteenth century to the pale plastic imitations popular as flower-pot holders in the late twentieth century may serve as a parallel and a warning.

The division between the rich and the poor was greater in the late empire than earlier; the rich may have used metal table services to a larger extent (Kent and Painter 1977), whilst the poor could not afford anything as fine as first-century terra sigillata. The reduced volume of late Roman trade must have made any imported fine pottery expensive. The inhabitants of a villa at San Giovanni di Ruoti in south Italy went over to regional ceramics in its later stages, turning their backs on traditional Mediterranean fine wares in the fourth century AD (Freed 1985, 185–186). A wide market may have existed only for lower-quality wares such as those made in Germany, or, as far as Britain was concerned, colour-coated pottery of the kind made in Oxfordshire. The peaks in the supply of terra sigillata to Britain coincide with the popularity of other fine wares, showing that these enjoyed the same periods of prosperity, rather than acting as competitors (Greene 1982).

ASSESSING THE ECONOMIC IMPLICATIONS OF POTTERY

Different categories of pottery must be examined very carefully if valid interpretations are to be made about the economy. For instance, amphorae are very interesting pots, which have been subjected to detailed typological research, and whose distributions have been extensively mapped (e.g. Panella 1981). In the final analysis it must be remembered that they were used as containers, and that what is being mapped is the trade in their perishable contents such as wine, oil or fish sauce, not a trade in pots. Attention has been focused upon them largely through the unintentional fact of their survival, whilst equally important trade in foodstuffs carried in barrels or sacks will have left virtually no traces in normal conditions of preservation.

Amphora studies have made a striking contri-

bution to our knowledge of ancient trade (Paterson 1982); it may be helpful to cite some examples of studies which present different kinds of information. A 'snapshot' of Spanish exports in the mid-first century AD is given by amphorae and other items of cargo from the shipwreck excavated at Port-Vendres (Colls et al. 1977). A longer-term pattern of shifting geographical contacts was revealed by amphorae imported into the Roman port of Ostia (fig. 4). An even wider perspective has been attempted by Keay (1983), who integrated his records of site-finds of amphorae from Spain into the history of west Mediterranean trade in general. Individual traders – some from aristocratic families well known from historical sources – are encountered on the stamps and ink inscriptions on amphorae, which also recorded details of their weight, contents and origins (Will 1979; Liou 1980; Rodriguez 1977). Lest too much emphasis should be placed on the agricultural motivation of the wine trade in its republican days, Tchernia has stressed the fact that it made a convenient high-status exchange medium for the purchase of slaves from barbarians (1983).

In contrast, the importance of the transportation of liquids in barrels is well known from carvings (Molin 1984), but its extent and directions cannot be studied by archaeologists. Although barrels are occasionally found in excavations, it is normally because they were re-used as ready-made linings for wells; their distribution is merely that of a particular method of well construction, and tells us little about their original function.

Other kinds of pottery may have travelled not because of any particularly notable qualities, but because large-scale trade in other items already took place from their production centres. A good example of this phenomenon is related to the question of amphorae which has just been discussed. Around the middle of the first century AD, there was a shortlived fashion for hemispherical cups and ovoid beakers in colour-coated fabrics, often decorated with delicate clay motifs; centres of production existed in Gaul, Germany, Italy and Spain (Greene 1979). The commonest ware was made in Lyon, but the widest distribution was achieved by vessels made in Spain, which reached sites all around the coasts of the west Mediterranean, and appeared more sporadically in France and on sites in Britain, Germany and Switzerland. This type of colour-coated ware was made in the province of Baetica in southern

Spain, probably in the valley of the river Guadal-cuivir (Greene 1979, 65–73; Mayet 1975).

Significantly, this was also the source of an enormous export of olive oil, marked by the distribution of the globular Dressel 20 amphorae in which it was transported (above p. 111). The obvious implication is that a few crates of the fine-ware drinking vessels travelled along with the amphorae, and thus incurred virtually no travel costs. The merchants in charge of the oil export may have included the occasional crate to fill a gap in a cargo, or traders in Spain may have paid them to add the pottery to the cargo. Underlying both possibilities was the knowledge that a taste for decorated colour-coated ware existed, and that some extra money could be gained by selling Spanish vessels. This interpretation was reinforced by the discovery of some fine-ware vessels in the Port-Vendres II shipwreck (fig. 72; Colls *et al.* 1977, 110–114), along with several varieties of amphorae from Baetica. It could not be argued that any serious trade in fine ware existed; the small quantities involved, and the adequate supplies of comparable vessels available from better-placed centres such as Lyon make this quite clear. In the late Roman period, Fulford has used similarly sparse distributions of pottery to indicate trade on a larger scale in perishable items (1977).

Some categories of pottery did of course achieve large-scale export because of their intrinsic qualities; fine wares such as terra sigillata and African red slip ware are obvious examples, although even with these there may have been advantages in accompanying other trade goods. The importance of north African grain, wine and oil exports was probably of great assistance to the trade in tableware (Carandini 1983), whilst metal exploitation in the Massif Central has been suggested as a supporting factor in the success of terra sigillata from La Graufesenque in the first century AD (Middleton 1980, 190). One specific type of vessel which was extensively traded was the mortarium, a heavy flanged bowl with internal grits for grinding up foodstuffs (Hartley 1973). Mortaria are among the few kinds of pottery which frequently bore name-stamps, indicating a rather more sophisticated level of production than was usual for coarse wares. Like terra sigillata production, there is evidence for diffusion of production over time; within 60 years of its conquest, centres in Britain made all of the province's mortaria, whereas earlier they had

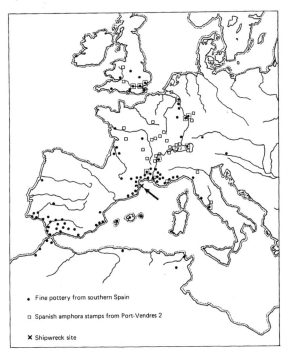

- Fine pottery from southern Spain

□ Spanish amphora stamps from Port-Vendres 2

✖ Shipwreck site

72. Trade in bulky agricultural products provided assistance for the distribution of other goods. Olive oil was shipped from southern Spain to the northern provinces in enormous quantities, and a small amount of fine pottery from the same source, which could not have been sold competitively on its own, reached the same markets. Oil amphorae and some of the fine drinking vessels were found together in a shipwreck at Port Vendres. Amphorae bearing the same name-stamps as those from the wreck are plotted on the map to indicate the likely destination of the lost cargo. It can be seen that in Britain and Germany, the fine pottery was sold in exactly the same areas. (Audio-Visual Centre, University of Newcastle; based on Mayet 1975, 157 carte 11, Greene 1979, 66, fig. 28, Colls *et al.* 1977, 136, fig. 53)

been imported from Italy, central Gaul and north-eastern Gaul. The mortarium makers who became established in south-eastern England had in some cases demonstrably moved from the Continent soon after the conquest (Hartley K. 1977).

Between the products of the major tableware producers and the local kitchenware makers lay a large number of regional fine wares, which underwent frequent changes of style during the Roman period. They were often associated with the table, in particular with drinking, as in the case of the Spanish colour-coated ware which has already been discussed. The long continuity in the use of red-slipped tableware has been stressed above; it is matched by the continuous availability of these 'auxiliary' table vessels. Cups, beakers, flagons, bowls and plates with a variety of surface finishes from lead-glazes to golden mica particles, and from metallic slips to mottled paint were produced throughout the duration of the Roman empire. They seem to have been seen as an adjunct to terra sigillata dinner services, and were much more susceptible to changes in fashion. Thus in the first century AD, deep cups were common in the Augustan period; hemispherical colour-coated cups and ovoid beakers around the mid-century; and beakers with a low girth after AD 70, when the fashion for cups in colour-coated ware came to an end (Greene 1978).

COARSE POTTERY

Attention has been concentrated so far upon finer classes of pottery which were intended for table use. The bulk of Roman pottery was far simpler, and was used in food preparation and for storage (fig. 70); the functions of glass jars and metal pans found in the kitchens of today were largely fulfilled by pottery during the Roman period. Such pottery was normally produced for a single region, and many of these unglazed earthenwares had very much smaller distributions. Being essentially functional, they were not so subject to fashion, and some basic forms survived little changed for centuries (Gillam 1957). These wares are usually termed coarse wares – even when comparatively fine – to distinguish them from fine wares and terra sigillata; American excavators refer to them less prosaically as kitchen wares.

Unless Roman pottery was introduced into an area where pottery had not previously been in use, it is very important to understand the local pre-Roman pottery traditions which were likely to continue with modifications into the Roman period. In practice, the coarse wares of Italy and the provinces are normally a straightforward extension of their pre-Roman counterparts. Standardisation and the extent of distribution might increase in the case of the better wares, but otherwise the character of native ceramic traditions remained little changed. The principle sign of 'Romanisation' is the appearance of vessel forms related to Roman eating, drinking and cuisine, such as mortaria and flagons, which were grafted onto the native repertoire as demand for them grew (Greene 1979b).

The mode and scale of pottery production undoubtedly ranged from a part-time activity which probably supplemented farming, to full-time employment for more specialised craft workers (Peacock 1983, 8–11). Even the latter may have had other occupations at some times of the year, for in areas with damp winters, pottery making and firing would have been essentially a summer activity. It must be emphasised that many establishments were very diverse in their output, and that even the terra sigillata manufacturers made other classes of vessels. For example, in the second century AD, an attempt was made to set up a terra sigillata workshop in Britain at Colchester, involving potters who had previously worked at Sinzig in Germany (Hull 1963). One potter stamped his name not only on terra sigillata, but on colour-coated vessels and mortaria too. In central Gaul, a major centre existed at Lezoux, but the surrounding region around the river Allier contained many other production sites making various combinations of coarse ware, colour-coated ware, glazed ware, terra sigillata and moulded figurines. The whole range was made in Lezoux, but how the different wares related to different workshops cannot be determined, although large-scale excavation of kiln sites could probably elucidate this question. Specialised production of coarse ware could exist, however; the clearest case is probably the black-burnished ware industry of south Dorset in England, which only included robust cooking vessels in its output (Farrar 1973).

THE MARKETING OF ROMAN POTTERY

The variety of different wares, distribution patterns, and modes of production which have been revealed by archaeological research must be interpreted not only in relation to each other, but in a more general theoretical framework of trade (Hodder 1974). It has been suggested above that a trade in pottery as such may have existed rarely, if ever. The mechanisms by which pottery was traded need to be explored, therefore, with the help of other evidence. At the lowest level, pottery made as a part-time household or peasant farming activity may have been used by its makers and exchanged locally for necessities without actually being sold. However, the scale of distribution of even the simplest wares suggests that they may have been sold at local rural or even urban markets in the same way as any cash-crop. Many potteries must have been located on land which formed part of villa estates, whether directly or as part of a tenancy. Again, pottery could have been treated in the same manner as agricultural products, although the managers of large estates would have had access to more widespread markets through the ownership of better and more frequently used means of transport such as carts and traction animals. What is quite clear is that most Roman pottery was traded rather than made in households or estates for their own consumption. The extent of this trade, even in remote rural areas of Italy well away from towns, has been restated by Dyson (1985), and contrasted with the pattern of medieval pottery from the same area. In late Roman Britain, the villa at Gatcombe (above p. 92) received 60 per cent of its pottery from sources over 100km (62 miles) away.

There is clear evidence that Roman pottery was sensitive to transport costs, which supports the view that it was largely sold in markets rather than being produced for internal use on estates or in the payment of official levies. For example, the late Roman New Forest industry in Britain was scattered over a wide rural area, and made a variety of products including ordinary coarse wares, mortaria, white flagons and bowls with dark red painted decoration known as 'parchment ware', colour-coated beakers and jugs, and colour-coated table ware whose forms reflected the terra sigillata tradition (Fulford 1975). Each category had different distribution patterns, which correlate well with their technical complexity and fineness (Fulford 1973). Elegant decorated beakers with glossy colour-coated surfaces are found up to almost 100km (62 miles) from the kilns, whilst coarse wares are restricted to within 40km ($24\frac{3}{4}$ miles). Between the two lay the distribution area of red colour-coated tableware, which was in direct competition with similar pottery made in the Oxford region (Young 1977). The most elaborate New Forest wares presumably commanded the highest prices, and could therefore absorb transport costs more successfully than the coarse wares, which would also have been heavier and more bulky. The clear implication is that a price-sensitive market still existed in the late Roman period, despite problems of inflation during the third century and the sup-posed decline in trade in the late empire.

The relationship between Oxford and New Forest ware has been explored further, using mathematical methods drawn from geographical analysis (Fulford and Hodder 1975). The tablewares produced in the two centres were very similar, and exactly contemporary, and therefore allow unusually direct comparisons of their distributions. The rival production centres are $c.$96km ($59\frac{1}{2}$ miles) apart, and their products would be expected, all things being equal, to have been present in equal quantities on sites located halfway between them. This is not the case, however, as Oxford products remain in the majority for 63km (39 miles) in the direction of the New Forest rather than 48 (fig. 73a). However, the scale of the Oxford industry seems to have been greater, the range of pottery fuller, and the quality better. Fulford and Hodder concluded that 'the relative importance of the two production concerns is reflected in the estimated areal size of the centres, and that the observed uneven pattern of distribution of the products in the area between the centres is the result of competition' (op. cit. 31). More detailed analysis of the pattern of finds of Oxford ware indicated that access to water transport may have been crucial in enhancing the success of its producers (fig. 73b), partly by giving access to the markets of the two large cities of Cirencester and London.

Transport was also a very important influence upon the location of terra sigillata kilns, although the presence of suitable clays was also essential. The establishment of branch workshops at Lyon in Gaul from production centres in Italy gave access to the network of rivers for which Gaul was rightly famous (above p. 30). South Gaulish terra sigillata was made beside the river Tarn in a valley in the Massif Central; the difficult seasonal river conditions do not seem to favour this location, but the valley led towards Toulouse, and thus gained access to the Atlantic via Bordeaux; Middleton has drawn attention to the possible importance of overland transport from La Graufesenque to the Mediterranean port of Narbo (1980). In Britain, heavy mortaria were transported over extensive inland areas, as well as by coastal shipping (Fulford 1982, 412, fig. 4). However, arrangements for transport may not have been the concern of potters, but of the merchants who purchased and distributed their products; this was certainly true of Italian pottery until the nineteenth century (Blake 1981).

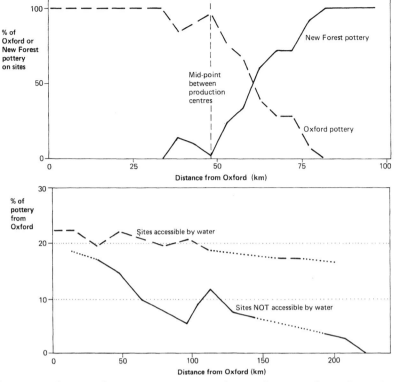

73a and b. If fragments of pottery found in excavations are studied with sufficient care, interesting information can emerge. This comparison between the products of rival production centres shows how fine wares and mortaria from kilns in the Oxford region dominated a larger area than their New Forest equivalents. Pottery from the two centres does not appear in equal quantities on sites until a point well beyond the half-distance between them is reached (fig. 73a). The reason for the greater success of the Oxford potters may be revealed by fig. 73b, which shows that high levels of their wares could be maintained on sites which could be reached by water, an opportunity which did not exist for the New Forest potters. (Audio-Visual Centre, University of Newcastle; based on data from Fulford and Hodder 1975)

Negotiatores cretarii

The commonest Latin word for a trader in the Roman period was *negotiator*, sometimes qualified by the name of a commodity such as wine, fish sauce or pottery. In some cases, a further geographical term is added, and we even have inscriptions from the Netherlands which refer to an individual as *negotiator cretarius Britannicianus*: trader in pottery with Britain (Hassal 1978, 43). It seems that *negotiatores* were fairly large-scale traders, who may have been involved in the organisation of trade rather than necessarily being personally involved (Rougé 1966, 274–283). Agents, other merchants, sailors and river-boatmen might all be employed in the process, and a degree of financial organisation would also have been necessary. It is inconceivable that each of the hundreds of terra sigillata workshops traded separately, and archaeology clearly demonstrates that their products are evenly spread around the entire distribution area of terra sigillata. On the other hand, Jacob and Leredde have warned against any tendency to impose ideas of craft-guilds derived from the medieval period onto the potters of the Roman period (1982).

In a recent survey, Peacock concluded that the activities of *negotiatores* were the most likely means of exporting pottery from dispersed and sub-divided rural industries (1983, 106, etc.); further support can be added because of evidence for the selection of particular products for distribution and not others. For example, terra sigillata and fine wares were made at both La Graufesenque in southern Gaul and Lezoux in central Gaul around the middle of the first century AD. In the case of terra sigillata, south Gaulish ware was exported very widely in great quantities, whilst the central Gaulish ware (not yet of robust quality) was scarcely exported at all until it improved by *c.*AD 100. However, an appreciable amount of green lead-glazed pottery and colour-coated ware was exported widely from Lezoux and other centres in central Gaul, whilst south Gaulish colour-coated wares remained rare; in fact, most colour-coated ware in this period came from Lyon rather than either of the terra sigillata production areas (Greene 1979).

Perhaps *negotiatores* based in an important centre like Lyon set up speculative or regular trading ventures, using agents to assemble terra sigillata from La Graufesenque, glazed wares from the Lezoux area, and colour-coated ware from Lyon into loads destined for Britain, or the cities and forts of the Rhine-Danube frontier, and arranged their transport. Other merchants may possibly have paid to place smaller cargoes of pottery on the same ships or river boats, and as has been stressed above, cargoes were unlikely to have consisted entirely of pottery.

The same kind of selection of pottery for trade can still be seen in the late second and third centuries, when terra sigillata and a remarkably fine black colour-coated ware were both made at Trier on the river Mosel in Germany (Greene 1978). The terra sigillata had a mainly regional distribution, whilst the colour-coated drinking vessels are encountered in large numbers from northern Britain to the Danube, and even in north Italy, where east Gaulish terra sigillata is unknown. Excavation has demonstrated that the two wares were made on the same site, using the same clay fired in different kiln atmospheres in order to produce the black surface of the colour-coated ware (above p. 159). It could be suggested that wine was the main interest of *negotiatores* based in Trier, and that the elegant colour-coated drinking vessels were an obvious item for inclusion in the cargoes of barrels which are known from carvings in the Mosel valley (Ellmers 1978, figs. 9, 12, 15 and 16a), just as Saintonge jugs came with wine from Bordeaux to Britain in the thirteenth century AD.

Except for occasions when the supply of local pottery was unsuitable, the Roman army seems to have relied upon the same sources as civilians; where military pottery-making took place, it was normally shortlived (Greene 1977; 1979b). The army must always have been an attractive market for traders, as soldiers were well-paid in cash. Bulk supplies of equipment such as clothing or food-stuffs are likely to have been handled by *nego-tiatores* who would have operated in the same manner as in civilian trade; to claim that the army determined the direction of trade and the location of traders (Middleton 1979) underestimates the size and demands of the civilian population. In Britain, the presence of garrisons along the northern frontier was never enough to cause the relocation of pottery production; indeed, much of the Roman army's cooking pottery came from Dorset, as far away from the frontier as it was possible to go. The production area was near the coast, and *negotiatores* may have conducted a variety of trading activities around the west coast seaways – metals, hides and slaves southwards, grain and pottery northwards, perhaps. Dorset black burnished ware (BB1) had a rival made on the Thames estuary (BB2), and shipped up the east coast to Hadrian's Wall and, when it was occupied, Scotland (Gillam 1976). The quantities found on sites along Hadrian's Wall in no way suggest official supply and distribution to specific sites, but rather competition and factors of price versus quality (Gillam and Greene 1981).

CONCLUSIONS

The absence of Roman pottery from serious discussion in the Roman literary and epigraphic sources demonstrates the importance of archaeology in expanding the range of information upon which an understanding of the economy can be based. The extensive geographical distribution of wares like terra sigillata and African red slip ware is matched by the extent of the social range of sites which they reached, including ordinary peasant farmsteads. The actual quantities involved are staggering: virtually every Romano-British site occupied in the second century AD received at least some central Gaulish ware. In a discussion of ceramics of Roman, medieval and post-medieval date in Italy, Blake concluded that in the Roman period: 'The ceramic structure (in terms of qualities and distribution) is unparalleled until the eighteenth century when the social structure of wealth and aspirations was remarkably similar to that portrayed in the Roman empire' (1978, 440). Also, 'Ancient historians need to look again at their scanty sources to see how their view of society and its attitudes can be modified to accommodate the dynamic economic structure implied by the study of pottery' (ibid. 439). In Britain too, it was not until the eighteenth or even nineteenth centuries that fine dinner services reappeared on the tables of ordinary farmers.

FURTHER READING

The Roman period features in most general histories of technology; it appears in volume 2 of the Oxford *History of technology*, which covers the period 700 BC to AD 1500 (Singer *et al.* 1956), and is included in Forbes' *Studies in ancient technology* (9 vols, 1955–1963). Both of these works are becoming rather dated, particularly in their archaeological content. Hodges' *Technology in the ancient world* (1970) is shorter and more archaeological, but the most up-to-date study is White's *Greek and Roman technology* (1984). Some books are more technical in their scope, such as Landels' *Engineering in the ancient world* (1978), or Drachman's *The mechanical technology of Greek and Roman antiquity* (1963); the latter concentrates on the literary sources rather than archaeology. A recent Italian conference consisted of papers relating technology to the Roman economy and society: *Tecnologia economia e società nel mondo romano* (1980).

Studies of the techniques of artists and craftworkers are available, such as *The muses at work*, edited by Roebuck (1969), or *Roman crafts*, edited by Strong and Brown (1976). The context of crafts is the subject of Burford's *Craftsmen in Greek and Roman society* (1972), whilst Petrikovits has combined a comprehensive list of Latin crafts and workers' names from Roman literature and inscriptions ('Die Spezialisierung des römischen Handwerks', in Jankuhn *et al.* 1981, 63–132). The capital of the empire is examined in Maxey's *The occupations of the lower classes in Roman society* (1938). The Greek background is explored in Hopper's *Trade and industry in classical Greece* (1979).

The long and complex development of the use of metals has been summarised in Tylecote's book *A history of metallurgy* (1976), and the beginnings of mining are explored in *Prehistoric mining and allied industries* by Shepherd (1980). Both subjects are brought together in Healy's *Mining and metallurgy in the Greek and Roman world* (1978), and Ramin's *La technique minière et métallurgique des anciens* (1977). A good account of lead, derived almost entirely from literary sources, is Boulakia's 'Lead in the Roman world' (*Amer. J. Archaeol.* 1972). Cleere has published many studies of ironworking, such as 'Ironworking in a Roman furnace' (*Britannia* 1971).

Roman architecture, which involved technology and the use of considerable quantities of stone, is comprehensively described in Boethius and Ward-Perkins' *Etruscan and Roman architecture* (1970). The origins of stone exploitation are examined in Ericson and Purdy's *Prehistoric quarries and lithic production* (1984). Quarrying, construction and decoration are featured in Adam's *La construction romaine* (1984), together with superb explanatory diagrams. The most highly-prized stone – marble – is dealt with in Gnoli's *Marmora romana* (1971). Bedon's *Les carrières et les carriers de la Gaule romaine* (1984) is a useful synthesis of quarries for a variety of types of stone.

Students of pottery are well served by Peacock's recent book *Pottery in the Roman world: an ethnoarchaeological approach* (1982), which explores technology, as well as the economics of production and marketing; in 1977, he edited a collection of papers whose discussions of trade were all based on the results of scientific analysis of pottery (*Pottery and early commerce*). Some of the recent research on amphorae has been reviewed by Paterson, in an article entitled 'Salvation from the sea' in the *Journal of Roman Studies* (1982) 146–157. The 1981 volume of the same journal contained an account of 'Pottery manufacture in Roman Egypt: a new papyrus', which underlines the importance of papyrus documents for information on matters ignored in literary texts. A well-preserved lamp workshop in Pompeii has been published by Irelli in *Instrumentum domesticum* (1977).

The mechanics of trade have been the subject of papers by Pleket and Whittaker in *Trade in the ancient empires*, edited by Garnsey *et al.* in 1983.

The development of technology since the Roman period is a subject with an enormous literature, with debates between those who see steady progress and those who detect sudden revolutionary advances. The flavour of the latter can be gained from collected papers of Lynn White, *Medieval religion and technology* (1978), whilst Braudel takes a characteristically broad evolutionary view in *The structures of everyday life: the limits of the possible* (1981). The neglected period before the eighteenth century is examined in Cipolla's *Before the Industrial Revolution: European society and economy, 1000–1700 (1981)*, and Coleman's *Industry in Tudor and Stuart England* (1975). The strength of the classical tradition may be judged from Parsons' *Engineers and engineering in the Renaissance* (1939). Hobsbawm's *Industry and empire: an economic history of Britain since 1750* (1968) is only one of dozens of excellent books which assess the effects of industrialisation and the mass-market in the last 250 years.

SEVEN

Conclusions

It is true that the *Romans* being Lords of the World, had the Command of the People, their Persons and their work, their Cattle and their Carriages; even their Armies were employ'd in these noble Undertakings . . . But now the Case is alter'd, Labour is dear, Wages high, no Man works for Bread and Water now; our Labourers do not work in the Road, drink in the Brook; so that as rich as we are, it would exhaust the whole Nation to build the Edifices, the Causways, the Aqueducts, Lines, Castles, Fortifications, and other publick Works, which the *Romans* built with very little Expence. (Defoe 1724–6, 520–1)

SUMMING UP THE ROMAN ECONOMY

It must not be forgotten that this book is a review of the contribution of archaeology to the study of the Roman economy, not an economic history. The relevance of archaeology to each chapter will therefore be summarised as concisely as possible.

Transport

Transport is the key to defining the physical limits to trade. Literary evidence of travel times and costs is important, and artistic representations are useful, but both sources are incomplete and geographically limited. Archaeology has certainly helped to underline the remarkable degree of trading which took place in the early empire, partly through the study of shipwrecks and their cargoes, and partly through the recognition of an enormous range of ships, boats and vehicles adapted to different conditions. Simple experiments have removed false notions about the supposed ineffectiveness of the steering of ships and the pulling of vehicles. It is clear that Roman transport was equal to the demands placed upon it, and that it was not excelled in scale or effectiveness until the advent of canal and railway networks and steam-powered ships. The archaeological study of the results of transport, such as the distributions of marble, wine or humble cooking pottery, demands the existence of a successful transport system; it also suggests that the transport costs derived from Roman sources may be too high. They are, after all, few in number and relate to the mountainous geography of the Mediterranean region, rather than the flatter fringes of the empire. From a technical point of view, the scale and size of Roman transport seems to have been limited by demand, not technology.

Coinage

Archaeology continues to be a major source of information by providing samples of coins recovered in controlled conditions through the excavation of sites of all kinds. These form a vital element in a numismatic approach, for they form a basis for comparison with hoards buried in the Roman period, or modern museum collections made up from scattered finds without firm details of provenance. Coin finds lend support to a view of the Roman economy involving comprehensive monetisation, although they cannot prove its existence on their own. I believe that the nature, quantity and distribution of Roman coins is more compatible with the evidence for monetisation derived from Roman literature (Apuleius: Millar 1975) and papyrus documents (Bowman 1980) than with the restricted needs of the state proposed by Crawford (1970; 1975). Furthermore, the extent and diversity of Roman trade in everyday items as well as luxuries add circumstantial weight to the concept of complex interactions facilitated by cash payments.

Every excavation on a site increases the overall statistical reliability of studies such as those by Casey and Reece, whilst laboratory analyses will advance our knowledge of the financial and technological aspects of coinage. However, the application of theoretical models of trade and exchange in different parts of the Roman empire may yet emphasise the plurality of economic systems within which coins were used. Sophisticated though the Augustan system of denominations may have been in comparison with the coinages of remarkably recent centuries, it does not seem to have been matched by methods of accounting, credit or banking, which were to be so important in the later Middle Ages. The real potential of the coinage may, therefore, never have been tapped.

Agriculture

The study of Roman agriculture can be undertaken at different levels, using different proportions of historical and archaeological evidence. There is undeniably a rich Roman literature on this subject, and important historical phenomena had their origins in agrarian politics. Archaeology has only just begun to supplement these documents with hard information derived from the numerous techniques employed by prehistorians, but already, bone and plant remains from sites far from the experience of Columella or Pliny have illustrated such matters as the butchery trade in towns, and the range of crops which were grown in the countryside. The recovery of suitable samples of these kinds from Roman sites is a fairly recent phenomenon, and will continue to provide more and more detail about this fundamental part of Roman life, particularly when enough reports are published to allow comparisons between sites of different social levels or in different geographical or chronological contexts. The results will have to be related to the general environmental context of weather and climate.

Settlement in the Roman empire

Agriculture and other forms of economic activity can only make sense in the setting of a clear perception of the form and extent of human occupation of the territory included in the empire. It seems that most fieldwork studies which are conducted reveal a surprisingly heavy but dispersed scatter of Roman rural sites, whilst the number of towns, most of which are already well known, remains static. The dynamics of this pattern reduce the notional importance of towns, particularly away from the Mediterranean; once again, it is difficult to conceive how such a dispersed but apparently prosperous rural population could have existed without good transport and exchange facilities. Perhaps the explosion of information derived from fieldwork studies, many of which are still in progress, is the single most significant archaeological contribution to the understanding of Roman economics. For this reason, it is vitally important that historians who wish to use this evidence should be fully aware of its variable quality and lack of precision; indistinct trends derived from statistically uncertain samples of ancient settlement patterns may too easily be forced into interpretations based upon scanty historical documents.

Metal, stone and pottery

The exploitation of the resources of the empire did not involve revolutionary technology; the consistent feature of mining, quarrying and pottery making is the extent of operations and the quantity of output. The Roman state constructed marble buildings on an unprecedented scale, and minted millions of gold, silver and bronze coins. Thousands of ordinary Roman farmers had more iron tools, architectural stonework and fine tableware than ever before, to an extent that would not be matched again until the post-medieval period. The technology applied to the extraction and processing of raw materials was evidently adequate to meet this high level of demand, at prices which could be afforded by a wide range of society. The combination of effective transport and appropriate coin denominations, which has been noted above, would obviously have helped to sustain trade in these materials, far beyond the requirements of the state and the army alone. Archaeology is of fundamental importance in examining all aspects of this phenomenon.

THE ROMAN ECONOMY IN AN ARCHAEOLOGICAL PERSPECTIVE

Quite simply, I believe that the level of economic activity, revealed by archaeological research makes the 'minimalist' approach of historians such as Finley untenable. The economy does not show signs of advance or evolution, simply an intensification of everything that already existed in Greek and Roman republican times. This may have been the result of territorial expansion through conquest, and the resources which it released; it might have reflected a brief period of favourable climate which allowed agriculture and transport to operate with unusual effectiveness.

These two factors may have coincided, and produced 'feedback' in the system, which was subsequently brought to a slow but sure end by external enemies and internal problems, quite possibly intensified by climatic deterioration.

What is absolutely clear is that no economic history of the Roman empire can ever be written again which does not give the same detailed attention to the results and technical problems involved in archaeology as it does to the textual criticism of Roman documentary sources. The balance is not even, of course, and in parts of Italy, archaeology is likely to remain firmly within the framework of Roman history, rather than providing an alternative structure. However, in areas more distant from the heart of the empire, the importance of archaeology rises as the number of relevant documents falls. The additional level of difficulties that are consequently posed in the formulation of hypotheses, and the assessment of interpretations, should be a source of excitement rather than depression.

Bibliography

Abel 1980: Abel W, *Agricultural fluctuations in Europe*. London

Abrams and Wrigley 1978: Abrams P. and Wrigley E. A. (ed), *Towns in societies*. Cambridge

Adam 1984: Adam J.-P., *La construction romaine*. Paris

Agache 1970: Agache R., *Détection aérienne de vestiges protohistoriques, gallo-romains et médiévaux*. Bull. Soc. Préhist. Nord 7. Amiens

Agache 1972: Agache R., 'New aerial research in Picardy and Artois', *Antiq.* 46, 117–123

Agache 1975: Agache R., 'La campagne à l'époque romaine dans les grandes plaines du nord de la France d'après les photographies aériennes', *Aufstieg Niedergang Röm. Welt* 2.4, 658–713

Agache 1978: Agache R., *La Somme pré-romaine et romaine*. Amiens

Agache and Bréart 1975: Agache R. and Bréart B., *Atlas d'archéologie aérienne de Picardie*. Amiens

Alföldy 1974: Alföldy G., *Noricum*. London

Allan and Richards 1983: Allan J. A. and Richards T. S., 'Use of satellite imagery in archaeological surveys', *Libyan Stud.* 14, 4–8

Amand 1984: Amand M., 'L'industrie, la taille et le commerce de la pierre dans le basin du Tournaisis à l'époque romaine', *Rév. du Nord* 66.260, 209–219

Ammerman 1985: Ammerman A. J., 'Modern land use versus the past: a case study from Calabria', in Malone and Stoddart 1985. Part 1, 27–40

Anderson and Anderson 1981: Anderson A. C. and Anderson A. S. (ed), *Roman pottery research in Britain and north-west Europe* (2 vols). Brit. Archaeol. Rep. S123. Oxford

Angell 1930: Angell N., *The story of money*. London

Applebaum 1975: Applebaum S., 'Some observations on the economy of the Roman villa at Bignor, Sussex', *Britannia* 6, 118–132

Arthur 1982: Arthur P., 'Amphora production in the Tripolitanian Gebel', *Libyan Stud.* 13, 61–72

Asgari 1973: Asgari N., 'Roman and early Byzantine marble quarries of Proconnesus', *Proc. 10th Int. Congr. Class. Archaeol.* 467–480

Ashtor 1976: Ashtor E., *A social and economic history of the Near East in the Middle Ages*. London

Atkinson 1914: Atkinson D., 'A hoard of samian ware from Pompeii', *J. Rom. Stud.* 4, 27–64

Aubin 1925: Aubin H., 'Der Rheinhandel in römische Zeit', *Bonn. Jb.* 130 1–37

Aufstieg Niedergang Röm. Welt: Temporini H. and Haase W. (ed), *Aufstieg und Niedergang der römischen Welt: Geschichte und Kultur Roms im Spiegel der neueren Forschung*. Berlin

Austin and Vidal-Naquet 1977: Austin M. M. and Vidal-Naquet P., *Economic and social history of ancient Greece: an introduction*. London

Bagwell 1974: Bagwell P. S., *The transport revolution from 1770*. London

Ball 1977: Ball J. N., *Merchants and merchandise: the expansion of trade in Europe 1500–1630*. London

Balmuth and Rowland 1984: Balmuth M. S. and Rowland R. J. (ed), *Studies in Sardinian archaeology*. Michigan

Barker 1978: Barker G., 'Dry bones: economic studies and historical archaeology in Italy', in Blake *et al.* 1978, 35–49

Barker 1981: Barker G., *Landscape and society: prehistoric central Italy*. London

Barker 1982: Barker G., 'The bones', in Whitehouse 1982, 81–91

Barker 1983: Barker G., 'Economic life at Berenice: the animal and fish bones, marine molluscs and plant remains', in Lloyd 1983, 1–49

Barker 1985: Barker G., 'Landscape archaeology in Italy', in Malone and Stoddart 1985 Part 1, 1–19

Barker 1985b: Barker G., 'Agricultural organisation in classical Cyrenaica: the potential of subsistence and survey data', in Barker *et al.* 1985, 121–134

Barker and Hodges 1981: Barker G. and Hodges R., *Archaeology and Italian society*. Brit. Archaeol. Rep. S102. Oxford

Barker and Jones 1980–1981: Barker G. W. W. and Jones G. D. B., 'The UNESCO Libyan valleys survey 1980', *Libyan Stud.* 12, 9–48

Barker and Jones 1982: Barker G. W. W. and Jones G. D. B., 'The UNESCO Libyan valleys survey 1979–1981: palaeoeconomy and environmental archaeology in the pre-desert', *Libyan Stud.* 13, 1–34

Barker and Jones 1984: Barker G. W. W. and Jones G. D. B., 'The UNESCO Libyan valleys survey VI: investigations of a Romano-Libyan farm, part I', *Libyan Stud.* 15, 1–70

Barker et al. 1978: Barker G., Lloyd J. and Webley D., 'A classical landscape in Molise', *Pap. Brit. School Rome* 33, 35–51

Barker et al. 1983: Barker G. W. W. et al., 'The UNESCO Libyan valleys survey V: sedimentological properties of Holocene wadi floor and plateau deposits in Tripolitania', *Libyan Stud.* 14, 69–85

Barker et al. 1985: Barker G., Lloyd J. and Reynolds J. (ed), *Cyrenaica in antiquity*. Brit. Archaeol. Rep. S236. Oxford

Barker P. 1977: Barker P. 1977 *Techniques of archaeological excavation*. London

Barley 1977: Barley M. W. (ed), *European towns: their archaeology and early history*. Leicester

Barrandon et al. 1980: Barrandon J.-N. et al., 'Analyses et numismatique', *Dossiers de l'archéologie* 42, 17–23

Barrandon and Brenot 1978: Barrandon J.-N. and Brenot C., 'Analyse de monnaies de bronze (318–340) par activation neutronique à l'aide d'une source isotopique de californium 252', in Dévaluations 1978, 123–144

Barrandon et al. 1980b: Barrandon J. N. et al., 'De la dévaluation de l'antoninianus à la disparition du sesterce: essai de modelisation d'un phénomène monétaire', *Colloque CNRS statistique et numismatique.* Paris

Bartoccini 1958: Bartoccini R., *Il porto romano di Leptis Magna*. Rome

Basch 1972: Basch L., 'Ancient wrecks and the archaeology of ships', *Int. J. Naut. Archaeol.* 1, 1–58

Bass 1972: Bass G. F. (ed), *A history of seafaring based on underwater archaeology*. London

Bateman and Milne 1983: Bateman N. and Milne G., 'A Roman harbour in London: excavations and observations near Pudding Lane, City of London 1979–82', *Britannia* 14, 207–226

Batović and Chapman 1985: Batović S. and Chapman J. C., 'The Neothermal Dalmatia project', in Macready and Thompson 1985, 158–195

Bedon 1984: Bedon R., *Les carrières et les carriers de la Gaule romaine*. Paris

Bell B. 1981: Bell B., 'Analysis of viticultural data by cumulative deviations' in Rotberg and Rabb 1981, 271–278

Bell 1981: Bell M., 'Valley sediments and environmental change', in Jones and Dimbleby 1981, 75–91

Bell 1982: Bell M., 'The effects of land-use and climate on valley sedimentation', in Harding 1982, 127–142

Belshaw 1965: Belshaw C. S., *Traditional exchange and modern markets*. Englewood Cliffs NJ

Besançon 1979: *Terres et paysans dépendants dans les sociétés antiques*. Colloquium, Université de Besançon 2–3 May

Binford 1978: Binford L. R., *Nunamiut ethnoarchaeology*. London

Binsfeld 1972: Binsfeld W., 'Eine Bierverlegerin aus Trier zu CIL XIII 450*', *Germania* 50, 256–8

Bintliff 1982: Bintliff J., 'Palaeoclimatic modelling of environmental changes in the east Mediterranean region since the last glaciation', in Bintliff and Zeist 1982, 485–527

Bintliff and Zeist 1982: Bintliff J. L. and Zeist W. van (ed), *Palaeoclimates, palaeoenvironments and human communities in the eastern Mediterranean region in later prehistory*. Brit. Archaeol. Rep. S133. Oxford

Bird 1972: Bird D. G., 'The Roman gold mines of north-west Spain', *Bonn. Jb.* 172, 36–64

Bird 1984: Bird D. G., 'Pliny and the gold mines of the north-west of the Iberian peninsula', in Blagg et al. 1984, 341–368

Birks 1981: Birks H. J. B., 'The use of pollen analysis in the reconstruction of past climates: a review', in Wigley et al. 1981, 111–138

Blackman 1973: Blackman D. J. (ed), *Marine archaeology*. Colston Papers 23. London

Blackman 1982: Blackman D. J., 'Ancient harbours in the Mediterranean', *Int. J. Naut. Archaeol.* 11, 79–104 (part 1), 185–211 (part 2)

Blackman and Branigan 1977: Blackman D. K. and Branigan K., 'An archaeological survey of the lower catchment of the Ayiofarango valley', *Ann. Brit. Sch. Athens* 72, 13–84

Blagg 1976: Blagg T. F. C., 'Tools and techniques of the Roman stonemason in Britain', *Britannia* 7, 152–172

Blagg 1980: Blagg T. F. C., 'Roman civil and military architecture in the province of Britain: aspects of patronage, influence and craft organization', *World Archaeol.* 12.1, 27–42

Blagg and Read 1977: Blagg T. F. C. and Read S., 'The Roman pewter-moulds from Silchester', *Antiq. J.* 57

Blagg et al. 1984: Blagg T. F. C., Jones R. F. J. and Keay S. J. (ed), *Papers in Iberian archaeology*. Brit. Archaeol. Rep. S193. Oxford

Blake 1978: Blake H. McK., 'Medieval pottery: technical innovation or economic change?', in Blake *et al.* 1978, 435–473

Blake 1981: Blake H., 'Pottery exported from northwest Italy between 1450 and 1830: Savona, Albisola, Genoa, Pisa, and Montelupo', in Barker and Hodges 1981, 99–124

Blake *et al.* 1978: Blake H. M., Potter T. W., and Whitehouse D. B. (ed), *Papers in Italian archaeology I: the Lancaster seminar.* Brit. Archaeol. Rep. S41. Oxford

Blazquez 1980: Blazquez J. Martinez (ed), *Produccion y comercio de aceite en la antigüedad: premier congreso internacional.* Madrid

Boethius and Ward-Perkins 1970: Boethius A. and Ward-Perkins J. B., *Etruscan and Roman architecture.* Harmondsworth

Böhner 1977: Böhner K., 'Urban and rural settlement in the Frankish Kingdom', in Barley 1977, 185–202

Bonatti 1970: Bonatti E., 'Pollen sequence in the lake sediments', in Hutchinson 1970, 26–31

Bonnard 1913: Bonnard L., *La navigation intérieure dans la Gaule romaine.* Paris

Boon and Williams 1966: Boon G. C. and Williams C., 'The Dolaucothi drainage wheel', *J. Rom. Stud.* 56, 122–127

Boserup 1965: Boserup E., *The conditions of agricultural growth.* London.

Boulakia 1972: Boulakia J. D. C., 'Lead in the Roman world', *Amer. J. Archaeol.* 76, 139–144

Bowen and Fowler 1978: Bowen H. C. and Fowler P. J. (ed), *Early land allotment in the British Isles: a survey of recent work.* Brit. Archaeol. Rep. 48. Oxford

Bowman 1980: Bowman A. K., 'The economy of Egypt in the earlier fourth century' in King 1980, 23–40

Bradford 1957: Bradford J., *Ancient landscapes: studies in field archaeology.* London

Brandt and Slofstra 1983: Brandt R. and Slofstra J. (ed), *Roman and native in the Low Countries: spheres of interaction.* Brit. Archaeol. Rep. S184. Oxford

Branigan 1977: Branigan K., *Gatcombe: the excavation and study of a Romano-British villa estate 1967–78.* Brit. Archaeol. Rep. 44. Oxford.

Braudel 1981: Braudel F., *Civilization and capitalism 15th–18th century 1: the structures of everyday life: the limits of the possible.* London

Braudel 1982: Braudel F., *Civilization and capitalism 15th–18th century 2: the wheels of commerce.* London

Braudel 1984: Braudel F., *Civilization and capitalism 15th–18th century 3: the perspective of the world.* London

Breglia 1950: Breglia L., 'Circolazione monetale e aspetti di vita economica a Pompei', *Pompeiana* 41–59. Naples

Brooke 1983: Brooke C. N. L. *et al.* (ed), *Studies in numismatic method presented to Philip Grierson.* Cambridge

Brown 1968: Brown A. C., *Catalogue of Italian terra sigillata in the Ashmolean Museum.* Oxford

Brown 1983: Brown A. E. (ed), 'Archaeology in Northamptonshire 1982', *Northamptonshire Archaeol.* 18, 171–183

Brown 1976: Brown D., 'Pottery', in Strong and Brown 1976, 74–91

Brown 1951: Brown F. E., 'Cosa I, history and topography', *Mem. Amer. Acad. Rome* 20, 5–113

Brown 1980: Brown F. E., *Cosa: the making of a Roman town.* Michigan

Burford 1960–1961: Burford A., 'Heavy transport in classical antiquity', *Econ. Hist. Rev.* 13, 1–18

Burford 1972: Burford A., *Craftsmen in Greek and Roman society.* London

Burnham and Johnson 1979: Burnham B. C. and Johnson H. B. (ed), *Invasion and response: the case of Roman Britain.* Brit. Archaeol. Rep. 73. Oxford

Campbell and Skinner 1976: Campbell R. H. and Skinner A. S. (ed), *Adam Smith: An inquiry into the nature and causes of the wealth of nations.* Oxford.

Carandini 1983: Carandini A., 'Pottery and the African economy', in Garnsey *et al.* 1983, 145–162

Carandini and Panella 1981: Carandini A. and Panella C., 'The trading connections of Rome and central Italy in the late second and third centuries: the evidence of the Terme del Nuotatore', in King and Henig 1981, 487–503

Carandini and Settis 1979: Carandini A. and Settis S., *Schiavi e padroni nell'Etruria romana: la villa di Settefinestre dallo scavo alla mostra.* Bari

Carandini and Tatton-Brown 1980: Carandini A. and Tatton-Brown T., 'Excavations at the Roman villa of "Sette Finestre" in Etruria, 1975–9: first interim report', in Painter 1980, 9–43

Carney 1975: Carney T. F., *The shape of the past: models and antiquity.* Kansas

Carte 1979: *Carte archéologique du Cher: pour une banque de données des sites archéologiques en France.* Annales Litt. Univ. Besançon 240. Paris

Carter *et al.* 1985; Carter L. *et al.*, 'Population and agriculture: Magna Graecia in the fourth century BC', in Malone and Stoddart 1985, Part 1, 281–312

Casey 1974: Casey J., 'The interpretation of Romano-British site finds', in Casey and Reece 1974, 37–51

Casey 1980: Casey J., *Roman coinage in Britain.* Aylesbury

Casey 1985: Casey J., 'Roman coinage of the fourth century in Scotland', in Miket and Burgess 1985, 295–304

Casey and Reece 1974: Casey J. and Reece R. (ed), *Coins and the archaeologist*. Brit. Archaeol. Rep. 4. Oxford

Casson 1950: Casson L., 'The Isis and her voyage', *Trans. Amer. Philol. Assoc.* 81, 43–56

Casson 1971: Casson L., *Ships and seamanship in the ancient world*. Princeton

Casson 1974: Casson L., *Travel in the ancient world*. London

Casson 1980: Casson L., 'The rôle of the state in Rome's grain trade', in D'Arms and Kopff 1980, 21–33

Castagnoli 1980: Castagnoli F., 'Installazione portuali a Roma', in D'Arms and Kopff 1980, 35–42

Chapman and Mytum 1983: Chapman J. and Mytum H. (ed), *Settlement in north Britain 1000 BC to 1000 AD*. Brit. Archaeol. Rep. 118. Oxford

Charleston 1955: Charleston R. J., *Roman pottery*. London

Charlesworth 1926: Charlesworth M. P., *Trade routes and commerce of the Roman empire*. Chicago

Chatterton and Chatterton 1984: Chatterton B. A. and L., 'Medicago – its possible rôle in Romano-Libyan dryfarming and its positive role in modern dryfarming', *Libyan Stud.* 15, 157–160

Cherry 1983: Cherry J. F., 'Frogs round the pond: perspectives on current archaeological survey projects in the Mediterranean region', in Keller and Rupp 1983, 375–416

Cherry and Shennan 1978: Cherry J., Gamble C. and Shennan S. (ed), *Sampling in contemporary British archaeology*. Brit. Archaeol. Rep. 50. Oxford

Chevallier 1974: Chevallier R. (ed), *Littérature gréco-romaine et géographie historique: mélanges offerts à Roger Dion*. Paris.

Chevallier 1976: Chevallier R., *Roman roads*. London

Chouquer 1982: Chouquer G. *et al.*, 'Cadastres, occupation du sol et paysages agraires antiques', *Annales* 37, 847–882

Christol 1971: Christol M., 'Remarques sur les naviculaires d'Arles', *Latomus* 30, 643–663

Cipolla 1956: Cipolla C. M., *Money, prices and civilization in the Mediterranean world*. Princeton

Cipolla 1981: Cipolla C. M., *Before the Industrial Revolution: European society and economy, 1000–1700*. London

Clack 1981: Clack P. A. G., 'The northern frontier: farmers in the military zone', in Miles 1982, 377–402

Clarke 1972: Clarke D. L. (ed), *Models in archaeology*. London

Clavel 1970: Clavel M., *Béziers et son territoire dans l'antiquité*. Paris

Cleere 1971: Cleere H., 'Ironmaking in a Roman furnace', *Britannia* 2, 203–217

Cleere 1976: Cleere H. F., 'Some operating parameters for Roman ironworks', *Bull. Inst. Archaeol. Univ. London* 13

Cleere and Crossley 1986: Cleere H. and Crossley D., *The iron industry of the Weald*. Leicester

CNRS 1977: Centre Nationale de la Recherche Scientifique, *Armées et fiscalité dans le monde antique*. Paris

Cockle 1981: Cockle H., 'Pottery manufacture in Roman Egypt: a new papyrus', *J. Rom. Stud.* 71, 87–97

Coleman 1975: Coleman D. C., *Industry in Tudor and Stuart England*. London

Collingwood and Richmond 1969: Collingwood R. G. and Richmond I. A., *The archaeology of Roman Britain*. London

Collingwood and Wright 1965: Collingwood R. G. and Wright R. P., *The Roman inscriptions of Britain*. Oxford

Colls *et al.* 1975: Colls D., Domergue C., Laubenheimer F. and Liou B., 'Les lingots d'étain de l'épave Port-Vendres II', *Gallia* 33.1, 61–94

Coltorti and Dal Ri 1985: Coltorti M. and Dal Ri L., 'The human impact on the landscape: some examples from the Adige valley', in Malone and Stoddart 1985, part 1, 105–134

Cope 1971: Cope L. H., 'Oxygen in Roman coinage metals and alloys', *Numis. Circ.* 79, 402–4

Cornell and Matthews 1982: Cornell T. and Matthews J., *Atlas of the Roman world*. Oxford

Crawford 1970: Craford M. H., 'Money and exchange in the Roman world', *J. Rom. Stud.* 60, 40–8

Crawford 1975: Crawford M., 'Finance, coinage and money from the Severans to Constantine', *Aufstieg Niedergang Röm. Welt* 2.2, 560–593

Crawford 1983: Crawford M. (ed), *Sources for ancient history*. Cambridge

Crawford 1983b: Crawford M. H., 'Numismatics', in Crawford 1983, 185–233

Crawford 1984: Crawford M., *Coinage and money under the Roman Republic*. London

Crook 1967: Crook J. A., *Law and life of Rome*. London

Cunliffe 1971: Cunliffe B. W., *Fishbourne: a Roman palace and its garden*, 2 vols. London

Cunliffe 1978: Cunliffe B. W., *Rome and her empire*. London

Cüppers 1982: Cüppers H., 'Ein Metzger in römischen Trier', *Trierer Z* 45, 289–292

Cüppers 1983: Cüppers H. (ed), *Die Römer an Mosel und Saar*. Mainz

Curle 1911: Curle J., *A Roman frontier post and its people: the fort of Newstead in the parish of Melrose*. Glasgow

Curtis 1978: Curtis R. I., *The production and commerce of fish sauce in the western Roman empire: a social and economic study*. Maryland

D'Arms 1970: D'Arms J. H., *Romans on the Bay of Naples: a social and cultural study of the villas and their owners from 150 BC to AD 400*. Harvard

D'Arms 1977: D'Arms J. H., 'M. I. Rostovtzeff and M. I. Finley: the status of traders in the Roman world', in D'Arms and Eadie 1977, 159–180

D'Arms 1981: D'Arms J. H., *Commerce and social standing in ancient Rome*. Cambridge, Mass.

D'Arms and Eadie 1977: D'Arms J. H. and Eadie J. W. (ed), *Ancient and modern: essays in honor of G. F. Else*. Ann Arbor

D'Arms and Kopff 1980: D'Arms J. H. and Kopff E. C. (ed), *The seaborne commerce of ancient Rome: studies in archaeology and history*. Mem. Amer. Acad. Rome 36. Rome

Darvill and McWhirr 1984: Darvill T. and McWhirr A., 'Brick and tile production in Roman Britain', *World Archaeol.* 15, 239–261

Dauphin and Schonfield 1983: Dauphin C. and Schonfield J., 'Preliminary reports on three seasons of survey of cities of the Roman and Byzantine periods in the Golan Heights', *Israel Explor. J.* 33, 189–206

Davaras 1974: Davaras C., 'Rock-cut fish tanks in eastern Crete', *Ann. Brit. Sch. Athens* 69, 87–93

Davies 1983: Davies J. L., 'Coinage and settlement in Roman Wales and the Marches: some observations', *Archaeol. Cambrensis* 132, 78–94

Day 1932: Day J., 'Agriculture in the life of Pompeii', *Yale Class. Stud.* 3, 165–208

Defoe 1724–1726: Defoe D. (ed G. D. H. Cole 1927), *A tour through the whole island of Great Britain*. London

Deman 1975: Deman A., 'Matériaux et réflexions pour servir à une étude de développement et du sous-développement dans les provinces de l'empire romain', *Aufstieg Niedergang Röm. Welt* 2.3, 3–97

Denton and Karlen 1973: Denton G. and Karlen W., 'Holocene climatic variations their pattern and possible cause', *Quaternary Res.* 3.2, 155–205

D'Escurac 1976: D'Escurac H. Pavis, *La préfecture de l'annone: services administratif impérial d'Auguste à Constantin*. Rome

Detsicas 1973: Detsicas A. P. (ed), *Current research in Romano-British coarse pottery*. Council Brit. Archaeol., Res. Rep. 10.

Dévaluations 1978: Ecole française de Rome, *Les 'dévaluations' à Rome: époque républicaine et impériale*. Rome

Dihle 1978: Dihle A., 'Die entdeckungsgeschichlticher Voraussetzungen des Indienhandels der römischen Kaiserzeit', *Aufstieg Niedergang Röm. Welt* 2.9, 546–580

Domergue 1966: Domergue C., 'Les lingots de plomb romains du musée archéologique de Carthagène et du musée naval de Madrid', *Archivo. Esp. Arqueol.* 39, 41–72

Domergue 1974: Domergue C., 'A propos de Pline, *Naturalis Historia* 33, 70–78, et pour illustrer sa description des mines d'or romaines d'Espagne', *Archivo Esp. Arqueol.* 47, 499–548

Domergue 1983: Domergue C., 'La mine antique d'Aljustrel (Portugal) et les tables de bronze de Vipasca', *Conimbriga* 22

Domergue and Hérail 1978: Domergue C. and Hérail G., *Mines d'or romaines d'Espagne*. Toulouse

Doorninck 1972: Doorninck F. Van, 'Byzantium, mistress of the sea: 330–642', in Bass 1972, 133–158

Dore and Greene 1977: Dore J. and Greene K. (ed), *Roman pottery studies in Britain and beyond*. Brit. Archaeol. Rep. S30. Oxford

Dossiers 1982: *Les voies romaines. Les dossiers d'histoire et archéologie* 67. Dijon

Drachmann 1963: Drachmann A. A., *The mechanical technology of Greek and Roman antiquity: a study of the literary sources*. Copenhagen

Drinkwater 1975: Drinkwater J. F., 'Lugdunum: 'natural capital' of Gaul?', *Britannia* 6, 133–140

Drinkwater 1983: Drinkwater J. E., *Roman Gaul: the three provinces 58BC – AD260*. Beckenham

Dunbabin 1978: Dunbabin K. M. D., *The mosaics of Roman north Africa: studies in iconography and patronage*. Oxford

Duncan-Jones 1974: Duncan-Jones R., *The economy of the Roman Empire: quantitative studies*. Cambridge; revised edition 1982

Duncan-Jones 1977: Duncan-Jones R. P., 'Giant cargo-ships in antiquity', *Class. Quart.* 27, 331–332

Dunn 1978: Dunn P., *Appropriate technology: technology with a human face*. London

Dušanić 1977: Dušanić S., 'Aspects of Roman mining in Noricum, Pannonia, Dalmatia and Moesia Superior', *Aufstieg Niedergang Röm. Welt* 2.6, 52–94

Dyos & Aldcroft 1971: Dyos H. J. and Aldcroft D. H., *British transport: an economic survey from the seventeenth century to the twentieth*. Leicester

Dyson 1978: Dyson S. L., 'Settlement patterns in the Ager Cosanus: the Wesleyan University Survey 1974–1976', *J. Field Archaeol.* 5, 251–268

Dyson 1981: Dyson S. L., 'Settlement reconstruction in the *ager cosanus* and the Albegna valley: Wesleyan university research 1974–1979', in Barker and Hodges 1981, 269–274

Dyson 1981b: Dyson S. L., 'Some reflections on the archaeology of south Etruria', *J. Field Archaeol.* 8, 79–83

Dyson 1981c: Dyson S. L., 'Survey archaeology: reconstructing the Roman countryside', *Archaeology* 34.3, 31–37

Dyson 1982: Dyson S. L., 'Archaeological survey in the Mediterranean basin: a review of recent research', *Amer. Antiq.* 47, 87–98

Dyson 1983: Dyson S. L., *The Roman villas of Buccino.* Brit. Archaeol. Rep. S187. Oxford

Dyson 1985: Dyson S. L., 'The villas of Buccino and the consumer model of Roman rural development', in Malone and Stoddart 1985, Part 4, 67–84

Eckoldt 1980: Eckoldt M., *Schiffahrt auf kleinen Flüssen Mitteleuropas in Römerzeit und Mittelalter.* Bremerhaven

Eckoldt 1984: Eckoldt M., 'Navigation on small rivers in Central Europe in Roman and medieval times', *Int. J. Naut. Archaeol.* 13, 3–10

Eddy 1981: Eddy J. A., 'Climate and the rôle of the sun', in Rotberg and Rabb 1981, 145–167

Ellison and Harris 1972: Ellison A. and Harris J., 'Settlement and land use in the prehistory and early history of southern England', in Clarke 1972, 910–62

Ellmers 1978: Ellmers D., 'Shipping on the Rhine during the Roman period: the pictorial evidence', in Taylor and Cleere 1978, 1–14

Ericson and Purdy 1984: Ericson J. E. and Purdy B. A. (ed), *Prehistoric quarries and lithic production.* Cambridge

Erim and Reynolds 1970: Erim K. and Reynolds J., 'The copy of Diocletian's Edict on Maximum Prices from Aphrodisias in Caria', *J. Rom. Stud.* 60, 120–141

Evenari 1971: Evenari M. *et al.*, *The Negev.* Harvard

Farrar 1973: Farrar R. A. H., 'The techniques and sources of Romano-British black-burnished ware', in Detsicas 1973, 67–103

Fentress 1979: Fentress E. W. B., *Numidia and the Roman army; social, military and economic aspects of the frontier zone.* Brit. Archaeol. Rep. S53. Oxford

Fentress *et al.* 1983: Fentress E. *et al.*, 'Excavations at Fosso della Crescenza 1962', *Pap. Brit. Sch. Rome* 51, 58–101

Finley 1965: Finley M. I., 'Technical innovation and economic progress in the ancient world', *Econ. Hist. Rev.* 18, 29–45

Finley 1970: Finley M. I., 'Metals in the ancient world', *J. Roy. Soc. Arts* 118, 597–607

Finley 1973: Finley M. I., *The ancient economy.* London

Finley 1976: Finley M. I. (ed), *Studies in Roman property.* Cambridge

Finley 1983: Finley M. I., *Economy and society in ancient Greece.* Harmondsworth

Flach 1982: Flach D., 'Die Pachtbedingungen der Kolonen und die Verwaltung der kaiserlichen Güter in Nordafrika', *Aufstieg Niedergang Röm. Welt* 2.10, 427–473

Flohn and Fantechi 1984: Flohn H. and Fantechi R. (ed), *The climate of Europe: past, present and future.* Dordrecht

Foerster 1984: Foerster F., 'New views on bilge pumps from Roman wrecks', *Int. J. Naut. Archaeol.* 13, 85–93

Forbes 1955–1963: Forbes R., *Studies in ancient technology*, 9 vols. Leiden

Fowler 1975: Fowler P. J. (ed), *Recent work in rural archaeology.* Bradford on Avon

Fowler 1983: Fowler P. J., *The farming of prehistoric Britain.* Cambridge

Fox 1958: Fox C., *Pattern and purpose: a survey of early Celtic art in Britain.* Cardiff

Frank 1927: Frank T., *An economic history of Rome.* London

Frank 1933–1940: Frank T. (ed), *An economic survey of ancient Rome*, 5 vols. Baltimore (reprinted 1975)

Frank 1933: Frank T., *An economic survey of ancient Rome 1: Rome and Italy of the Republic.* Baltimore

Frank 1936: Frank T. (ed), *An economic survey of ancient Rome 2: Roman Egypt.* Baltimore

Frank 1937: Frank T. (ed), *An economic survey of ancient Rome 3: Britain, Spain, Sicily, Gaul.* Baltimore

Frank 1937b: Frank T., 'Notes on Roman commerce', *J. Rom. Stud.* 27, 74–5

Frank 1938: Frank T. (ed), *An economic survey of ancient Rome 4: Africa, Syria, Greece, Asia Minor.* Baltimore

Frank 1940: Frank T., *An economic survey of ancient Rome 5: Rome and Italy of the Empire.* Baltimore

Fraser 1972: Fraser P. M., *Ptolemaic Alexandria.* Oxford

Frayn 1979: Frayn J. M., *Subsistence farming in Roman Italy.* Fontwell

Frayn 1984: Frayn J. M., *Sheep-rearing and the wool trade in Italy during the Roman period.* Liverpool

Frederiksen 1975: Frederiksen M. W., 'Theory, evidence and the ancient economy', *J. Rom. Stud.* 65, 164–171

Freed 1985: Freed J., 'San Giovanni di Ruoti: cultural discontinuity between the early and late Roman empire in southern Italy', in Malone and Stoddart 1985, Part 4, 179–193

French 1980: French D. H., 'The Roman road system of Asia Minor', *Aufstieg Niedergang Röm. Welt* 2.7.2, 698–729

Fulford 1973: Fulford M. G., 'The distribution and dating of New Forest pottery' *Britannia* 4, 160–178

Fulford 1975: Fulford M., *New Forest Roman pottery.* Brit. Archaeol. Rep. 17. Oxford

Fulford 1977: Fulford M., 'Pottery and Britain's foreign trade in the late Roman period', in Peacock 1977, 35–84

Fulford 1977b: Fulford M. G., 'The location of Romano-British pottery kilns: institutional trade and the market', in Dore and Greene 1977, 301–306

Fulford 1978: Fulford M. G., 'Coin circulation and mint activity in the later Roman empire', *Archaeol. J.* 135, 67–114

Fulford 1978b: Fulford M., 'The interpretation of Britain's late Roman trade: the scope of medieval historical and archaeological analogy', in Taylor and Cleere 1978, 59–69

Fulford 1982: Fulford M., 'Town and country in Roman Britain – a parasitical relationship?', in Miles 1982, 403–419

Fulford and Hodder 1975: Fulford M. and Hodder I., 'A regression analysis of some late Romano-British pottery: a case study', *Oxoniensia* 39, 26–33

Fulford and Peacock 1984: Fulford M. G. and Peacock D. P. S., *The Avenue du President Habib Bourgiba, Salammbo: the pottery and other ceramic objects from the site. Excavations at Carthage: the British Mission* I, 2. Sheffield

Gabelmann 1983: Gabelmann H., 'Ein Wagenrelief in Pesaro', in Metzler 1983, 145–152

Gaitzsch 1980: Gaitzsch W., *Eiserne römische Werkzeuge.* Brit. Archaeol. Rep. S78. Oxford

Galbraith 1975: Galbraith J. K., *Money: Whence it came, where it went.* London

Galliou 1981: Galliou P., 'Western Gaul in the third century', in King and Henig 1981, 259–286

Garnsey 1979: Garnsey P. D. A., 'Where did Italian peasants live?', *Proc. Cambr. Phil. Soc.* 25, 1–25

Garnsey 1983: Garnsey P., 'Grain for Rome', in Garnsey *et al.* 1983, 118–130

Garnsey *et al.* 1983: Garnsey P., Hopkins K. and Whittaker C. R. (ed), *Trade in the ancient economy.* London

Gechter 1979: Gechter M., 'Die Anfänge des niedergermanischen Limes', *Bonn. Jb.* 179, 1–129

Gennaro and Stoddart 1982: Gennaro F. di and Stoddart S., 'A review of the evidence for prehistoric activity in part of south Etruria', *Pap. Brit. School Rome* 50, 1–21

Giaccherro 1974: Giacchero M., *Edictum Diocletiani et Collegarum de Pretiis Rerum Venalium.* Genoa

Giardina 1981: Giardina A., 'Allevamento ed economia della selva in Italia meridionale: transformazioni e continuita', in Giardina and Schiavone 1981, 87–113

Giardina and Schiavone 1981: Giardina A. and Schiavone A. (ed), *Societa romana e produzione schiavistica I: l'Italia: insediamenti e forma economiche.* Rome

Giardina and Schiavone 1981 2: Giardina A. and Schiavone A. (ed), *Societa romana e produzione schiavistica II: Merci, mercati e scambi nel Mediterraneo.* Rome

Gilbertson *et al.* 1984: Gilbertson D. D. *et al.*, 'The UNESCO Libyan valleys survey VII: an interim classification and functional analysis of ancient wall technology and land use', *Libyan Stud.* 15, 45–70

Gillam 1957: Gillam J. P., 'Types of Roman coarse pottery vessels in northern Britain', *Archaeol. Aeliana* 35, 180–251

Gillam 1976: Gillam J. P., 'Coarse fumed ware in northern Britain', *Glasgow Archaeol. J.* 4, 57–80

Gillam and Greene 1981: Gillam J. P. and Greene K., 'Roman pottery and the economy', in Anderson and Anderson 1981, 1–23

Glodariu 1976: Glodariu I., *Dacian trade with the Hellenistic and Roman world.* Brit. Archaeol. Rep. S8. Oxford

Glodariu 1977: Glodariu I., 'Die Landwirtschaft im römischen Däkien, *Aufstieg Niedergang Röm. Welt* 2.6, 950–989

Gnoli 1971: Gnoli R., *Marmora romana.* Rome

Goethert-Polaschek 1977: Goethert-Polaschek K., *Katalog der römischen Gläser des Rheinischen Landesmuseums Trier.* Mainz

Goffart 1974: Goffart W., *Caput and colonate: towards a history of late Roman taxation.* Toronto

Gorges 1979: Gorges J.-G., *Les villas hispano-romaines: inventaire et problématique archéologiques.* Paris

Graeve 1981: Graeve M.-C. de, *The ships of the ancient Near East c 2000–500 BC.* Orientalia Lovaniensia Analecta 7.

Green 1980: Green S. W., 'Toward a general model of agricultural systems', in Schiffer 1980, 311–355

Greene 1973: Greene K., 'The pottery from Usk', in Detsicas 1973, 25–37

Greene 1977: Greene K., 'Legionary pottery, and the significance of Holt', in Dore and Greene 1977, 113–132

Greene 1978: Greene K., 'Roman trade between Britain and the Rhine provinces: the evidence of pottery to *c.*AD 250', in Taylor and Cleere 1978, 52–58

Greene 1978b: Greene K., 'Apperley Dene Roman fortlet: a re-examination', *Archaeol. Aeliana* 6, 29–59

Greene 1979: Greene K., *Report on the excavations at Usk 1965–1976: the pre-Flavian fine wares.* Cardiff

Greene 1979b: Greene K., 'Invasion and response: pottery and the Roman army', in Burnham and Johnson 1979, 99–106

Greene 1982: Greene K., 'Terra sigillata: imitations and alternatives', *Acta Rei Cretariae Romanae Fautorum* 21–22, 71–78

Greene 1983: Greene K., *Archaeology: an introduction.* London

Greene 1984: Greene K., 'The Roman fortress at Usk, Wales, and the processing of Roman pottery for publication', *J. Field Archaeol.* 11, 405–412

Greenhill 1976: Greenhill B., *The archaeology of the boat: a new introductory study*. London

Greenhill 1980: Greenhill B., *The life and death of the merchant sailing ship 1815–1965*. London

Gren 1941: Gren E., *Kleinasien und der Ostbalkan in der wirtschaftlichen Entwicklung der römischen Kaiserzeit*. Uppsala/Leipzig

Grenier 1937: Grenier A., 'La Gaule romaine', in Frank 1937, 379–644

Gribbin 1978: Gribbin J. R. (ed), *Climatic change*. Cambridge

Gribbin and Lamb 1978: Gribbin J. R. and Lamb H. H., 'Climatic change in historical times', in Gribbin 1978, 68–82

Grierson 1959: Grierson P., 'Commerce in the Dark Ages: a critique of the evidence', *Trans. Royal Hist. Soc.* 9, 123–40

Grigson and Clutton-Brock 1984: Grigson C. and Clutton-Brock J. (ed), *Animals and archaeology: 4. Husbandry in Europe*. Brit. Archaeol. Rep. S227. Oxford

Gsell 1901: Gsell S., *Les monuments antiques de l'Algérie*. Paris

Guy 1954: Guy P. L. O., 'Archaeological evidence of soil erosion and sedimentation in Wadi Musrara', *Israel Explor. J.* 4, 77–87

Hagenow 1982: Hagenow G., *Aus der Weingarten der Antike*. Mainz

Hall and Kenward 1976: Hall R. A. and Kenward H. K., 'Biological evidence for the usage of Roman riverside warehouses at York', *Britannia* 7, 274–276

Harding 1982: Harding A. F. (ed), *Climatic change in later prehistory*. Edinburgh

Harris 1980: Harris W. V., 'Roman terracotta lamps: the organization of an industry', *J. Rom. Stud.* 70, 126–145

Hartley 1969: Hartley B. R., 'Samian ware or terra sigillata', in Collingwood and Richmond 235–251

Hartley 1972: Hartley B. R., 'The Roman occupation of Scotland: the evidence of samian ware', *Britannia* 3, 1–55

Hartley 1977: Hartley B. R., 'Some wandering potters', in Dore and Greene 1977, 251–261

Hartley K. 1973: Hartley K. F., 'The marketing and distribution of mortaria', in Detsicas 1973, 39–51

Hartley K. 1977: Hartley K. F., 'Two major potteries producing mortaria in the first century AD', in Dore and Greene 1977, 5–18

Hassall 1978: Hassall M., 'Britain and the Rhine provinces: epigraphic evidence for Roman trade', in Taylor and Cleere 1978, 41–48

Hayes 1972: Hayes J. W., *Late Roman pottery*. London; see also supplement published in 1980

Healy 1978: Healy J. F., *Mining and metallurgy in the Greek and Roman world*. London

Hedeager 1977: Hedeager L., 'A quantitative analysis of Roman imports in Europe north of the limes (0–400 AD)', in Kristiansen and Palaudan-Muller 1977, 191–216

Heinen 1976: Heinen H., 'Grundzüge der wirtschaftlichen Entwicklung des Moselraumes zur Römerzeit', *Trier Z.* 39, 75–118

Helen 1975: Helen T., *Organisation of Roman brick production in the first and second centuries AD*. Helsinki

Herz and Wenner 1981: Herz N. and Wenner D., 'Tracing the origins of ancient marble', *Archaeol.* 34.5, 14–21

Higgins 1961: Higgins R. A., *Greek and Roman jewellery*. London

Higgs 1972: Higgs E. S. (ed), *Papers in economic prehistory*. Cambridge

Higgs and Vita-Finzi 1972: Higgs E. S. and Vita-Finzi C., 'Prehistoric economies: a territorial approach', in Higgs 1972, 27–36

Higham and Jones 1975: Higham N. J. and Jones G. D. B., 'Frontiers, forts and farmers: Cumbrian aerial survey 1974–5', *Archaeol. J.* 132, 16–53

Hobsbawm 1968: Hobsbawm E. J., *Industry and empire: an economic history of Britain since 1750*. London

Höckmann 1983: Höckmann O., '"Keltisch" oder "römisch"? Bemerkungen zur Typgenese der spätrömischen Rüderschiffe von Mainz', *Jb. Röm.-Germ. Zentralmus. Mainz* 30, 403–434

Hodder 1974: Hodder I., 'Some marketing models for Romano-British coarse pottery', *Britannia* 5, 340–359

Hodder 1979: Hodder I., 'Pre-Roman and Romano-British tribal economies', in Burnham and Johnson 1979, 189–196

Hodder 1982: Hodder I., *The present past: an introduction to anthropology for archaeologists*. London

Hodder and Hassall 1971: Hodder I. R. and Hassall M. W. C., 'The non-random spacing of Romano-British walled towns', *Man* 6, 391–407

Hodder and Millett 1980: Hodder I. and Millett M., 'Romano-British villas and towns: a systematic analysis', *World Archaeol.* 12, 69–76

Hodder and Orton 1976: Hodder I. and Orton C., *Spatial analysis in archaeology*. Cambridge

Hodges 1970: Hodges H., *Technology in the ancient world*. London

Hodges 1973: Hodges H. W. M., 'Archaeology and the history of medieval technology' in Strong 1973, 265–273

Hodges 1982: Hodges R., *Dark Age economics*. London

Hodges and Whitehouse 1983: Hodges R. and Whitehouse D., *Mohamed, Charlemagne and the origins of Europe*. London

Hogg 1943: Hogg A. H. A., 'Native settlements of Northumberland', *Antiquity* 17, 136–147

Hopkins 1978: Hopkins K., 'Economic growth and towns in classical antiquity', in Abrams and Wrigley 1978, 35–79

Hopkins 1978b: Hopkins K., 'Rules of evidence', *J. Rom. Stud.* 68, 178–186

Hopkins 1978c: Hopkins K., *Conquerors and slaves*. Cambridge

Hopkins 1980: Hopkins K., 'Taxes and trade in the Roman empire (200 BC – AD 400)', *J. Rom. Stud.* 70, 101–125

Hopkins 1982: Hopkins K., 'The transport of staples', *Technical change, employment and investment: eighth international economic history congress Budapest 1982*. Budapest 81–87

Hopkins 1983: Hopkins K., 'Introduction', in Garnsey *et al.* 1983, ix–xxv

Hopkins 1983b: Hopkins K., 'Models, ships and staples', in Garnsey *et al.* 1983, 84–109

Hopper 1979: Hopper R. J., *Trade and industry in classical Greece*. London

Hughes 1977: Hughes M. J., 'The analysis of Roman tin and pewter ingots', in Oddy 1977, 41–50

Hull 1963: Hull M. R., *The Roman potters' kilns of Colchester*. Rep. Res. Comm. Soc. Antiq. London 21. Oxford

Hurst 1979: Hurst H., 'Excavations at Carthage, 1977–8: fourth interim report', *Antiq. J.* 59, 19–49

Hutchinson 1970: Hutchinson G. E., 'Ianula – an account of the history and development of the Lago di Monterosi, Latium, Italy', *Trans. Amer. Philos. Soc.* 60, pt 4

Instrumentum 1977: *L'instrumentum domesticum di Ercolano e Pompei nella prima età imperiale*. Rome

Irelli 1977: Irelli G. Cerulli, 'Una officina di lucerne fittili a Pompei', in Instrumentum 1977, 53–72

Jackson *et al.* 1973: Jackson D. A., Biek L. and Dix B. F., 'A Roman lime kiln at Weekley, Northants', *Britannia* 4, 128–140

Jacob and Leredde 1982: Jacob J.-P. and Leredde H., 'Un aspect de l'organisation des centres de production céramique: le mythe du "cartel"', *Acta Rei Cretariae Romanae Fautorum* 21/22, 89–94

James 1977: James E., *The Merovingian archaeology of south-west Gaul*. Brit. Archaeol. Rep. S25. Oxford

Jankühn *et al.* 1981: Jankühn H., Jannssen W. *et al.* (ed), *Das Handwerk in vor- und frühgeschichtlicher Zeit*. Göttingen

Jarman *et al.* 1982: Jarman M. R., Bailey G. N. and Jarman H. N. (ed), *Early European agriculture*. Cambridge

Jashemski 1979: Jashemski W. F., *The gardens of Pompeii*. New York

Jenkins 1980: Jenkins N., *The boat beneath the Pyramid: King Cheops' royal ship*. London

Jobey 1974: Jobey G., 'Notes on some population problems in the area between the two Roman walls', *Archaeol. Aeliana* 2, 17–26

Johns 1963: Johns C., 'Gaulish potters' stamps', *Antiq. J.* 43, 288–289

Johns 1971: Johns C. M., *Arretine and samian pottery*. London

Jones 1952–1953: Jones A. H. M., 'Inflation under the Roman empire', *Econ. Hist. Rev.* 5, 293–318

Jones 1963: Jones G. D. B., 'Capena and the Ager Capenas: Part II', *Pap. Brit. Sch. Rome* 31, 100–158

Jones 1974: Jones A. H. M., *The Roman economy: studies in ancient economic and administrative history*. Oxford

Jones 1980: Jones G. D. B., 'The Roman mines at Rio Tinto', *J. Rom. Stud.* 70, 146–165

Jones 1981: Jones M., 'The development of crop husbandry', in Jones and Dimbleby 1981, 95–127

Jones and Dimbleby 1981: Jones M. and Dimbleby G. (ed), *The environment of man: the Iron Age to the Anglo-Saxon period*. Brit. Archaeol. Rep. 87. Oxford

Jones and Walker 1983: Jones G. D. B. and Walker J., 'Either side of the Solway: towards a minimalist view of Romano-British agricultural settlement in the north-west', in Chapman and Mytum 1983, 185–204

Judson 1983: Judson S., 'Alluviation and erosion', in Fentress *et al.* 1983, 70–72

Kapitän 1983: Kapitän G., 'A toothed gear and water-drawing pendulum from the Mahdia wreck', *Int. J. Naut. Archaeol.* 12, 145–153

Katzev 1972: Katzev M. L., 'The Kyrenia ship', in Bass 1972, 50–52

Keay 1981: Keay S. J., 'The Conventus Tarraconensis in the third century AD: crisis or change?', in King and Henig 1981, 451–486

Keay 1983: Keay S. J., *Late Roman amphorae in the western Mediterranean: a typology and economic study*. Brit. Archaeol. Rep. S196. Oxford

Keay 1984: Keay S. J., 'Decline or continuity? The coastal economy of the Conventus Tarraconensis from the fourth century until the late sixth century' in Blagg *et al.* 1984, 552–577

Kehoe 1982: Kehoe D. P., *The economics of food production on Roman imperial estates*. PhD. Michigan

Keller and Rupp 1983: Keller D. R. and Rupp D. W. (ed), *Archaeological survey in the Mediterranean area*. Brit. Archaeol. Rep. S155. Oxford

Kent 1978: Kent J. P. C., *Roman coins*. London

Kent and Painter 1977: Kent J. P. C. and Painter K. S. (ed), *Wealth of the Roman world*. London

Keppie 1983: Keppie L., *Colonisation and veteran settlement in Italy 47–14 BC*. London

Kewley 1974: Kewley J., 'A Roman stone-mason's workshop at Chester-le-Street and Lanchester (Co. Durham)', *Antiq. J.* 54, 53–65

King 1981: King A., 'The decline of samian ware manufacture in the north west provinces: problems of chronology and interpretation', in King and Henig 1981, 55–78

King and Hedges 1974: King C. E. and Hedges R. E. M., 'An analysis of some 3rd century Roman coins for surface silvering and silver percentage of their alloy content', *Archeometry* 16, 189–200

King and Henig 1981: King A. and Henig M. (ed), *The Roman west in the third century*. Brit. Archaeol. Rep. S109. Oxford

Knight 1984: Knight D., *Late bronze age and iron age settlement in the Nene and great Ouse basins*. Brit. Archaeol. Rep. 130. Oxford

Knörzer 1970: Knörzer K.-H., *Novaesium IV: Römerzeitliche Pflänzenfunde aus Neuss*. Berlin

Knörzer 1981: Knörzer K.-H., *Römerzeitliche Pflänzenfunde aus Xanten*. Cologne

Kolendo 1976: Kolendo J., *Le colonat en Afrique sous le haut-empire*. Besançon

Kolendo 1980: Kolendo J., *L'agricoltura dell'Italia antica*. Rome

Krämer 1958: Krämer W. (ed), *Neue Ausgrabungen in Deutschland*. Berlin

Kristiansen and Palaudan-Mulle 1977: Kristiansen K. and Palaudan-Muller C. (ed), *New directions in Scandinavian archaeology*. Lyngby

Künow 1980: Künow J., *Negotiator et Vectura: Händler und Transport im freien Germanien*. Marburg

La Marche 1974: La Marche V. C., 'Palaeoclimatic inferences from long tree-ring records', *Science* 183, 1043–1048

Lagadec 1983: Lagadec J.-P., 'Le flotteur de radeau de Flavigny-sur-Moselle (Meurthe et Moselle)', *Gallia* 41, 201–207

Lamb 1977: Lamb H. H., *Climate: present, past and future, 2: climatic history and the future*. London

Lamb 1981: Lamb H. H., 'Climate from 1000 BC to 1000 AD', in Jones and Dimbleby 1981, 53–65

Lamb 1982: Lamb H. H., *Climate, history and the modern world*. London

Landels 1978: Landels J. G., *Engineering in the ancient world*. Berkeley

Lang and Hughes 1984: Lang J. and Hughes M. J., 'Soldering Roman silver plate', *Oxford J. Archaeol.* 6.3, 77–107

Lasko 1971: Lasko P., *The kingdom of the Franks*. London

Laubenheimer-Leenhardt 1973: Laubenheimer-Leenhardt F., *Recherches sur les lingots de cuivre et de plomb d'époque romaine*. Paris

Lawson 1975: Lawson A. J., 'Shale and jet objects from Silchester', *Archaeologia* 105, 241–276

Le Roy Ladurie 1971: Le Roy Ladurie E., *Times of feast, times of famine; a history of climate since the year 1000*. New York

Le Roy Ladurie and Baulant 1981: Le Roy Ladurie E. and Baulant M., 'Grape harvests from the fifteenth through the nineteenth centuries', in Rotberg and Rabb 1981, 259–269

Leday 1980: Leday A., *La campagne à l'époque romaine dans le centre de la Gaule: villas, vici et sanctuaires dans la cité des Bituriges Cubi*. Brit. Archaeol. Rep. S73. Oxford

Lefebvre des Noëttes 1931: Lefebvre des Noëttes, *L'attelage, le cheval de selle à travers les âges*. Paris

Lehmann-Hartleben 1923: Lehmann-Hartleben K., *Die antiken Hafenanlagen des Mittelmeeres*. Klio Beiheft 14. Leipzig

Leighton 1972: Leighton A. C., *Transport and communication in early medieval Europe*. Newton Abbot

Leveau 1975: Leveau P., 'Paysans maures et villes romaines en Maurétanie Césarienne centrale', *Mél. École Franç. Rome* 87, 857–871

Leveau 1982: Leveau P., 'Caesarea de Maurétanie', *Aufstieg Niedergang Röm. Welt* 2.10, 683–738

Leveau 1984: Leveau P., *Caesarea de Maurétanie: une ville romaine et ses campagnes*. Rome

Levick 1984: Levick B., *The government of the Roman empire: a sourcebook*. London

Lewis 1983: Lewis N., *Life in Egypt under Roman rule*. Oxford

Lewis and Jones 1969: Lewis P. R. and Jones G. D. B., 'The Dolaucothi gold mines, I: the surface evidence', *Antiq. J.* 49, 244–72

Lewis and Jones 1970: Lewis P. R. and Jones G. D. B., 'Roman gold-mining in north-west Spain', *J. Rom. Stud.* 60, 169–185

Lewis and Reinhold 1966: Lewis N. and Reinhold M., *Roman civilization. Sourcebook II: the empire*. New York

Liebeschutz 1972: Liebeschutz J. H. W. G., *Antioch: city and imperial administration in the later Roman empire*. Oxford

Limbrey 1975: Limbrey S., *Soil science and archaeology*. London

Liou 1980: Liou B., 'Les amphores à huile de l'épave Saint-Gervais 3 à Fos-sur-mer; premières observations sur les inscriptions peintes', in Blazquez 1980, 161–175

Lloyd 1983: Lloyd J. (ed), *Excavations at Sidi Krebish, Benghazi (Berenice), 2. Libya Antiqua* Supp. 5. Tripoli

Lloyd and Barker 1981: Lloyd J. and Barker G., 'Rural settlement in Roman Molise: problems of archaeological survey', in Barker and Hodges 1981, 289–304

Lo Cascio 1981: Lo Cascio E., 'State and coinage in the late republic and early empire', *J. Rom. Stud.* 71, 76–86

Loane 1938: Loane H. J., *Industry and commerce of the city of Rome (50 BC–200 AD)*. Baltimore

Loeschcke 1932: Loeschcke S., 'Römische Denkmaler vom Weinbau an Mosel, Saar und Ruwer', *Trier. Z.* 7, 1–60

Lopez 1976: Lopez R. S., *The commercial revolution of the middle ages*. Cambridge

Luff 1982: Luff R.-M., *A zooarchaeological study of the Roman north-western provinces.* Brit. Archaeol. Rep. S137. Oxford

Luzon 1968: Luzon J. M., 'Los sistemos de desague en minas romanas del suroeste peninsular', *Archivo. Esp. Arqueol.* 41, 101–120

MacPhail 1981: Macphail R., 'Soil and botanical studies of the "dark earth"', in Jones and Dimbleby 1981, 309–331

Macready and Thompson 1985: Macready S. and Thompson F. H. (ed), *Archaeological field survey in Britain and abroad*. London

Magny 1982: Magny M., 'Atlantic and Sub-boreal: dampness and dryness?', in Harding 1982, 33–43

Maiuri 1958: Maiuri A., 'Navalia pompeiana', *Rendiconti della Accademia di Archeologia di Napoli* 33, 7–34

Malinowski 1922: Malinowski B., *Argonauts of the western Pacific: an account of native enterprise and adventure in the archipelagoes of Melanesian New Guinea*. London

Malone and Stoddart 1985: Malone C. and Stoddart S. (ed), *Papers in Italian archaeology IV: Part i, the human landscape; Part iv, classical and medieval archaeology*. Brit. Archaeol. Rep. S243, S246. Oxford

Maltby 1984: Maltby J. M., 'Animal bones and the Romano-British economy', in Grigson and Clutton-Brock 1984, 125–138

Manacorda 1978: Manacorda D., 'The Ager Cosanus and the production of the amphorae of Sestius', *J. Rom. Stud.* 68, 122–131

Manacorda 1980: Manacorda D., 'L'ager cosanus tra tard repubblica e impero: forme di produzione e assetto della proprieta', in D'Arms & Kopff 1980, 173–184

Manacorda 1981: Manacorda D., 'Produzione agricola, produzione ceramica e proprietari nell'ager cosanus nel I ac', in Giardina and Schiavone 1981, 3–54

Manning 1975: Manning W. H., 'Roman military timber granaries in Britain', *Saalburg Jb.* 32, 105–29

Manning 1976: Manning W. H., *Catalogue of Romano-British ironwork in the Museum of Antiquities, Newcastle upon Tyne*. Newcastle upon Tyne

Marsden 1972: Marsden P., 'Ships of the Roman period and after in Britain', in Bass 1972, 113–132

Martin 1971: Martin R., *Recherches sur les agronomes latins et leurs conceptions économiques et sociales*. Paris

Martino 1979: Martino F. de, *Storia economica di Roma antica*. Florence

Maxey 1938: Maxey M., *The occupations of the lower classes in Roman society*. Chicago

Mayet 1975: Mayet F., *Les céramiques à parois fines dans la péninsula ibérique*. Paris

McGowan 1981: McGowan A., *Tiller and whipstaff: the development of the sailing ship 1400–1700*. London

McGrail 1981: McGrail S., *Rafts, boats and ships from prehistoric times to the medieval era*. London

McGrail 1985: McGrail S., 'Towards a classification of water transport', *World Archaeol.* 16.3, 289–303

McWhirr 1979: McWhirr A. (ed), *Roman brick and tile: studies in manufacture, distribution and use in the western empire*. Brit. Archaeol. Rep. S68. Oxford

Meiggs 1960: Meiggs R., *Roman Ostia*. Oxford

Meiggs 1982: Meiggs R., *Trees and timber in the ancient Mediterranean world*. Oxford

Merzagora 1929: Merzagora M., 'La navigazione in Egitto nell'età greco-romana', *Aegyptus* 10, 105–48

Metzler 1983: Metzler D. (ed), *Antidoron: Festschrift für Jürgen Thimme*. Karlsruhe

Middleton 1979: Middleton P., 'Army supply in Roman Gaul: an hypothesis for Roman Britain', in Burnham and Johnson 1979, 81–97

Middleton 1980: Middleton P., 'La Graufesenque: a question of marketing', *Athenaeum* 58, 186–191

Miket and Burgess 1985: Miket R. and Burgess C. (ed), *Between and beyond the Walls: essays on the prehistory and history of north Britain in honour of George Jobey*. Edinburgh

Miles 1982: Miles D. (ed), *The Romano-British countryside: studies in rural settlement and economy*. Brit. Archaeol. Rep. 103. Oxford

Millar 1964: Millar F., 'The aerarium and its officials under the Empire', *J. Rom. Stud.* 54, 33

Millar 1981: Millar F., 'The world of the Golden Ass', *J. Rom. Stud.* 71, 63–75

Millet 1981: Millett M., 'Aspects of Romano-British pottery in west Sussex', *Sussex Archaeol. Collect.* 118

Mills 1981: Mills N. T. W., 'Luni: settlement and landscape in the Ager Lunensis', in Barker and Hodges 1981, 261–268

Milne 1985: Milne G., *The port of Roman London*. London

Mitchell 1976: Mitchell S., 'Requisitioned transport in the Roman empire: a new inscription from Pisidia', *J. Rom. Stud.* 66, 106–131

Mitchell 1980: Mitchell S., 'Population and the land in Roman Galatia', *Aufstieg Niedergang Röm. Welt* 2.7.2, 1053–1081

Modena 1984: Commune di Modena, *Misura la terra: centuriazione e coloni ne mondo romano*. Modena

Moeller 1976: Moeller W. O., *The wool trade of ancient Pompeii*. Leiden

Molin 1984: Molin M., 'Quelques considérations sur le chariot des Vendanges de Langres', *Gallia* 42, 97–114

Morel 1965: Morel J.-P., *Céramique à vernis noir du Forum romain et du Palatin*. Paris

Morel 1981: Morel J.-P., 'La produzione della ceramica campana: aspetti economici e sociali', in Giardina and Schiavone 1981, 2, 81–97

Morris 1979: Morris P., *Agricultural buildings in Roman Britain*. Brit. Archaeol. Rep. 70. Oxford

Morrison 1980: Morrison J., *Long ships and round ships: warfare and trade in the Mediterranean 3000 BC–500 AD*. London

Mossé 1969: Mossé C., *The ancient world at work*. London

Mrozek 1977: Mrozek S., 'Die Golbergwerke im römischen Däzien', *Aufstieg Niedergang Röm. Welt* 2.6, 95–109

Navigation 1978: *La navigation dans l'antiquité. Les dossiers de l'archéologie* 29. Dijon

Noeske 1977: Noeske H.-C., 'Studien zur Verwaltung und Bevölkerung der däkischen Goldbergwerke in römischer Zeit', *Bonn. Jb.* 177, 271–416

Oates 1953: Oates D., 'The Tripolitanian Gebel: settlement of the Roman period', *Pap. Brit. School Rome* 21, 81–117

Oddy 1977: Oddy W. A. (ed), *Aspects of early metallurgy*. Sheffield

Oswald and Pryce 1920: Oswald F. and Pryce T. D., *An introduction to the study of terra sigillata*. London

Painter 1977: Painter K. S., 'Gold and silver in the Roman world', in Oddy 1977, 135–158

Painter 1980: Painter K. (ed), *Roman villas in Italy: recent excavations and research*. Brit. Mus. Occ. Papers 24. London

Palmer 1926–1927: Palmer R. E., 'Notes on some ancient mine equipment and systems', *Trans. Institution Mining Metallurgy* 36, 299–336

Panella 1981: Panella C., 'La distribuzione e i mercati', in Giardina and Schiavone 1981, 2, 55–80

Parker 1973: Parker A. J., 'The evidence provided by underwater archaeology for Roman trade in the Western Mediterranean', in Blackman 1973, 361–379

Parker 1984: Parker A. J., 'Shipwrecks and ancient trade in the Mediterranean', *Archaeol. Rev. Cambridge* 3:2, 99–113

Parker and Painter 1979: Parker A. J. and Painter J. M., 'A computer-based index of ancient shipwrecks', *Int. J. Naut. Archaeol.* 8, 69–70

Parsons 1968: Parsons W. B., *Engineers and engineering in the Renaissance*. Cambridge, Mass.

Paterson 1982: Paterson, J., 'Survey article: 'Salvation from the sea': amphorae and trade in the Roman West', *J. Rom. Stud.* 72, 146–57

Peacock 1977: Peacock D. P. S. (ed), *Pottery and early commerce: characterization and trade in Roman and later ceramics*. London

Peacock 1980: Peacock D. P. S., 'The Roman millstone trade: a petrological sketch', *World Archaeol.* 12(1), 43–53

Peacock 1982: Peacock D. P. S., *Pottery in the Roman world*. London

Pekary 1968: Pekary T., *Untersuchungen zu den römischen Reichsstrassen*. Bonn

Percival 1975: Percival J., *The Roman villa: an historical introduction*. London

Petrikovits 1981: Petrikovits H. von, 'Die Spezialisierung des römischen Handwerks', in Jankühn 1981, 63–132

Peyras 1975: Peyras J., 'Le fundus Aufidianus: étude d'un grand domaine romain de la région de Mateur (Tunisie du Nord)', *Antiq. Afric.* 9, 181–222

Phillips 1970: Phillips C. W. (ed), *The Fenland in Roman times*. Roy. Geog. Soc. Res. Ser. 5. London

Piggott 1983: Piggott S., *The earliest wheeled transport from the Atlantic coast to the Caspian Sea*. London

Platt 1978: Platt C., *Medieval England: a social history and archaeology from the Conquest to AD 1600*. London

Pleket 1973: Pleket H. W., 'Technology in the Graeco-Roman world', *Talanta* 5, 1973, 6–47

Pleket 1983: Pleket H. W., 'Urban élites and business in the Greek part of the Roman Empire', in Garnsey et al. 1983, 131–144

Polanyi et al. 1957: Polanyi K., Arensberg C. M. and Pearson H. W. (ed), *Trade and market in the early empires*. Glencoe, Illinois

Pomey and Tchernia 1978: Pomey P. and Tchernia A., 'Le tonnage maximum des navires de commerce romains', *Archaeonautica* 2, 233–251

Ponsich 1974: Ponsich M., *Implantation rurale antique sur le Bas-quadalcuivir I*. Paris

Ponsich 1979: Ponsich M., *Implantation rurale antique sur le Bas-Quadalcuivir II*. Paris

Ponsich and Tarradell 1965: Ponsich M. and Tarradell M., *Garum et industries de salaison dans la Méditerranée occidentale*. Paris

Pope and Andel 1984: Pope K. O. and Andel T. H. van, 'Late Quaternary alluviation and soil formation in the southern Argolid: its history, causes and archaeological implications', *J. Archaeol. Science* 11, 281–306

Porter 1981: Porter H., 'Environmental change in the third century', in King and Henig 1981, 353–362

Porter S. 1981: Porter S. C., 'Glaciological evidence of Holocene climatic change' in Wigley *et al.* 1981, 82–110

Postan 1973: Postan M. M., *Essays on medieval agricultural and general problems of the medieval economy*. Cambridge

Potter 1976: Potter T. W., 'Valleys and sediment: some new evidence', *World Archaeol.* 8, 207–219

Potter 1978: Potter T. W., 'Population hiatus and continuity: the case of the south Etruria survey', in Blake *et al.* 1978, 99–116

Potter 1979: Potter T. W., *The changing landscape of south Etruria*. London

Potter 1980: Potter T., 'Villas in south Etruria: some comments and contexts', in Painter 1980, 73–81

Précheur-Canonge 1961: Précheur-Canonge Th., *La vie rurale en Afrique romaine d'après les mosaïques.*

Price 1983: Price M. J., 'Thoughts on the beginning of coinage', in Brooke *et al.* 1983, 1–10

Pryor 1977: Pryor F. K., *The origins of the economy: a comparative study of distribution in primitive and peasant economies*. New York

Pucci 1981: Pucci G., 'La ceramica italica (terra sigillata)', in Giardina and Schiavone 1981, 2, 99–121

Rackham 1976: Rackham O., *Trees and woodland in the British landscape*. London

Raepsaet 1979: Raepsaet G., 'La faiblesse de l'attelage antique: la fin d'un mythe?', *L'Antiq. Class.* 48, 171–6

Raepsaet 1982: Raepsaet G., 'Attelage antiques dans le nord de la Gaule: les systèmes de traction par équides', *Trier. Z.* 45, 215–273

Ramin 1974: Ramin J., 'L'éspace économique en Gaule: les documents concernant les mines', in Chevallier 1974, 417–437

Ramin 1977: Ramin J., *La technique minière et métallurgique des anciens*. Bruxelles

Rapp and Aschenbrenner 1978: Rapp G. and Aschenbrenner S. E., *Excavations at Nichoria in southwest Greece I: site, environs, and techniques*. Minneapolis

Raschke 1978: Raschke M. G., 'New studies in Roman commerce with the East', *Aufstieg Niedergang Röm. Welt* 2.9, 604–1361

Rathbone 1981: Rathbone D. W., 'The development of agriculture in the 'Ager Cosanus' during the Roman republic: problems of evidence and interpretation', *J. Rom. Stud.* 71, 10–23

RCHM 1975: Royal Commission on Historical Monuments (England), *An inventory of the historical monuments in the county of Northampton 1: archaeological sites in north-east Northamptonshire*. London

RCHM 1979: Royal Commission on Historical Monuments (England), *An inventory of the historical monuments in the county of Northampton 2: archaeological sites in south-east Northamptonshire*. London

RCHM 1980: Royal Commission on Historical Monuments (England), *Northamptonshire: an archaeological atlas*. London

RCHM 1981: Royal Commission on Historical Monuments (England), *An inventory of the historical monuments in the county of Northampton 3: archaeological sites in north-west Northamptonshire*. London

RCHM 1982: Royal Commission on Historical Monuments (England), *An inventory of the historical monuments in the county of Northampton 4: archaeological sites in south-west Northamptonshire*. London

RCHM 1983: Royal Commission on Historical Monuments (England), 'West Park Roman villa, Rockbourne, Hampshire', *Archaeol. J.* 140, 129–150

Reece 1972: Reece R., 'A short survey of the Roman coins found on fourteen sites in Britain', *Britannia* 3, 269–276

Reece 1973: Reece R., 'Roman coinage in the western empire', *Britannia* 4, 227–51

Reece 1973b: Reece R., 'Wages and prices', in Strong 1973, 239–45

Reece 1979: Reece R., 'Roman monetary impact', in Burnham and Johnson 1979, 211–217

Reece 1980: Reece R., 'Town and country: the end of Roman Britain', *World Archaeol.* 12.1, 77–92

Reece 1984: Reece R., 'The use of Roman coinage', *Oxford J. Archaeol.* 3, 197–210

Rees 1979: Rees S. E., *Agricultural implements in prehistoric and Roman Britain*. Brit. Archaeol. Rep. 69. Oxford

Renfrew 1972: Renfrew C., *The emergence of civilization: the Cyclades and the Aegean in third millennium BC*. London

Renfrew 1973: Renfrew C., *Before civilization; the radiocarbon revolution and prehistoric Europe*. London

Renfrew and Wagstaff 1982: Renfrew C. and Wagstaff J. M. (ed), *An island polity: the archaeology of exploitation in Melos*. Cambridge

Renfrew J. 1973: Renfrew J., *Palaeoethnobotany: the prehistoric food plants of the Near East and Europe*. London

Reynolds 1979: Reynolds P. J., *Iron age farm: the Butser experiment*. London

Reynolds and Langley 1979: Reynolds P. J. and Langley J. K., 'Romano-British corn-drying ovens: an experiment', *Archaeol. J.* 136, 27–42

Richardson 1976: Richardson J. S., 'The Spanish mines and the development of provincial taxation in the second century BC', *J. Rom. Stud.* 66, 139–152

Rickman 1980: Rickman G., *The corn supply of ancient Rome*. Oxford

Riley 1981: Riley J. A., 'Italy and the eastern Mediterranean in the Hellenistic and early Roman periods: the evidence of coarse pottery', in Barker and Hodges 1981, 69–78

Robinson 1975: Robinson H. Russell, *The armour of imperial Rome*. London

Robinson 1981: Robinson M., 'The Iron Age to early Saxon environment of the upper Thames terraces', in Jones and Dimbleby 1981, 251–277

Röder 1958: Röder J., 'Antike Steinbrüche in der Vorder-Eifel', in Krämer 1958, 268–285

Rodriguez 1977: Rodriguez J. Remesal, 'La economia oleicola betica: nuevas formas de analisis', *Archivo Esp. Arqueol.* 50, 87–142

Rodwell and Rowley 1975: Rodwell W. and Rowley T. (ed), *The 'small towns' of Roman Britain*. Brit. Archaeol. Rep. 15. Oxford

Roebuck 1969: Roebuck C. (ed), *The muses at work: arts, crafts and professions in ancient Greece and Rome.* Cambridge, Mass

Röring 1983: Röring C. W., *Untersuchungen zu römischen Reisewagen*. Koblenz

Rossiter 1978: Rossiter J. J., *Roman farm buildings in Italy*. Brit. Archaeol. Rep. S52. Oxford

Rostovtzeff 1957: Rostovtzeff M. (revised Fraser P. M.), *Social and economic history of the Roman empire*. Oxford

Rotberg and Rabb 1981: Rotberg R. I. and Rabb T. K. (ed), *Climate and history: studies in interdisciplinary history*. Princeton

Rothenberg and Blanco-Freijero 1981: Rothenberg B. and Blanco-Freijero A., *Studies in ancient mining and metallurgy in south-west Spain*. London

Rougé 1964: Rougé J., 'Les relations de Lyon avec la mer, à propos de CIL XIII 1942', *Actes 89e Congrès Nat. Soc. Savantes* 137–152. Lyon

Rougé 1966: Rougé J., *Recherches sur l'organisation du commerce maritime en Méditerranée sous l'empire romain*. Paris.

Rougé 1975: Rougé J., *La marine dans l'antiquite*. Paris

Rougé 1981: Rougé J., *Ships and fleets of the ancient Mediterranean*. Middletown

Rowland 1984: Rowland R. J., 'The countryside of Roman Sardinia', in Balmuth and Rowland 1984, 285–300

Rupprecht 1984: Rupprecht G. (ed), *Die Mainzer Römerschiffe: Berichte uber Entdeckung, Ausgrabung und Bergung*. Mainz

Ryder 1983: Ryder M. L., *Sheep and man*. London

Salway 1981: Salway P., *Roman Britain*. Oxford

Sanders 1976: Sanders I. F., 'Settlement in the Hellenistic and early Roman periods on the plain of the Mesara, Crete', *Ann. Brit. Sch. Athens* 71–137

Sanquer and Galliou 1972: Sanquer R. and Galliou P., 'Garum, sel et salaisons en Armorique gallo-romaine', *Gallia* 30, 199–273

Schiffer 1980: Schiffer M. B. (ed), *Advances in archaeological method and theory 3*. New York

Schlippschuch 1974: Schlippschuch O., *Die Händler im römischen Kaiserreich in Gallien, Germanien und den Donauprovinzen Rätien, Noricum und Pannonien*. Amsterdam

Schmiedt 1981: Schmiedt G., 'Les viviers romains de la côte tyrrhènienne', *Dossiers de l'Archéologie* 50, 28–45

Schnurbein 1982: Schnurbein S. von, *Die unverzierte terra sigillata aus Haltern*. Bodenaltertümer Westfalens 19. Munster

Schumacher 1973: Schumacher E. F., *Small is beautiful: a study of economics as if people mattered*. London

Scott 1983: Scott E., 'Romano-British wheat yields', in Chapman and Mytum 1983, 221–222

Selkirk 1983: Selkirk R., *The Piercebridge formula: a dramatic new view of Roman history*. Cambridge

Setälä 1977: Setälä P., *Private domini in Roman brick stamps of the empire, a historical and prosopographical study of landowners in the district*. Helsinki

Severin 1978: Severin T., *The Brendan voyage*. London

Sevink 1985: Sevink J., 'Physiographic soil surveys and archaeology', in Malone and Stoddart 1985, 41–52

Shackley 1982: Shackley M., *Environmental archaeology*. London

Shackley 1985: Shackley M., *Using environmental archaeology*. London

Shaw 1981: Shaw B. D., 'Climate, environment, and history: the case of Roman North Africa', in Wigley et al. 1981, 379–403

Shaw 1984: Shaw B. D., 'Water and society in the ancient Maghrib: technology, property and development', *Antiq. Afric.* 20, 121–173

Shaw 1972: Shaw J. W., 'Greek and Roman harbourworks', in Bass 1972, 87–112

Shepherd 1980: Shepherd R., *Prehistoric mining and allied industries*. London

Sheridan and Bailey 1981: Sheridan A. and Bailey G. (ed), *Economic archaeology: towards an integration of ecological and social approaches*. Brit. Archaeol. Rep. S96. Oxford

Simmons 1979: Simmons B. B., 'The Lincolnshire Car Dyke: navigation or drainage?', *Britannia* 10, 183–196

Singer et al. 1956: Singer C., Holmyard E. J. and Williams T. I. (ed), *A History of technology, 2: the Mediterranean civilizations and the middle ages c.700 BC to AD 1500*. Oxford

Sion 1935: Sion J., 'Quelques problèmes de transport dans l'antiquité: le point de vue d'un géographe méditerranéan', *Annales* 7, 628–633

Smith 1776: Smith A., *An inquiry into the nature and causes of the wealth of nations* (ed Campbell and Skinner 1976). Oxford

Smith 1978: Smith G. H., 'Excavations near Hadrian's Wall at Tarraby Lane 1976', *Britannia* 9, 19–57

Smith 1977–1978: Smith N. A. F., 'Roman canals', *Trans. Newcomen. Soc.* 49, 75–86

Snell 1984: Snell D. C., *Ledgers and prices: early Mesopotamian merchant accounts*. Yale

Snodgrass 1982: Snodgrass A. M., 'La prospection archéologique en Grèce et dans le monde méditerranéan', *Annales* 37, 800–812

Sölter 1979: Sölter W., *Römische Kalkbrenner im Rheinland*. Düsseldorf

Spaar 1981: Spaar S. L., *The ports of Roman Baetica: a study of provincial harbors and their functions from an historical perspective*. PhD Univ. of Colorado, Boulder

Sperber 1977: Sperber D., 'Aspects of agrarian life in Roman Palestine I: agricultural decline in Palestine during the later principate', *Aufstieg Niedergang Röm. Welt* 2.8, 397–443

Spruytte 1983: Spruytte J., *Early harness systems: experimental studies: contribution to the study of the history of the horse*. London

Spurr 1983: Spurr S., 'The cultivation of millet in Roman Italy', *Pap. Brit. School Rome* 51, 1–15

Squarciapino n.d.: Squarciapino M., *Civiltà romana: artigianato e industria*. No date or place of publication

Sterpos 1970: Sterpos D., *The Roman road in Italy*. Rome

Strong 1966: Strong D. E., *Greek and Roman silver plate*. London

Strong 1973: Strong D. E. (ed), *Archaeological theory and practice*. London

Strong 1976: Strong D. E., *Roman art*. Harmondsworth

Strong and Brown 1976: Strong D. E. and Brown D. (ed), *Roman crafts*. London

Sutherland 1973: Sutherland C. H. V., *English coinage 600–1900*. London

Sutherland 1974: Sutherland C. H. V., *Roman coins*. London

Swan 1984: Swan V. G., *The pottery kilns of Roman Britain*. London

Taylor 1974: Taylor C., *Fieldwork in medieval archaeology*. London

Taylor 1975: Taylor C., 'Roman settlements in the Nene Valley: the impact of recent archaeology', in Fowler 1975, 107–120

Taylor 1983: Taylor C., *Village and farmstead: a history of rural settlement in England*. London

Taylor and Cleere 1978: Taylor J. du P. and Cleere H. (ed), *Roman shipping and trade: Britain and the Rhine provinces*. London

Tchalenko 1953: Tchalenko G., *Villages antiques de la Syrie du nord; le massif de Bélus à l'époque romaine 1–2*. Paris

Tchernia 1983: Tchernia A., 'Italian wine in Gaul at the end of the Republic', in Garnsey *et al.* 1983, 87–104

Tchernia *et al.* 1978: Tchernia A., Pomey P., Hesnard A. *et al.*, *L'épave romaine de la Madrague de Giens (Var)*. *Gallia* Supp. 34. Paris

Tecnologia 1980: *Tecnologia, economia e societa nel mondo romano*. Como

Teichert 1984: Teichert M., 'Size variation in cattle from Germania Romana and Germania Libra', in Grigson and Clutton-Brock 1984, 93–103

Tengström 1974: Tengström E., *Bread for the people: studies of the corn-supply of Rome during the late empire*. Stockholm

Ternes 1976: Ternes C.-M., 'Die Provincia Germania Superior im Bilde der jüngeren Forschung', *Aufstieg Niedergang Röm. Welt* 2.5, 721–1260

Thirgood 1981: Thirgood J. V., *Man and the Mediterranean forest: a history of resource depletion*. London

Thompson 1952: Thompson E. A., *A Roman inventor and reformer*. Oxford

Tranoy 1981: Tranoy A., *La Galice romaine: recherches sur le nord-ouest de la péninsule ibérique dans l'antiquité*. Paris

Tylecote 1976: Tylecote R. F., *A history of metallurgy*. London

Ucelli 1950: Ucelli G., *Le navi di Nemi*. Rome

Unger 1980: Unger R., *The ship in the medieval economy*. London

Varène 1974: Varène P., *Sur la taille de la pierre antique, médiévale et moderne*. Dijon

Veen 1980–1981: Veen M. van der, 'The Ghirza plant remains: Romano-Libyan agriculture in the Tripolitanian pre-desert', in Barker and Jones 1980–1981, 45–48

Vegas 1969–1970: Vegas M., 'ACO-Becher', *Acta Rei Cretariae Rom. Fautorum* 11–12, 107–124

Venedikov 1960: Venedikov I., *Trakijskata kolesniza'* Sofia

Viereck 1975: Viereck H. D. L., *Die römische Flotte: classis romana*. Herford

Vigneron 1968: Vigneron P., *Le cheval dans l'antiquité gréco-romaine*. Nancy

Vilar 1976: Vilar P., *A history of gold and money*. London

Villefosse 1914: Villefosse H. de, 'Deux armateurs narbonnais', *Mem. Soc. Nat. Antiq. France* 74, 153–180

Vita-Finzi 1961: Vita-Finzi C., 'Roman dams in Tripolitania', *Antiq.* 35, 14–20

Vita-Finzi 1969: Vita-Finzi C., *The Mediterranean valleys*. Cambridge

Vita-Finzi 1978: Vita-Finzi C., *Archaeological sites in their setting*. London

Waateringe 1983: Waateringe W. Groenman-van, 'The disastrous effect of the Roman occupation', in Brandt and Slofstra 1983, 147–157

Waelkens 1977; Waelkens M., 'Phrygian votives and tombstones as sources of the social and economic life in Roman antiquity', *Ancient Soc.* 8, 277–315

Wagstaff 1981: Wagstaff J. M., 'Buried assumptions: some problems in the interpretation of the 'Younger Fill' raised by recent data from Greece', *J. Archaeol. Sci.* 8, 247–264

Walda and Walker 1984: Walda H. and Walker S., 'The art and architecture of Lepcis Magna: marble origins by isotopic analysis', *Libyan Stud.* 15, 81–92

Walker 1976–1978: Walker D. R., *The metrology of the Roman silver coinage I-III*. Brit. Archaeol. Rep. S5, S22 and S40. Oxford

Walker 1981: Walker S., 'La campagne lyonnaise du 1er siècle av JC jusqu'au 5ème siècle ap JC', in Walker, 1981b, 279–329

Walker 1981b: Walker S. (ed), *Récentres recherches en archéologie gallo-romaine et paléochretienne sur Lyon et sa région*. Brit. Archaeol. Rep. S108. Oxford

Walker 1984: Walker S., 'Marble origins by isotopic analysis', *World Archaeol.* 16.2, 204–221

Ward-Perkins *et al.* 1986: Ward-Perkins B., Delano-Smith C., Gadd D. and Mills, 'Luni and the *ager lunensis*: the rise and fall of a Roman town', *Pap. Brit. School Rome* 54

Ward-Perkins 1971: Ward-Perkins J. B., 'Quarrying in antiquity: technology, tradition and social change', *Proc. Brit. Acad.* 62. 137–158

Ward-Perkins 1980: Ward-Perkins J. B., 'Nicomedia and the marble trade', *Pap. Brit. School Rome* 48, 23–69

Warmington 1974: Warmington E. H., *The commerce between the Roman empire and India*. London

Watrous 1982: Watrous L. V., *Lasithi, a history of settlement in a highland plain in Crete*. Hesperia Suppl. 18. Princeton

Watson 1983: Watson A. M., *Agricultural innovation in the early Islamic world*. Cambridge

Webb 1981: Webb T., 'The reconstruction of climatic sequences from botanical data', in Rotberg and Rabb 1981, 169–192

Webster 1955: Webster G., 'A note on the use of coal in Roman Britain', *Antiq. J.* 35, 199–217

Weerd 1978: Weerd M. de, 'Ships of the Roman period at Zwammerdam/Nigrum Pullum, Germania Inferior', in Taylor and Cleere 1978, 15–21

Wheeler and Locker 1985: Wheeler A. and Locker A., 'The estimation of size in sardines (sardina pilchardus) from amphorae in a wreck at Randello, Sicily', *J. Archaeol. Sci.* 12.2, 97–100

White 1967: White K. D., *Agricultural implements of the Roman world*. Cambridge

White 1967b: White K. D., 'Gallo-Roman harvesting machines', *Latomus* 26, 634–647

White 1967c: White K. D., 'Latifundia. A critical review of the evidence', *Bull. Inst. Class. Stud.* 14, 62–79

White 1970: White K. D., *A bibliography of Roman agriculture*. Reading

White 1975: White K. D., *Farm equipment of the Roman world*. Cambridge

White 1977: White K. D., *Country life in classical times*. London

White 1984: White K. D., *Greek and Roman technology*. London

White 1978: White L. T., *The transformation of the Roman world: Gibbon's problem after two centuries*. Berkeley

Whitehouse 1981: Whitehouse D., 'The Schola Praeconum and the food supply of Rome in the fifth century AD', in Barker and Hodges 1981, 191–195

Whitehouse 1982: Whitehouse D., 'The Schola Praeconum I: the coins, pottery, lamps and fauna', *Pap. Brit. School Rome* 50, 53–101

Whitehouse 1985: Whitehouse D., 'Raiders and invaders: the Roman Campagna in the first millennium AD', in Malone and Stoddart 1985, part 4, 207–213

Whiting 1971: Whiting J. R. S., *Trade tokens: a social and economic history*. Newton Abbott

Whittaker 1983: Whittaker C. R., 'Late Roman trade and traders', in Garnsey *et al.* 1983, 163–180

Wiedemann 1981: Wiedemann T., *Greek and Roman slavery*. Beckenham

Wightman 1969: Wightman E. M., *Roman Trier and the Treveri*. London

Wightman 1981: Wightman E. M., 'The lower Liri valley: problems, trends and peculiarities', in Barker and Hodges 1981, 275–287

Wightman 1985: Wightman E. M., *Gallia Belgica*. London

Wigley *et al.* 1981: Wigley T. M. L., Ingram M. J. and Farmer G. (ed), *Climate and history*. Cambridge

Wild 1970: Wild J. P., *Textile manufacture in the northern Roman provinces*. Cambridge

Wild 1975: Wild J. P., 'Roman textiles from the Walbrook (London)', *Germania* 53, 138–143

Will 1979: Will E. L., 'The Sestius amphoras; a reappraisal', *J. Field Archaeol.* 6, 339–350

Will 1984: Will E. L., 'Ähnlichkeiten zwischen Stempeln auf Amphoren und auf arretinischen Gefässen', *Acta Rei Cretariae Rom. Fautorum* 23–24, 9–11

Wilson 1981: Wilson A. T., 'Isotope evidence and climate', in Rotberg and Rabb 1981, 215–232

Wilson 1974: Wilson D. R., 'Romano-British villas from the air', *Britannia* 5, 251–261

Wilson 1981: Wilson R. J. A., 'Mosaics, mosaicists and patrons', *J. Rom. Stud.* 71, 173–177

Wilson 1985: Wilson R. J. A., 'Changes in the pattern of urban and rural settlement in Roman, Byzantine and Arab Sicily', in Malone and Stoddart 1985, part 1, 313–344

Yeo 1946: Yeo C. A., 'Land and sea transportation in imperial Italy', *Trans. Amer. Philol. Assoc.* 77, 221–244

Young 1977: Young C. J., *The Roman pottery industry of the Oxford region.* Brit. Archaeol. Rep. 43. Oxford

Young 1980: Young C. J. (ed), *Guidelines for the processing and publication of Roman pottery from excavations.* Dept Envir. Occ. Pap. 4. London

Zimmer 1983: Zimmer G., *Römische Berufsdarstellung.* Berlin

Index